Through the Eye of a Needle

Through the Eye of a Needle

Theological Conversations over Political Economy

Edited by

John Atherton
and Hannah Skinner

 EPWORTH

Copyright © John Atherton and Hannah Skinner 2007

The Authors have asserted their right under the Copyright, Designs
and Patents Act, 1988, to be identified as the Authors of this Work

British Library Cataloguing in Publication data

A catalogue record for this book is available
from the British Library

978 0 7162 0626 2

First published in 2007
by Epworth
4 John Wesley Road
Werrington
Peterborough PE4 6ZP

Printed and bound in Great Britain by
William Clowes Ltd, Beccles, Suffolk

Contents

vi

Acknowledgements

This project reflects the connections developed by the William Temple Foundation with the ecumenical body Churches Together in Britain and Ireland, and its sponsoring denominational bodies. We are grateful for their support as reflected in the Foreword and on the back cover. Above all, as a collaborative project, it is profoundly a joint effort of the twelve contributors. Thank you to them, to St Michael's College, Llandaff for hosting our residential consultation, and to the Church of England's Mission and Public Affairs Council for funding it. Above all, we have been very dependent on Manchester Cathedral's Joanne Hooper for seeing this book into print, and on the support of our editor Natalie Watson.

Hannah Skinner and John Atherton

Foreword

The publication by Churches Together in Britain and Ireland of *Prosperity with a Purpose*, ahead of the 2005 General Election, was a signal that western Christians should no longer, albeit subconsciously, regard a relatively comfortable life in their affluent societies as somehow inherently suspect and sinful, perpetuating the massive injustice of human poverty and masking the time-bomb of environmental degradation.

Readers of that publication will recall the cover picture featuring the laden camel that amazingly appears to have gone through the eye of the needle, recalling the vivid rabbinic picture that Jesus paints of a rich man hardly managing to enter the kingdom of heaven. To our modern minds the more surprising feature of that story is that the disciples were themselves surprised! Did they really say, 'Then who can be saved?', assuming that the rich somehow got into heaven first? On that issue Jesus certainly put them right. But neither then nor since have Christians universalized the instruction to the rich man to 'sell all you have, give to the poor, and then follow me'. Perhaps there were contemporary examples of comparatively rich people helping to build the kingdom (for example Luke 8.3). And I like to think the rabbi's eyes twinkled as he conceded that even a rich man might be saved! (Mark 10.27).

This book takes up the fresh approach of *Prosperity with a Purpose*, which reminds us that guilt is no basis for personal or societal renewal, contrary to what many preachers still assume. Guilt without good news will generate contempt or even hostility toward the messenger and eventual apathy to the message, both of which are evident in our own society. This is why charity – and certainly not professional, competitive charity – will not do. Deep down we feel the approach is aimed at our guilt, and sometimes at our guilt rather than actually at the problem.

So what is the good news? – to quote the title of Bishop Richard Harries' 1992 book *Is there a Gospel for the Rich?* For a start, no one is saying 'greed is good; mammon has won'. But there are creative ways forward, even for the powerful, which re-state the teaching of Christ and church leaders through the centuries. And we are all powerful now, albeit more as consumers than citizens. *Prosperity with a Purpose* began to unpack the implications for personal life-style and public policy of faith in our world as it actually is, rather than as we wish it were or, conversely, the world as it is painted, riddled with competing vested interests, media half-truths, politicians seeking re-election and church leaders wringing their hands as their institutions crumble.

You will find neither such cynicism nor fantasy in this volume. Rather you will find an ecumenical realism, an honest sharing of contrasting views leading to a clear conclusion that we must and can offer the good news of God relevantly in these times of unparalleled economic prosperity, which is so dominant as to be electorally self-justifying, hardly needing a purpose.

All the contributors agree that we dare not assume the analyses, nor repeat the mantras, of previous decades, whether theologically liberal or conservative, politically of the right or left, obscurely theoretical or simplistically specious, emotionally cool or hot. They have all 'moved significantly' in recent years, to quote John Atherton's conclusion, and all recognize 'the need for faith traditions and faith communities to occupy a more central position in the reformulation of religion in the West including in its conversation with economics'. And these are people you would wish to talk with on such matters.

True ecumenism does not muddle through, whether seeking false consensus, submerging minority voices or huddling together for warmth in the face of a common 'enemy'. This volume is an authentic contemporary ecumenical enterprise, robust yet sensitive, challenging but not condemnatory, well-researched, seeing both the wood and the trees in broad brush and detailed argument. What makes it authentic is the common loyalty to the task, to the calling, of trying to bring the reality of life and the reality of God into the same discussion. As such it deserves to be called prophetic and as such it demands and deserves the attention of faith communities and political economists alike.

Peter Brain
Moderator of the Church and Society Forum of Churches
Together in Britain and Ireland and Minister of the United
Reformed Church

The Contributors

John Atherton, now retired canon theologian of Manchester Cathedral, has a long-standing interest in the relationship between Christian social ethics and economic affairs. He continues to work as Secretary of the William Temple Foundation, and part-time lecturer in the Department of Religions and Theology, University of Manchester. His publications include *Christianity and the Market* (SPCK, 1992), *Marginalization* (SCM Press, 2003) and forthcoming *Religion and Transcendence of Capitalism* (SCM Press, 2008). He co-edits *Crucible* with Peter Sedgwick. He is Doctor of Sacred Theology, *honoris causa*, of the University of Uppsala, Sweden.

Chris Baker is the Research Director of the William Temple Foundation in Manchester and part-time lecturer in the Department of Religions and Theology at Manchester University. He writes and researches extensively on faith-based engagement within cities and civil society within the UK. His book *The Hybrid Church in the City: Third Space Thinking* is published by Ashgate Press in April 2007. He is also a member of the Scargill community in North Yorkshire.

Malcolm Brown is Principal of Eastern Region Ministry Course within the Cambridge Theological Federation. He was formerly an industrial missioner and Executive Secretary of the William Temple Foundation. His publications include: (ed. with Peter Sedgwick) *Putting Theology to Work* (CCBI/WTF, 1998), *After the Market: Economics, Moral Agreement and the Churches' Mission* (Peter Lang, 2004) and (with Paul Ballard) *The*

Churches and Economic Life: A Documentary Study: 1945 to the Present (Epworth, 2006).

Peter Heslam is Carts Fellow and Director of Transforming Business, Divinity Faculty, University of Cambridge (www. transformingbusiness.net). He is also Associate Tutor at Ridley Hall in Cambridge and Research Associate at the London Institute for Contemporary Christianity. His writings include *Creating a Christian Worldview: Abraham Kuyper's Lectures on Calvinism* (Eerdmans, 1998), *Globalization: Unravelling the New Capitalism* (Grove, 2002) and *Globalization and the Good* (SPCK, 2004).

Zahid Hussain is a founder director of a Manchester faith-based social enterprise that specializes in community regeneration. He studied business with information technology, before undertaking a postgraduate diploma in European management. He recently wrote an article for *Enterprising*, Manchester's social enterprise magazine.

John Kennedy is a Methodist minister. He has worked chiefly on the east coast of Sri Lanka and in the East End of London. He was the Secretary for Political Affairs for the Methodist Church for 12 years and performed a similar task for Churches Together in Britain and Ireland for 6 years. He edited and contributed to *Prosperity with a Purpose: Exploring the Ethics of Affluence* (CTBI, 2005). His main interests have been the morality of markets in relation to the environment. He is currently a minister in Hampshire.

Michael Northcott is Reader in Christian Ethics in the University of Edinburgh and Associate Priest at the Episcopal Church of St James, Leith. He is also Canon Theologian of Liverpool Cathedral. He is the author of *The Environment and Christian Ethics* (CUP, 1996), *Life After Debt: Christianity and Global Justice* (SPCK, 1999), and *An Angel Directs the Storm: Apocalyptic Religion and American Empire* (SCM Press, 2007).

The Contributors

Patrick Riordan SJ is Associate Director of the Heythrop Institute for Religion, Ethics and Public Life. He teaches political philosophy at Heythrop College, University of London. His main areas of research are religion in public life, citizenship and the common good. His publications include *Philosophical Perspectives on People Power* (Ateneo de Naga University Press, 2001), and *A Politics of the Common Good* (Institute of Public Administration, Dublin, 1996).

Peter Sedgwick is Principal of St Michael's College, Llandaff and Ministry Officer for the Church in Wales. He is also Dean of the Collegiate Faculty of Religious and Theological Studies at Cardiff University. He has worked in social responsibility for many years and published widely in economics and theology. His last book (with Andrew Britton) was *Economic Theory and Christian Belief* (Peter Lang, 2003). He co-edits *Crucible* with John Atherton.

Hannah Skinner is Economic Affairs Adviser to the William Temple Foundation and the Mission and Public Affairs Unit of the Church of England. Her work involves contributing to the William Temple Foundation's ongoing research into the faith-based contributions to society and social capital, as well as writing reports and briefings on economic affairs for use within the Church of England and its ecumenical partners. Publications include co-authoring *Faith in Action: The Dynamic Connection between Spiritual and Religious Capital* (WTF, 2006) and *A Place of Refuge: A Positive Approach to Asylum Seekers and Refugees in the UK* (Church House Publishing, 2005).

Ian Steedman is Professor Emeritus of Economics at Manchester Metropolitan University. Educated in London, Cambridge and Manchester, he has a long-standing interest in micro-economic theory, the history of economic thought, and the borderlines between economics and other areas of thought.

Wilf Wilde is a development economist who studied at Durham and the National Institute of Development Studies, Sussex

University. He worked in the oil industry for 3 years and then as a stockbroker for 12 years at Wood Mackenzie, on utilities privatizations at Merrill Lynch and on emerging markets at ING-Barings. He has co-founded a Christian-led interfaith regeneration agency working with Black majority churches, migrants to London and in Afghanistan. His publications include *Crossing the River of Fire: Mark's Gospel and Global Capitalism* (Epworth, 2006).

Introduction

Developing Faith Traditions and Economic Wellbeing: The Task Before Us All

Theological engagement with the economic affairs so central to human living has been bedevilled by simplistic pronouncements, often supported by particular passages plucked from Holy Scripture. With such arguments and methods, it can and has been argued that they question the commitment to wealth creation and material advancement. The famous passage in the Gospels in which Jesus declares 'how hard it will be for those who have riches to enter the Kingdom of God. . . . It is easier for a camel to go through the eye of a needle than for a rich man to enter the Kingdom of God'[1] is an example of this mindset. It is therefore used as the title of this project and book essentially as a provocative act. It is a reminder of the tradition, splendidly embodied in the work of F. D. Maurice in the turbulent middle of the nineteenth century and its deep engagement with the historic emergence of a modern economy. For he chose to connect what most regarded as the unconnectable, as Christian Socialism, as a deep challenge to both unsocial Christians and unChristian socialists.[2] *Through the Eye of a Needle* is similarly a challenge both to the wealth creation of economics and the lack or distortion of it. It is also a reminder to us that in ways different from Islam and Hinduism, Christianity has therefore endured a profoundly ambiguous relationship to economic processes. That is profoundly necessary given the empirically verifiable contribution of economic growth to human wellbeing but also of the damage such processes have done to individual human lives and communities. Commentators who argue for modern wealth creation as essential for reducing poverty invariably do not argue from the perspective of those who have suffered unimaginable damage historically and contemporarily. However, simplistic appeals to particular passages in sacred writings can also do as much harm as good. Like R. H. Tawney introducing a lecture on Marx, such quoted passages suffer the fate of all great writing, petrifaction by the elect or dilution by the world.[3] For Jesus' words to the rich young man certainly challenged him to face up to the fact that his 'obsessive attachment to possessions was the enemy of his true freedom and therefore, of his true happiness, in this life as well as the next.'[4] Recent research into happiness would, as explained later, confirm that judgement. The continuing pursuit of material goods does not produce full prosperity or wellbeing at all. Yet to make that an excuse to condemn wealth creation wholesale is quite misleading if not fatuous. For it is equally clear, as Jesus concluded his parable, that 'with God all things are possible.' For in a framework of social justice, we must no longer equate the pursuit of Mammon (of economic wealth as an ultimate) as essentially and intrinsically a rival to the worship and service of God but as an aid to it, subject to being tested and rigorously measured by its fruits – the promotion of human flourishing and the reduction of poverty. This is a dramatic corrective to those who suggest wealth creation is inherently bad, but equally to those who view it as always intrinsically good. For the pursuit of justice is unequivocally and inextricably central to Christian belief. It is an ethical demand or divine imperative which must engage, and be seen to engage, with wealth creation. That is why this book is concerned to engage constructively with political economy by requiring the pursuit of an ethically adequate political economy for the twenty-first century in which all will share. Equally, for Christian social ethics, the pursuit of material wellbeing is never the end but profoundly the means to that goal of human flourishing in God. That makes this exercise even more necessary and worthwhile, and even more relevant to our world.

Introduction

The significance of this project, therefore, is its encouraging a conversation between faith and economy-based understandings and initiatives. It has become of strategic importance for both given the nature and threat of such global problematics as marginalization, security and environment. Importantly, it is strongly related to secular and religious contexts which are increasingly interacting, hopefully for their mutual benefit. The task of this project is to reflect on these understandings and overlaps and to promote their interconnections as a contribution both to an ethically adequate political economy for the twenty-first century and to the development of Christian social ethics. While the integrity of each context should always command respect, we are greatly aware of the benefits to be gained from promoting their interaction. The secular context reminds us of the continuing centrality of economics and economies to human living on this planet, and particularly their role in contemporary globalization processes, and how these are impacting on us all through globalized localities. The religious context, in contrast, is reminding us of the growing awareness of the public as well as personal significance of religion, not least since the events of 11 September 2001 in the USA and 7 July 2005 in the UK, but equally through the growing recognition of the actual and potential contribution of faith communities to the public good. These trends stand in marked contrast to the decline of mainstream churches in Europe and their increasing marginalization from the public square and mind, partly fostered by the intentional and unintentional processes of a secularization so deeply and ideologically rooted in government, academy and media.

It is against this backcloth of the actual and potential overlap between these contexts, as the promotion of faith-based involvements in economics and economies locally and globally, that this project emerges, as reflecting and promoting such interacting contexts and trends for the benefit of churches, faiths and society.

The early fruits of this process are evident, for example, in the recent outburst of Christian reflections on economic affairs.

These both encompass a Christian spectrum from denominational and ecumenical reports, regional Christian and interfaith enquiries, to books by individuals, but also a spectrum reflecting diverse understandings of a greatly changing economic life deeply affecting local, national and global living. The titles and authorships often embody these features. For example, they include denominationally, the Roman Catholic reports *The Common Good* (English and Welsh Bishops, 1996) and *Prosperity with a Purpose* (Irish Bishops' paper, 1999), the Salvation Army's reports *The Paradox of Prosperity* (1999) and *The Responsibility Gap* (2004), the Church of England's *Developing the Tradition of Economic Affairs: Mapping the Agenda* (private paper, Mission and Public Affairs Council, 2005) and the Commission on Urban Life and Faith report (CULF) *Faithful Cities: A Call for Celebration, Vision and Justice* (Methodist Publishing House and Church House Publishing, 2006), and ecumenically, *Unemployment and the Future of Work* (CCBI, 1997) and *Prosperity with a Purpose: Christians and the Ethics of Affluence* (CTBI, 2005); a recognition of the significance of the Church's engagement with the regions, as part of interfaith enquiries, is demonstrated by the reports *Faith in England's Northwest: The Contribution Made by Faith Communities to Civil Society in the Region* (NWRDA, 2003) and *Faith in England's Northwest: Economic Impact Assessment* (NWRDA, 2005); and from Christian non-governmental organizations (NGOs) the William Temple Foundation's reports *Telling the Stories: How Churches are Contributing to Social Capital* (2005), and *Faith in Action: The Dynamic Connection between Spiritual and Religious Capital* (2006). Supporting these initiatives, there are the contributions of individuals including *The Church and Economic Life: a Documentary Study, 1945 to the Present* (Malcolm Brown and Paul Ballard, Epworth, 2006), and representing radical faith-based critiques of mainstream political economy and Christian ethics, including *An Angel Directs the Storm: Apocalyptic Religion and American Empire* (Michael Northcott, I B Tauris, 2004) and *Crossing The River of Fire: Mark's Gospel and Global Capitalism* (Wilf Wilde, Epworth, 2006).

Such a substantial body of work confirms both the importance of and the agenda for this project. For we began with the most current ecumenical report, *Prosperity with a Purpose*, and particularly its accompanying volume of essays, *Prosperity with a Purpose: Exploring the Ethics of Affluence* (CTBI, 2005), taken essentially as a collecting or summary point for all these interactions of faith communities and traditions with economic life. From this base we have sought to develop contributions to an evolving tradition of Christian public theology and its search for necessary features of a model of an ethically adequate political economy for the twenty-first century. Using *Prosperity with a Purpose* as a springboard, each contributor to the project therefore addresses the question, what, from your religious tradition's or discipline's perspective, are the defining principles and ideas for the contours of an ethically adequate political economy for the twenty-first century?

In many ways, therefore, our project acts as a bridge between *Prosperity with a Purpose* and the future. Some of the issues we address are common to both enterprises, for example globalization, the paradox of prosperity and poverty, and the environment. Yet there are important differences, including the processes involved. So although our project does address the increasingly crucial global issue of the environment, *Prosperity with a Purpose* rightly pays more attention to it. This difference reveals our limitations. Essentially, we are 12 people contributing our individual perspectives on political economy from our particular experiences and current research interests. That means some key topics, like the environment and technology, are not sufficiently addressed. Yet despite these deficiencies the coverage provided by the contributors impresses by its breadth and quality. For example, the quite crucial debate over global capitalism, imperialism and market economies is faced up to, and not avoided either by intentional or unintentional neglect or by the profound reductionism of a too easy yet quite misleading polarization. Economic and political empires particularly have done at least as much harm as good throughout history, and the present excursions politically and religiously are likely to be no exception to this judgement. As important, for a project addressing political economy from an ethical/theological position, are the detailed studies beyond such larger agendas which are at least as important. For whichever political system is adopted in the contemporary world, issues relating to the mechanisms for the production, distribution and exchange of goods, services and finance, and particularly through market mechanisms, cannot be avoided for too long. Nor can the formative role of governments, companies, trade and poverty reduction. This is why we prefer to use the wider and original concept of political economy in the sense of addressing 'the functioning of entire socioeconomic systems'.[5] Yet the cumulative effect of such contributions or endeavours is not yet another book on globalization. We have deliberately shunned the pretensions of some theologians to produce essentially grand narratives either glibly supporting globalization or promoting alternatives that are almost invariably likely to be more damaging than existing regimes not least because they are so ill-thought-out. Rather, we represent a variety of perspectives certainly British in origin, yet increasingly seeking to interpret and connect with an increasingly global context. Our promotion of global localities therefore reflects our commitment to being both local and engaging with the global.

The difference between our work and *Prosperity with a Purpose* (indeed, with most of recent Church and Christian work in this field, including as noted above) may well therefore be as much to do with process as product. For we have clearly followed the route of bringing together twelve contributors, representing different skills, experiences and religious traditions. That is what the world is like, and we regard that as more of a cause for thanksgiving than of contrition (without in any way reducing the real necessity of the latter). Yet the recognition and celebration of diversity so politically right at this time, is no longer sufficient, and it never has been. For it has been, and still is, often equally a cause of unproductive and sometimes appalling conflict, including religiously. More importantly, the accelerating growth of problems with a global reach increasingly require extensive and intensive collaboration. So we have engaged with this global and contemporary need by adopting a number of procedures for developing a collaborative way of working. For example, we each addressed the same question – given *Prosperity with a Purpose*, what are the key features of an emerging political economy from your perspective (as experience and tradition)? We circulated all the draft contributions so we could prepare ourselves for an intensive 24-hour consultation at St Michael's College, Llandaff. Here, we each briefly introduced our contribution, and engaged in a critical but constructive conversation with each other in order to enable a fruitful redrafting. As important, we all considered a draft extended conclusion which sought to reflect on the very different contributions in order to identify and reflect on the directions which began to emerge for a political economy in the early twenty-first century as viewed from the vantage point of Christian social ethics. In doing so, it also suggested significant new routes for Christian social ethics, particularly its implications for developing interfaith social ethics. As a result, we certainly began to sense that future work in such fields would most profitably need to embody equally both a variety of different perspectives and traditions *and* shared perspectives, with the one never being allowed to crowd out the other. It is as though the cumulative effect of a spectrum of different religious traditions and interpretations of economic affairs, and the collaborations between them, begins to highlight the directions required for a reformulation of both economic affairs and Christian social ethics for the benefit of people and their environments.

That sense of urgency and excitement is reinforced by our sharp awareness that 2007 encompasses a quite crucial marker, the two hundredth anniversary of the abolition of the slave trade, and so of the continuing journey to greater human freedom. The historic and celebrated role of faith in that earlier liberation has empowered today's faith endeavours in promoting more faithful political economy, whether through the struggle of Jubilee 2000 for the debt relief of the world's poorest nations, or the more recent faith involvement in the struggle to

Make Poverty History. With all their weaknesses as well as strengths, as some of our contributors have crisply commented, the commitment to the ongoing liberation of the human continues apace. What we are most agreed on is the central and increasingly significant contribution which a more ethically sustainable political economy must make to that task. Our concern is to continue to develop the contributions of faiths to that visionary programme. It becomes, therefore, a promotion and celebration of a public theology and Church for today and tomorrow.

Given these introductory reflections on this endeavour as process and product, the book itself is divided into two main parts. The first and biggest part brings together, after consultation together and consequent revisions, the twelve individual contributions. This is the jewel of the project, not least because they represent a great wealth of experience in church, mosque, local communities, industry and academy. For example, they include different Christian denominations as well as the commitment to work ecumenically. An active sign of this is the endorsement by Peter Brain's foreword of the Churches Together in Britain and Ireland through its Church and Society Forum. The actual contributions are rooted in a variety of Christian traditions, including Methodist, Roman Catholic and Anglican, and cover a variety of spectrums from liberal, through post-liberal, to a Hauerwasian – Yoderian – radical orthodoxy position. Although the faiths represented are predominantly Christian, the active involvement of a Muslim is no token gesture to interfaith ethics, but rather represents what will hopefully become a substantial interfaith dialogue around issues of economy and finance. (This is no wishful thinking. A modest programme on these matters has been occurring in Manchester for nearly two years including three of our contributors.) And finally, the contributors include the active participation of a professional academic economist, as a recognition of the importance of interdisciplinary convictions, in that his involvement ensured we all sought to gain the respect of economists if not their agreement. It is also a reminder to economists of the historic importance of ethical economics and the role of the faith dimension in it.

For ease of comprehension and management, we have organized this large first part of the book into three sections, beginning with an introductory essay by Hannah Skinner. The first section addresses the theoretical relations between faith (as theology) and economics. This is a recognition of the profound importance of theory both to economics and religion. Any conversations between them must address this dimension. The second section recognizes our divisions, like the rest of the world, into for and against the capitalist market economy as wealth-creator. This is a recognition that faiths cannot avoid such divisions but must embrace them but then work through them into various forms of collaboration. The third brings together theological reflection on practice, as the location of personal experiences. This is a recognition that we certainly all inhabit the global context, but that we do so as individuals including in localities, as places in which we live and are neighbours, in which we work and volunteer.

The second part is a long concluding essay resulting from the reflections of one of the editors, John Atherton, shared with the other contributors at the residential consultation, and redrafted in the light of their comments and suggestions. It is both a summary of our achievements and hopefully a basis for further and future endeavours, and of work in progress.

Notes

1 Mark 10.25ff (and Matthew 19.24ff, Luke 18.25f).

2 F. Maurice, *The Life of Frederick Denison Maurice*, London, Macmillan, 1884, vol. 2, p. 550.

3 R. H. Tawney, *The Attack and Other Essays*, London, Allen and Unwin, 1953, p. 158.

4 *Prosperity with a Purpose: Christians and the Ethics of Affluence*, London, CTBI, 2005, p. 23.

5 Branko Harvat, 'political economy', in P. Deane and J. Kuper (eds), *A Lexicon of Economics*, London, Routledge, 1988, p. 299.

Part 1

Paying Attention to Detail:
Contributions to the
Debate between Theology and
Political Economy

1. Going Public with Public Theology: Developing Meaningful Discourse with the Wider World

HANNAH SKINNER

We live in a world in which the traditional boundaries of time and space that have separated peoples, cultures, countries and cultures are rapidly disintegrating. . . .We have the power, authority and responsibility to participate in the current political and social discourses that continue to shape the face of globalization in our world. God does not afford us the luxury of opting out of moral responsibility.[1]

These processes of disintegration are happening right now in the UK, and within this context the paradoxical situations of prosperity and poverty are being played out. The symptoms of each of these conditions as they exist within the UK create a number of challenges for Christians. Are we acting on the *responsibility* to respond to these challenges? Are we really in a position to speak and act with *authority*? And, in the UK context where Church membership is declining and the faiths are increasingly marginalized from public life, do we really have any *power* to respond to these challenges at all?

Our context is powerfully created by, and inseparably linked to, continuing economic change. Economics, on global, national, regional and local levels, is the determining reality of contemporary life and society – and so engagement with economics and the political economy is imperative in order to respond to the political and social discourses which shape our world. Joining with economists such as Sen in strengthening connections between ethics and economics is a key way in which the faiths can contribute to the macro-economic processes which shape our global context, as well as the local, personal, micro-economic factors that shape day-to-day life. Within this opening chapter:

- the situations of prosperity and poverty within the UK will be outlined,
- some distinctive potential and actual faith contributions to economics will be examined,
- followed by a brief look at two barriers which can prevent these religious contributions.

Prosperity and poverty within the UK[2]

Our context is one of, on one bejewelled and manicured hand, soulless, individualistic prosperity, where some are rich in possessions and status but increasingly find that this is not the magic formula for happiness that many thought it might be. As people are getting richer it is becoming clear that they are not getting any happier, and while they may have everything material they could wish for – 78 per cent of British people agreeing that 'there are no material comforts missing from my life' – this is only serving to increase levels of fear, anxiety and a sense of life's meaninglessness.[3] Meanwhile, on the other hand – this one bare with distinctly grubby fingernails – some live in poverty which marginalizes them from engagement in the social, physical, educational and cultural standards that are available to others in the UK.[4] Living in a wealthy society, but excluded from the benefits of this – through a number of social, financial, physical or other reasons – these people live in UK poverty which is exhausting, rife with uncertainty and anxiety, and dehumanizes and marginalizes.

These multifaceted, and often geographically neighbouring, contexts present Christians (and those of other faiths) with the need to develop a strong, confident public theology that engages with and speaks coherently and powerfully to these economic and social situations. A publicly articulated theology that is rooted in deep concern for all those experiencing the situations described above, and understands and engages with the economic, political and social processes that create them, has something distinctive to offer.

Distinctive contributions of religions to economics

This section will outline four distinctive elements of religious (particularly Christian) contributions to economic thought. The distinctiveness can, in part, be attributed to the motivation, value base and beliefs that inform these contributions, but often actions and processes are also distinctive to, or at least prominent in, religious contributions to economics and wider society.

1 *Christological beliefs and biblical basis*

An aspect of Christian public theology which informs all its contributions is its Christological beliefs and biblical basis. Proclaiming the life and message of Jesus should be an uncontroversial role of the Church, and this underpinning will affect the theology which engages with the public domain. In a sense, this is our non-negotiable – our distinctive edge. The radical teaching and example of Jesus – applying to areas including economics, politics, social justice and giving priority to the needs of the most vulnerable and marginalized – informs, inspires and energizes a Christian contribution to economics.

To the twenty-first-century UK situation, however, this truth alone is not enough. For our secular and often cynical society Christians and theologians need to prove the worth of a contribution rooted in faith. We need to show that this truth inspires us enough not just to accept it and expect others to follow suit, but that it motivates us to engage in a way that is powerfully informed and inspired by the truth of the Gospels. As Archbishop Sentamu said in his inauguration sermon, the commanding voice of Jesus must 'capture our hearts and turn us into radical disciples' – content not just with a 'life-enhancing' faith, but instead having a 'life-changing' faith which guides our response to social, political and economic realities.[5]

Similarly, there are a number of biblical imperatives that leave Christians with no alternative but to engage with the processes of injustice and marginalization:

- The fall of humankind in terms of the presence of sin and finitude, and the resulting consequence that we must live within and address the contingencies and shortcomings of a broken context.
- The belief in the sacred worth of all – all people are made in the image of God and are to be valued equally.
- The realization that we are actors in the *eschaton* – awaiting the coming Kingdom, while participating in the signs of its breaking through into the present age.
- The belief that the most vulnerable are of special significance, and Christians have a special responsibility to these people.
- The belief that the world was created by God and that we are custodians of it.

All of these factors motivate Christian public theology to engage seriously with the current context, and so to apply to it biblical imperatives along with lived experience. This leads to a cycle in which faith-based understandings and practical experience reinforce and energize each other: 'this model of knowledge is more than merely cognitive, it is a knowledge that arises from an engaged effort to change the world'.[6]

In terms of engaging politically, simply declaring the lordship of Jesus issues a profound political challenge to the current global and national powers. To say 'He is King' is to say that others are not. This challenge was lived out powerfully in the life of Christ, and continues to challenge the Church to speak prophetically and, when necessary, subversively. The cross of Christ revolutionized the world order when Jesus overcame death, and a Christian public theology has a responsibility to continue the agenda of the cross today through a considered critique of the economic issues that impact so profoundly the lives of many. Any policies which cause suffering or further marginalization for the poorest are unacceptable for Christians, and a publicly articulated theology will engage with those in policy making positions to condemn injustice and offer alternatives.

2 *The vision of shalom versus prosperity without a purpose*

A second contribution of publicly articulated theology to the contemporary UK context of wealth and poverty is the vision of shalom in critical conversation with prosperity without a purpose. The Hebrew word 'shalom' is often used to refer simply to the concept of peace, but this disguises the fact that true shalom is actually much bigger than this. Shalom is a powerful concept that describes God's societal harmony, order, blessing and prosperity. It describes the biblical vision of 'the good life'. It covers total wellbeing in all aspects of life and describes a situation of abundance in which people have more than they need and communities live in peace. The first period of the reign of King Solomon is described in Old Testament writings as a time of shalom for Israel, a time of abundance, celebration, multiplication and peace.[7] Every person is happy and healthy under their own vine and fig tree, and prosperity is understood holistically as applying to physical, spiritual, emotional and environmental wellbeing:

> God promised Abraham that Israel would be like the sand on the seashore; under Solomon it began to happen . . . It was party time – God's party. They were tasting the Messianic banquet, living to the full and prospering because Solomon's reign reflected God's rule.[8]

Taking this understanding of prospering and concept of shalom as a paradigm, public theology has a powerful ideal to use in critique of existing systems and situations. This takes it to the heart of economic and political debates, setting out a radical vision of shalom in which prosperity is experienced in all its fullness. An example of such a critique is found in Peters's *In Search of the Good Life* when she suggests three questions to interrogate the moral vision of globalization theories: 'What is our context for moral decision making? What is the telos of human life? What constitutes human flourishing?'[9] This utopian ideal also calls for Christians' actions to reflect their desire to see it realized, creating glimpses of God's will being done on earth as it is in heaven.[10]

A question to be asked when comparing shalom with the contemporary context is 'How does our current experience of prosperity match this vision?' This, in turn, raises questions about what it really means to prosper. Shalom incorporates abundance and the security of lacking nothing, but this provision is shared – *all* the people ate, drank and were happy.[11] This contrasts with our global situation, in which billions live in desperate poverty and terrible numbers of people die daily from preventable causes as a result. Shalom also incorporates safety and peace. In the UK context, while we may be materially wealthier than ever before, people's sense of fear and mistrust of others has increased – 'Concern about issues such as crime . . . is recorded at levels that outweigh the actual risk entailed'.[12] In addition, shalom as understood by the Hebrews affected every aspect of life – your health, family, relationships with neighbours, crops, herds, vines, fruit trees, the weather, feasts, worship and celebration.[13] Again, this contrasts with contemporary understandings of prosperity, where material possessions and individualistic experiences and choices are prized above other more holistic and community oriented markers of wellbeing.

Comparing the UK situation to the vision of shalom, it is clear that we have a *fractured image of prosperity*. Glossy advertising and images of wealth and happiness surround us – gorgeous couples reading Sunday papers, stretched out on the wooden floor of their city-centre apartment, drinking coffee from designer machines out of tiny, cute cups. Grotesque parodies of prosperity are paraded by celebrities and those affluent enough to emulate them; the hair extensions of foot-baller's wives – sometimes grown, cut off and sold by Eastern European women to cater for their basic needs, leading hair care experts to report the 'mystery' surrounding the origins of the human hair used for extensions and citing female Russian prisoners as a common source.[14] Meanwhile, a report by the *Guardian* newspaper highlights that collagen lip-plumping injections and skin smoothing creams are being made from the proteins removed from the skin, muscles and bones of Chinese aborted foetuses and executed prisoners.[15] The vision of shalom could not seem further removed from such examples of the perversions perpetrated in pursuit of prosperity. Such gruesome illustrations of the way in which we strive for prosperity, or at least the outward appearance of wealth, feeds off the poor, vulnerable and marginalized, highlight a striking link between narcissism and consumerism. Connections between current understandings of prosperity and personal image are explicit, and it could be argued that there is an almost cannibalistic edge in the examples given above. It appears that in the vain and self-absorbed pursuit of the image of prosperity, people and com-panies are sometimes willing to exploit and plunder the bodies of those who cannot defend themselves.

The falsity of contemporary understandings of prosperity is revealed when considering Layard's conclusions that increasing standards of living in Britain has not resulted in increasing happiness.[16] Job, health, money and relationship related stress all contribute to people from all levels of the income scale reaching crisis point: 'As life-pressures such as job insecurity, working hours and private provision continue to exert their influence, it is likely that stress figures will rise along with drug and alcohol dependency . . . 82% of the UK population claim to suffer from stress'.[17] Using the vision of shalom as a tool, public theologians have a powerful starting point from which to address the issue of true prosperity.

3 *The societal and individual benefits of religious faith*

A third contribution of religion and theology, including Christianity, can be described as the societal and individual benefits of religious faith – a working definitional title for this could be *Religious Capital*.[18] While this is not always the case, and there are recent examples in the UK where it is evident that religion has been used as a way of certain groups bonding and separating themselves from engagement with wider society, people who belong to a religion are generally bucking the trend of disconnection from political processes and community. For example, people who belong to any faith are 10 per cent more likely to vote in political elections than non-believers.[19] In addition, in terms of philosophy of life and ethics, there is a growing recognition that a belief in and commitment to something 'other' and beyond the individual contributes to a person's happiness.[20] A recent survey of young people (aged 13–15) found that those with a religious affiliation were more likely to feel a sense of purpose in life, which in turn positively affected their wellbeing in other areas of life.[21] Communities are also often strengthened by religious groups working and worshipping within them. The government recognizes this, calling the 'tremendous force for good' within all faith communities 'part of the 'glue' that binds us together.[22] This links to issues of trust, and resonates strongly in the prosperity debate as declining happiness is linked to declining levels of trust. John Atherton notes how deteriorating levels of trust have coincided with the decline of mainstream churches and their sidelining from public influence.[23]

This exploration of religious capital as a broadening of the definition of social capital is of great importance in wider debates about the nature of happiness, wellbeing, community and prosperity. The important part that faith, belief and theological identity plays in the actions of faith groups within civil society is highly significant. It is becoming increasingly clear that faith, or *why* religious groups do what they do, cannot be separated from action, or *what* religious groups do.[24] Ensuring that policy makers recognize this significance should be an important contribution of public theology in the twenty-first century as it addresses the paradoxes of prosperity and poverty.

4 *Offering critique and alternatives*

In addition to having much to offer to twenty-first-century public debate, a public theology should also be active in opposing and critiquing political and economic processes that it sees as further harming the marginalized and damaging the environment or are inherently unjust. This duty to speak prophetically and critically is a powerful responsibility of the Church and public theology. It calls not for party politics or the adoption of entrenched positions of left or right, conservative or radical. Instead, we find ourselves standing between these positions, not on neutral middle ground, but on Kingdom ground. Kingdom ground transcends all earthly allegiances and patterns of relating, and Kingdom people will therefore feel free to embrace from left, right or centre whatever social truths are compatible with biblical understandings. At Point A therefore, the Kingdom will make us radical, and at Point B conservative.[25] Chief Rabbi Sacks describes religious involvement in politics thus:

> Religion has a role in politics, but not in party politics. Religion is important in creating the environment in which party politics takes place. It's a major force for altruism, concern for the common good, building of families and communities, the sense of citizenship and responsibility – and those sound to me like political values. Without them you can't have a polis – a society.[26]

For Christians, being involved politically by opposing (or supporting) certain policies or processes requires the understanding that biblical imperatives, such as the call in Micah to 'do justice, and to love kindness, and to walk humbly with your God', apply not just to personal choices and actions.[27] Instead such challenges call Christians and public theologians to engage meaningfully with society. Christian public theology can learn much from Islam here, which does not draw a distinction between faith and other aspects of a believer's life. For Islam, as well as Christianity, 'One cannot compartmentalize [religious] teachings . . . into different areas. Whether it's the social aspect of your life, economic activity or political participation'.[28]

However, public theology cannot simply oppose unjust policies and economic systems. Instead, it must work, along with partners from other disciplines, to offer credible alternatives to what is on offer. While much of the global West offers a politics of blame and fear, public theology and the Church must seek to offer an alternative politics of hope, peace and justice. Many examples of economic alternatives offered and operated (predominantly) by faith groups are available, from credit unions that offer financial services to those excluded from mainstream banking, to micro-credit schemes set up in countries such as Bangladesh to help the rural poor start up small businesses and earn their way out of poverty, to interest-free Islamic banking systems.

Barriers to faith engagement with economics

Having examined a number of the distinctive responses of the faiths and public theology to economics, it is necessary to outline some of the barriers to these contributions. Looking particularly at the Christian faith, I will highlight two specific barriers which are inhibiting engagement with economics.

1 *Image*

> the narrow-minded, stultifying reality of most English churches hardly matches the dynamic, revolutionary image they're trying to push. If they spent more time helping the poor, campaigning for social justice, doing the things they're supposed to be doing and less time serving stale biscuits and weak tea to defenceless pensioners, they might find things work out a whole lot better for them.[29]

This was Toby from Canterbury, 'speaking' on a recent BBC online discussion board about church image.

While Toby's opinions are not universally held or sustainable, neither is he alone in his view of the Church. The *image* of the Church, both the way it is portrayed popularly in the media as well as its self-image and sense of worth, is creating a major obstacle to the voice of Christian theology being heard amidst the clamouring competitors for society's allegiance. Society is becoming increasingly image aware, and as consumers we are used to being offered a slick, glossy presentation of the goods and services we may wish to fill our lives with. Meanwhile, if the dominant image of the Church is of a disconnected, disinterested and irrelevant institution, then it and public theology face the inevitable prospect of increasing marginalization from public life and consciousness.

There are some signs of a growing awareness of the public and personal significance of religion, not least since the events of September 11 in the USA and 7 July in the UK, but also through the increasing recognition, among politicians and others, of the actual and potential contribution of faith communities to the public good. However, these trends stand in marked contrast to the decline of mainstream churches in Europe and their increasing marginalization from the public square and mind, partly fostered by the intentional and unintentional processes of secularization so deeply and ideologically rooted in government, academy and media. If current trends continue, the number of Muslims attending prayers at British mosques on Friday will be double the number of Christians at church on Sunday by 2040.[30]

It is interesting to note that in 2005, Archbishop Sentamu described many Christians as 'consumers of religion', pick-n-mixing the bits of religious faith that enhance their lives, rather than accepting the challenge of a life-changing discipleship. Lord Carey similarly highlighted that if the Church were a business it would have collapsed.[31] Both of these observations are significant for the Church is not a business, but is full of consumers. Despite the contributions that public theology has to make to the contemporary economic situation, these will be of no use unless they can be delivered effectively into wider dialogue and public consciousness. However, the image of the Church, and often the Christian religion as a whole, often marginalizes these contributions.

One cannot help but be constantly aware of cultural signs and pointers warning us off religion, as well as its norms and values. The idea of God and spirituality may be thriving, but institutional religions are mocked, derided and generally warned against. A song entitled 'Judgement Day' by Ms Dynamite, a British R+B performer, shows how recent scandals within the Church have further scarred its public image. Bearing in mind that this medium reaches millions of young people in a way which the Church does not, it is not hard to see why people have such low estimation of the Church:

> You claim you're doing God's work, greet the family with a
>   smile,
> When all the while you been raping that child,
> You're a priest but you still can't wash the blood from your
>   hands . . .
> I wonder what you going to do when He comes for you? . . .
> I wonder what you're going to say when that day comes –
> when Judgement Day comes.[32]

Likewise, an exchange in one episode of the American drama series, *Sex and the City,* in which a leading character's baby is to be baptized, described it as 'not about religion, and not about God . . . its just water on a kid's head', therefore highlighting popular feelings of scorn towards religion; '[I want you to be Godmother] . . . Officially, you provide the baby with spiritual guidance. Unofficially, you stand up there with me so I have somebody to roll my eyes at.'[33]

Some argue that the image of Christianity and theology is irrelevant, arguing that faith and the insights it brings are a personal, inward matter. The argument goes that religion is not selling a product, and should not be shaped by post-modernity, trying to convince people to like it and listen to what it has to say. This argument is right to the extent that it would not be right of public theology to attempt to pander to ideas that the only thing worth valuing is something that can be neatly packaged up and consumed. Let us face it, we could never sell the idea that theologians spend their time lounging on designer floors anyway. But what is the value of theology that no one knows or cares about? Public theology must be public, a voice in the (crowded) market-place of ideas.

Looking at the example of Jesus we find he constantly found ways to get people to listen to his message. Addressing the needs and situations of the contemporary context can only happen if public theology is prepared to speak in language that people listen to. This provides a continuing challenge for the Church; in the current climate of overwhelming choice, the Church and theology is competing for attention in a very crowded market. In this climate of public insecurity about what is trustworthy and real, public theology must show clearly to the wider world that what it offers is solid and significant.

Part of the challenge to accept and exercise the God-given power, authority and responsibility to engage with and confront the problems of prosperity and poverty, is to find new ways to communicate. Even if the product is strong, if delivery is weak then the contributions of the religions and public theology to economic thought and life will fail to engage. The challenge to find new ways to communicate with a secular world about religion's contributions has already been taken up locally, nationally and globally by many churches and groups, but the work done so often seems to go unnoticed – just ask Toby from Canterbury.

2 *Fear or complacency*

Linking powerfully to issues of image and the low public perception of the Church, a feeling of fear or under-confidence can also at times inhibit contributions. Christian campaigners, theologians and activists are often dismissed by the secular media as do-gooders who do not understand the issues they are attempting to engage with. Some Christian organizations attempt to distance themselves from their beliefs and value base in order to be taken more seriously by the wider world, and avoid the attitudes of disregard and derision that some sections of the media often level at Church or Christian-based groups. An interesting observation in some recent William Temple Foundation research was the almost unanimous rejection by church groups of being labelled religious. Participants in the research tended to view the word 'religious' as denoting a 'Pharisee faith' and referring to institutional, organized religion rather than a dynamic personal faith.[34]

Meanwhile, it is interesting to note that secular advertisers frequently use religious themes and imagery to sell their products. For example GHD Hair Straighteners will create 'Urban Angels – Made not Born' and allow users to 're-write your own set of beliefs . . . Be part of the new religion in hair and baptize yourself into a whole new world'.[35] In contrast, advertisements for Church or Christian-based 'products' often dare not mention religion, or do so in a very self-deprecating way. For example, even the Alpha Course advertisements make no reference to God, religion or Christianity, while the slogan on the newest Church campaign reads: 'Church: It's not as churchy as you think'.[36]

Entering into economic debate is a terrifying prospect for most Christians. After all, bringing Christian-inspired ethics to this discourse means flying in the face of neo-classical economic thought:

> Political economy is . . . a science, not an art or a department of ethical enquiry. It is described as standing neutral between social schemes. It furnishes information as to the probable consequences of given lines of action, but does not itself pass moral judgements.[37]

For the average Christian lay person this can sometimes feel like a losing battle. How does one enter into very complex issues such as international trade or debt with no hope of a level playing-field? This prospect can become even more terrible when faced with the prospect of being branded reactionary or infantile by other, specialist Christian thinkers. How does the average Christian, aware of injustice on a local, national and global level, and accepting power, authority and responsibility to act as part of a Christian desire to protect the vulnerable, begin to go about it?

There have been some splendid examples recently of how one might begin to do this. For example mass involvement occurred with non-governmental organizations for the Jubilee 2000 and Make Poverty History campaigns. These collaborations proved effective in their aims and showed the power that an average Christian can have in partnership with others. However, despite these recent examples, the situations that Christians wish to challenge can seem so big, and we so small, that it is easy to be gripped by fearful paralysis. This applies not only on an individual scale, but it is easy to feel that a public Christian theological voice would be drowned out by the scale of the issues it is addressing:

> As we race into a future of economic globalisation, ruthless domination, and commercial conquest on a scale never seen before, it is difficult to believe that there is a force in heaven or on earth that can challenge the principalities and powers behind McWorld.[38]

However, Christian public theology must not be silenced or worn down. As will be outlined within following chapters of this book, there are crucial contributions to wider discourses which public theology must not be ashamed to make. 'Without the broadening of neoclassical economics by reinforcing an ethical dimension, it will be found wanting at the bar of history. The stakes of marginalisation . . . are so high'.[39]

Equally, while we must not let low self-esteem or fearfulness hold back the contributions of theology to the public domain, we cannot afford to be complacent. It is no good announcing that we have the answers, expecting everyone to come flocking. We must be prepared to acknowledge that we do not have all the answers, but, as Chief Rabbi Sacks observes, one contribution of religion is at least to be asking the right questions.[40]

There is clearly a tension here: while Christian public theology must not be silenced by fear, it must also guard against any creeping complacency. Starting from a Christian position of concern for the marginalized, especially the most marginalized, as well as a concern that true prosperity reflects God's design for humanity, we have a distinctive role to play in dialogue about the changing world we inhabit. If we believe this contribution to be important, then we must find a way to present it that engages with the wider world.

Conclusions

The contributions that public theology can make to economics are both distinctive and important. Finding creative new ways to overcome the barriers to these contributions is vital, so that public theology for the twenty-first century may continue in the tradition of the Christian and other religiously based social ethicists throughout history who have called for justice and offered alternatives to the unjust systems of their time. A dynamic public theology with profound concern for strengthening connections between ethics and economics and creating social justice is a crucial way in which the Church can reflect to society that it, as Christ's body, is accepting the challenge to speak meaningfully to the current UK and global context. Public theology's contributions must be made confidently, unashamed of its belief and value undergirding, in partnership with others and must be embedded in praxis. If we lack conviction in power, authority or responsibility we will never achieve this.

Notes

1 Rebecca Todd Peters, *In Search of the Good Life: The Ethics of Globalisation*, New York, Continuum International Publishing Group, 2004, p. 4.

2 Inverted commas will be used around the word 'prosperity' in this context to denote the contested understanding of prosperity as used in this chapter. While many have understood prosperity to refer to the accumulation of material goods and status, I am arguing that true prosperity is much deeper and more nuanced than this. True prosperity will also include a number of less tangible aspects of wellbeing and happiness.

3 The Salvation Army/The Henley Centre, *The Paradox of Prosperity* (online). Available at <http://www1.salvationarmy.org.uk/uki/www_uki.nsf/0/1F6911511A0E8DEB80256F970051C8DC/$file/Library-ParadoxOfProsperity.pdf> Date of publication, 1999.

4 UK poverty is defined relatively to the global scene as less than 60 per cent of average disposable income. Author unknown, *The Facts about Poverty in the UK* (online). Available at http://www.oxfamgb.org/ukpp/poverty/thefacts.htm#2. April 2003.

5 John Sentamu. Sermon preached by the Archbishop of York at his inauguration (online). Available at <http://www.cofe.anglican.org/news/pr9205.html> 30 November 2005.

6 Peters, *In Search of the Good Life*, p. 7.

7 1 Kings 4 (NRSV Anglicized Version).

8 Derek Morphew, *Breakthrough: Discovering the Kingdom*, South Africa, Vineyard International Publishing, 1991. p. 19.

9 Peters, *In Search of the Good Life*, p. 31.

10 Hannah Skinner, *A Place of Refuge*, London, Church House Publishing, 2005, p. 6.

11 1 Kings 4.20 (NRSV Anglicized Version).

12 Salvation Army, *Paradox of Prosperity*, p. 12.

13 Morphew, *Breakthrough*, p. 20.

14 Author unknown, 'Beckham's hair feeds off Russian poverty' (online). Available at <http://www.contactmusic.com/new/xmlfeed.nsf/mndwebpages/beckham.s%20hair%20feeds%20off%20russian%20poverty> Date of publication February 2004; and Perriann Rodriguez, 'Synthetic Fibre Hair Extensions create choice hair styles for hair loss and fashion clients' (online). Available at <http://hairguide.info/News/30284-Synthetic-Fiber-Hair-Extensions-Create-Choice-Hair-Styles-for-Hair-Loss-and-Fashion-Clients.asp>.

15 Ian Cobain and Adam Luck, 'The beauty products from the skin of executed Chinese prisoners, London', *Guardian*, 13 September 2005.

16 Richard Layard Lecture at London School of Economics, 'Income

and Happiness: rethinking economic policy' (online). Available at
<http://cep.lse.ac.uk/events/lectures/layard/RL040303.pdf> Date of
Lecture 27 February 2003, p. 3.

17 Salvation Army, *Paradox of Prosperity*, p. 21.

18 Chris Baker and Hannah Skinner, *Telling the Stories: How
Churches are Contributing to Social Capital*, Manchester, William
Temple Foundation, 2005.

19 *God and the Politicians*, BBC 2 documentary. Broadcast 28
September 2005.

20 John Atherton, *Prosperity, Poverty and Purpose: Christian Con-
tributions to Urban Political Economy* (unpublished), commissioned
and acknowledged source in Commission on Urban Life and Faith,
Faithful Cities: A Call for Celebration, Vision and Justice, London and
Peterborough, Church House Publishing and Methodist Publishing
House, 2006, p. 8.

21 Gwyther Rees, Leslie J. Francis and Mandy Robbins, *Spiritual
Health and the Well-being of Urban Young People* (online). Available at
<http://culf.org/papers/uypreport.pdf> Date of publication July 2005,
p. 33. See also Leslie J. Francis and Mandy Robbins, *Urban Hope and
Spiritual Health: The Adolescent Voice*, Peterborough, Epworth, 2006.

22 Quote from Paul Goggins, MP for Wythenshawe and Sale East. In
God and the Politicians.

23 John Atherton, *Prosperity, Poverty and Purpose*.

24 Chris Baker and Hannah Skinner, *Faith in Action: The Dynamic
Connection between Spiritual and Religious Capital*, Manchester,
William Temple Foundation, 2006.

25 Michael Cassidy, 'The Power of Standing on Kingdom Ground',
in *Out of Africa* (African Enterprise magazine), March 2005.

26 Quote from Sir Jonathan Sacks, Chief Rabbi of the United
Hebrew Congregations of the Commonwealth. In *God and the
Politicians*.

27 Micah 6.8 (NRSV Anglicized Version).

28 Quote from Sir Iqbal Sacranie, head of the Muslim Council of
Britain. In *God and the Politicians*.

29 Online public discussion board. 'By your adverts ye shall be
known . . .' (online). Available at <http://news.bbc.co.uk/1/hi/magazine/
4244958.stm> Date of publication 14 September 2005.

30 Peter Brierley (ed.), *The Future of the Church*, quoted in the
Church of England Newspaper, Issue no. 5786. 'Bleak future predicted
for declining churches' (online). Available at <http://www.churchnews-
paper.com/englandonsunday/index.php?read=on&number_key=5786
&title=Bleak%20future%20predicted%20for%20declining%20churc
hes> Date of publication 16 September 2005.

31 John Sentamu, Inaugural Sermon; and Lord Carey quoted in *Church of England Newspaper,* Issue no. 5790. 'Lord Carey urges church to back Fresh Expressions' (online). Available at: <http://www.churchnewspaper.com/news.php?read=on&number_key=5790&title=Lord%20Carey%20urges%20Church%20to%20back%20Fresh%20Expressions>, 14 October 2005.

32 Lyrics from 'Judgement Day', by Ms Dynamite. Full lyrics available online at <http://www.lyricsmania.com/lyrics/ms_dynamite_lyrics_232/lyrics_1152/lyrics_1152/judgement_day_lyrics_196641.html>.

33 Quote from *Sex and the City* (HBO), written by Cindy Chupack. Season 5: episode 68: 'Unoriginal Sin'.

34 Baker and Skinner, *Faith in Action.*

35 GHD Hair Straighteners website (online). Available at <http://www.ghdhair.com/index.php?co.uk>.

36 Stephen Tomkins, 'By your adverts ye shall be known' (online).

37 John Neville Keynes (father of John Maynard Keynes) as quoted in Johnston, *Wealth or Health of Nations*, Cleveland, Pilgrim Press, 1998, p. 5.

38 Tom Sine, *Mustard Seed versus McWorld: Reinventing Life and Faith for the Future*, Grand Rapids, Baker Books, 1999, p. 174.

39 John Atherton, *Marginalization*, London, SCM-Canterbury Press, 2003, p. 147.

40 Quote from Sir Jonathan Sacks, Chief Rabbi of the United Hebrew Congregations of the Commonwealth. In *God and the Politicians.*

Section 1

The Task is to Change the World: The Importance of Theory in the Relations between Theology and Economics

2. Common Good or Selfish Greed?

PATRICK RIORDAN SJ

Stranger, anonymous, the masses. Sometimes the negative connotations of these terms are emphasized, when we are invited to contrast the contact with the anonymous stranger with the experience of acceptance in a known and knowing community, the isolation of feeling lost in an immense crowd with the sense of belonging in a family or parish. But the story does not have to be told that way. It is also possible to wonder in amazement and appreciation at the fact that people who might have reason to fear each other as enemies and threats can nonetheless meet in a context of mutual respect. Another telling of the story could evoke astonishment and gratitude that anonymous strangers, in large numbers, can co-operate with each other to a high degree of reliability and honesty so as to produce benefit for so many others, also unknown.

There is a tendency in religious circles to tell one story and to overlook or even be unaware of the other. We can be so intent on fostering and sustaining relationships of intimacy and familiarity that we ignore the bonds we have with millions of unknown others. We take for granted this reality of inter-dependence and co-operation precisely because it is not face-to-face. It is there, in the background, delivering its benefits, and not attracting attention.

Jane Jacobs has drawn attention to it.[1] She associates it with the basic human activity of trading. As she tells the story, it is the human propensity to trade which has enabled the emergence of a distinctive mindset with its characteristic openness to the stranger and the willingness to enter into a deal even with a risk of loss. She contrasts the trading mindset with another rooted in survival activities associated with taking. Hunting and gathering are obvious examples of the taking strategy of survival, but so too is agriculture. Resources available from nature are relied upon to sustain life, and this fact remains the case even if there is a sophisticated processing of the resources in manufacture. Accordingly, the perspective of taking is highly territorial and land is a major focus of attention. The mindsets associated with taking and trading include distinctive moral perspectives with characteristic values and virtues. Jacobs writes of these as moral syndromes, suggesting the amalgam of elements and indicators which together present a picture. In the moral syndrome linked to taking the moral imperatives stress the urgency of holding on to what is possessed, to its defence against predators and to sustaining the cohesion of the community which must be relied upon both to defend but also to exploit the resource. The values of this syndrome are loyalty, honour, cunning and military prowess. From within this syndrome the stranger is perceived as a threat, the risk undertaken in trade is a gamble with the resources of the community, and the individual's desire to try something different jeopardizes the cohesion of the group. Might there be grounds for suspecting that the allegation of selfish greed as the motivation for wealth generation requires the background of this syndrome in order to appear plausible?

Wealth based on greed?

It is a commonplace in certain kinds of literature to bemoan the fact that our prosperity is predicated on greed. Greed is assumed to be ethically suspect, since greed or covetousness is traditionally one of the vices familiarly known as the seven deadly sins.[2] A useful example is Clive Wright's book, *The Business of Virtue*. In it he boldly poses the paradox that something good is produced by motivational drives that are bad. Can we will the good without at the same time willing the bad that is the means to the good? And how does that stand to the familiar ethical injunction in Christian tradition that 'evil may not be done so that good may come of it'?[3]

Another example is taken from Alasdair MacIntyre who argues in his major trilogy that our moral thinking is rooted in some tradition, and that the history of thought reveals a variety and range of such traditions.[4] The continuity of language for speaking of the good and the right, virtue and vice, can deceive us into assuming that all those who speak about virtue are speaking about the same thing. What counts for virtue in one context can be considered a vice in a different tradition. As an example MacIntyre points to *pleonexia* or acquisitiveness, which he suggests is acknowledged in our contemporary world as key to the motivation for economic activity, but which counted for the Greeks as vice. '(T)he tradition of the virtues is at variance with central features of the modern economic order and more especially its individualism, its acquisitiveness and its elevation of the values of the market to a central social place.'[5]

The wealth created in this system is welcomed as contributing to the quality of life enjoyed by many people and as removing the drudgery associated with work in the past. Wealth is further approved of because of the many worthwhile projects which it makes possible, including provision for education, culture, health and welfare. However, it is assumed by the critics that the process of wealth creation is not motivated by the worthwhileness of these goods, but by individuals' greed for returns to themselves. For my present purposes it is not necessary to pursue further the distinction suggested here that a complete treatment of the topic would require. To focus on greed as a significant motive common to market activity requires that one abstract from the great range of goods that can be appealed to in order to make sense of the activities of market participants. The goods they pursue fit into life projects that are socially rooted and frequently shared. These goods ground the answers that explain why people do what they do. To have a meal, make a home, provide education and health care for one's family, take part in sport, enjoy the benefits of cultural life in the city, join with co-religionists in worship and in cultivation of the shared vision, engage in the campaigning and debate that will lead to a rejuvenated local council, all of these projects can make sense of people's economic activity. But to abstract from the goods they pursue and the projects in which they are located in order to focus on greed as a common factor in their motivation runs the risk of misunderstanding because the grounds of intelligibility are systematically excluded from consideration.

Even though these considerations give us good reasons for considering the challenge to be misplaced, I will accept for the sake of argument that there is a case to be answered. I will allow the presupposition that greed does play a significant role in the motivation of economic agents, but I will deny the implication that because there is greed in the motivation which generates wealth that the ensuing prosperity is thereby morally compromised. To make my case I will rely on a particular understanding of the nature of systems of social rules. First of all, I will clarify the challenge. Second I will take one philosophical account of economic theory which is prepared to concede that greed is located among its postulates. Third I will draw on recent work that explains systems of rules as providing solutions to problems of coordination. This approach demonstrates the irrelevance of the putative element of greed in the motivation of agents, by offering a useful distinction between two forms of ethical discourse. In a fourth section I will illustrate the argument in terms of Thomas Aquinas's discussion of property, and finally apply this to the contemporary situation with regard to intellectual property. I note further how the argument in relation to rule systems appeals to the human good, understood in a complex way, so that the appropriateness of rule systems is determined in terms of the achievement of human goods that would otherwise not be possible. These goods require analysis in terms of public good, a restricted domain of the common good.

The challenge

The argument that prosperity is based on greed is made in different ways and so it is useful to distinguish these for clarity of focus.

1 The theoretical model relied upon in economics presupposes greed in its description of the economic agent, even if it does not condone it.
2 There is a link between the analysis offered in terms of an abstract model and how people learn to think of themselves in terms of this model. People adjust their behaviour to the standards of rationality presented in the model.
3 The operation of the market and the prosperity it makes possible require that consumers desire and demand the products and services on offer.
4 There is an additional activity of advertising and promotion which fosters demand for and consumption of products and services which are superfluous, and for which there would be no demand without the marketing.

I will concentrate on the first challenge. The motivations of people in practice may be complex and greed or acquisitiveness may be part of anyone's motivation in pursuing economic goals. But the challenge is made not in terms of what happens in practice, but what is in principle the case. Is our prosperity founded in principle on greed, at least in part? If that is the case, is it regrettable?

Greed a postulate of economics

Among the philosophers of economics there are some who are prepared to admit that greed is one of the postulates of the theory. An important and much reprinted book on the philosophy of economics underlines the way in which economics goes beyond utility theory as used in other disciplines. Daniel Hausman reformulates this postulate as 'consumerism' although he admits it might equally be termed greed despite the pejorative loading of the term.[6] The theory of consumer choice relied upon in explaining market demand depends on three behavioural postulates, which Hausman calls rationality, consumerism, and diminishing marginal rates of substitution. The rationality postulate is that people have complete, transitive and continuous preferences, and do not prefer any available (affordable) option to the one they choose. The consumerism or greed postulate is:

> (1) The objects of every individual i's preferences are bundles of commodities consumed by i, (2) there are no interdependencies between the preferences of different individuals, and (3) up to some point of satiation (that is typically unattained), individuals prefer larger commodity bundles to smaller. Bundle y is larger than bundle x if y contains at least as much of every commodity or service as does x and more of some commodity or service. Consumerism implies self-interest.[7]

The third postulate is that the more one has of anything, the more of it one will be willing to exchange for a unit of something else.

The formulation of the second postulate underlines the fact that the economic agent is presumed to be concerned only with her own preferences, and it does not belong to her preferences that another succeed. Only her own satisfactions through her own consumption matter to her. And 'enough' is not part of her vocabulary; she always wants more. Hausman maintains that economic theory goes beyond the usual assumptions associated with the rational agent in utility theory. While altruism is consistent with rational agency, the consumerist model in economic theory excludes altruism, according to Hausman. Materialist acquisitiveness, greed, is assumed to be the motivator. Hausman insists that this is not intended as a description of how people actually are. If it were, it would be a 'libel on our species that is not seriously endorsed by even the most misanthropic economist. Obviously consumerism is not intended as the literal truth'.[8]

Hausman is clear on the exaggeration imported in this model. While models as such do not purport to make claims about the state of the world, they enable theories that do make such statements, so that there is a relevance to explanation. The verbal distinction being made here between models and theories is deliberate:

> Models are definitions of kinds of systems. The assumptions of models are clauses in definitions and not true or false assertions about the world. The investigation of models is a fully defensible part of science, for one crucial component of science is the articulation of new concepts in terms of which to theorize. When one offers a general theoretical hypothesis asserting that a model is true of some realm of reality, then one is offering a theory; and in offering the theoretical hypothesis one is committed to treating what were the assumptions of the model as assertions about the world.[9]

Relying on Hausman's account, therefore, we can accept for the sake of argument that greed is one of the postulates of the discipline in constructing models to be used in formulating theory, which in turn is applied to explaining and possibly shaping the world of experience. And so the question raised at the beginning by the critics we have quoted is not trivial: does our prosperity depend on greed?

Ethics and economics

The question whether prosperity depends on greed raises the further question of the relationship between ethics and economics. For this question the recent work of a German economist is particularly helpful. Karl Homann distinguishes between two levels of discourse in ethics – *Handlungsdiskurs* and *Regeldiskurs* – discourse on actions and on rules.[10] The former considers the specific actions that will be permitted, required or prohibited by operative rules in particular situations. Focus on actions presupposes a context of rules. In another form of ethical reflection, the attention is directed at the rules themselves, and what they ought to be. The shaping of rules generates institutions that provide the parameters for human interaction, and create grounds for expectation of others' actions and reactions. Ethical reflection on rules was always relevant, but, Homann maintains, it becomes increasingly relevant as societies become more anonymous and complex. In small-scale societies the prevalence of face-to-face encounters of people who know one another ensures immediate sanction enforcing conformity. In anonymous modern society, there is need for a comparable element of control, but that is one which requires a rule system.

Homann defends the model of the rational economic agent, *homo oeconomicus*, in economic analysis as a theoretical construct with a purpose. It can be useful for handling certain questions, but not for others. It is not intended as a depiction of human nature, it is not an anthropology. Homann argues that the model is useful for the analysis and construction of institutions given that actors in the institutions are motivated by individual interest. Game theoretic models such as The Prisoners Dilemma and the tragedy of the commons depict situations in which there is a dilemma arising from the tension between individual rationality and the impossibility of achieving the best communal outcome from within individual rationality.[11]

The purpose of rules in dealing with such situations is to generate security of expectation. Reliability of expectations depends on the adequacy of the rule system – only those rules will be followed that assure benefit for all, so accordingly it only makes sense to adopt those rules that assure benefit for all. Benefit for all is a precondition for co-operation since in any dilemma an individual is capable of undermining co-operation whenever it no longer provides him with benefit, understood in the widest sense. When a system of rules is established that fosters benefit for all, then each one can conform without having to engage in moral deliberation.

The model of *homo oeconomicus* at the heart of neo-classical economic theory enables the generation of such a system. Because it operates from the minimalist postulate about the motivation of agents it is able to express the rationality of stake-holders who continue to collaborate even in competitive systems in which they might have to face stiff opposition. The consideration of the benefit to humankind in general, and to society, in terms of public order, efficiency and innovation, warrants the creation and maintenance of norm systems which abstract from individuals' motivation even to the extent of being compatible with morally suspect motives.

I will illustrate and test this analysis by considering how it has been operative in traditional Christian social ethics. Thomas Aquinas's treatment of property reveals a parallel to Homann's distinction of the ethics of actions and the ethics of rules, and the adoption of a system of rules that abstracts from the motivation of the people who conform.

Aquinas on property

Aquinas distinguished two elements of property, namely, the two kinds of activity involved in owning.[12] One set of activities of owning has to do with administration, management and care. The other set of activities has to do with use, enjoyment and consumption. Aquinas considered that on balance the first set of activities was best allocated in a society to private individuals. He gave three reasons for this view. The first has to do with the best care of the things owned; where everybody is responsible nobody actually does the work, leaving it for others with the result that matters are neglected. Clear allocation of responsibility for the management of things works best. The second related idea points to the confusion and chaos that could arise if everyone were responsible for any one thing, or for everything. How many hours of meetings would be required of the nation's farmers to decide what to plant where, when to manure and irrigate, and when to harvest. Greater social order is achieved if each one can decide for himself in the care of what is allocated to him. And the third reason notes the potential for social peace when the possible conflict associated with the confusion about responsibility is avoided.

It is important to note how contingent these comments are. Aquinas does not appeal to anything that might be translated into a modern discourse as absolute rights to property. The claim to hold property privately is contingent on an arrangement for social order that sees the benefit for society in having administration and responsibility clearly divided among individuals. It is also important to note how he can reflect on the social outcome of inefficiency, confusion and conflict without having to consider the moral character of those whose action or inaction would contribute to the social consequence. Their laziness, greed, envy, avarice or arrogance are not relevant to Aquinas's argument. He considers, not the moral worthiness of individuals' motivation, but the best arrangement for social order. His reflections are contingent and tentative. It is conceivable that in other circumstances alternative arrangements would be preferable. It should be acknowledged, of course, that the tentativeness of Aquinas's defence of private property was overlooked in more recent presentations of Catholic social teaching responding to the threat of communism.[13] Far from asserting a moral fact (property rights) which should be incorporated in civil legal regulation, he considers rather what is conducive to social peace given the factors that can lead to disorder. This is what the designers of a system of rules should take into account. What Homann describes as *Regeldiskurs* is exemplified in Aquinas's discussion of private property.

Of course, it should also be mentioned that Aquinas engages in the ethical discussion of action as well. While he is willing to allow the management of material things to be in private hands, he also insists that private owners must so administer their property that it benefits all, especially those who are needy. This theme has not been neglected in the tradition and has formed a continuous strand in Catholic teaching on the obligations of ownership. Also in his treatment of theft and associated vices Aquinas demonstrates his ability to discuss the morality of action relative to established norms.

Intellectual property

The modern discussion of intellectual property, and of the usefulness of instituting intellectual property rights with copyright protections, provides another example of what was implicit in Aquinas's analysis. In this discussion the question focuses, not on the rights and wrongs of individual motivation and action, but on what the law should be so as to facilitate the life of society. That intellectual goods might be considered property would be shocking to medieval philosophers. For them intellectual goods are inherently public, not private. While a material good like a loaf of bread can be divided among a very limited number of people and at some point the bread is consumed and nothing is left, an idea can be shared endlessly without any necessary diminution of the idea. As Herbert McCabe has written, theologians like Aquinas saw the spiritual and intellectual as inherently common and public; what individuates and privatizes is the material, and the particular. Ever since Descartes, we are more likely to think of this contrast in the reverse direction, considering the spiritual in the sense of self-awareness as especially private, and the bodily, being visible and tangible to others, as especially public.[14]

Why might it be a good thing to institute intellectual property rights and allow people to derive profit by excluding others from the enjoyment of what is essentially common? One set of arguments in favour of intellectual property rights relies on the importance of fostering innovation. Unless those who develop new technologies, new medicines and new products are permitted to earn a return on their investment, they will not be prepared to bear the costs involved in development of their ideas. This argument is clearly very different from asserting some supposedly absolute moral claim to a spiritual good to the exclusion of others, 'my claim to my ideas'. It begins instead with a view of a social whole, which is considered as having an interest in fostering innovation. Innovation is to be fostered because it is assumed that society as a whole benefits from developments in technology of all kinds from electronics to pharmaceuticals. This does not preclude that there are harms to society and to the environment resulting also from the development. On balance, innovation is to be fostered because of its potential to find solutions to problems, or simply improve the quality of life. A new way of communicating cheaply and efficiently, a new way of controlling infection, a method for reducing CO_2 emissions, a new game (Sudoku!), a more drought-resilient strain of maize, an encryption device for protecting privacy of electronic messaging and so on, all contribute in various ways to improving human life. They can be recognized as such because we implicitly recognize that the human good is irreducibly complex. Even attempts to gain an overview of this complexity by listing values or basic forms of good must acknowledge their abstraction and the open-ended nature of the project. Knowledge, life, play, friendship and so on are dimensions of the human good. It does not reduce to some one factor such as desire-satisfaction, preference-satisfaction, pleasure or utility.[15] As I argued above, this point is relevant to denying that there is any such thing as generic greed or acquisitiveness. Even if one wanted to point to money as a universal carrier of value and means of exchange, it is only of use as such because of what it can buy, and that range of goods and services reflects the complexity of the human good.

Innovation is valued. The conditions for fostering innovation are valued. Risk is a major factor: managing risk is essential to fostering innovation. Incentives must counterbalance the disincentives that are linked to risk. Conditions for research that allow investors and researchers the possibility of making profits from their discoveries are more likely to foster the occurrence of innovation than conditions that increase the risks and costs of exploration. However, that is only half the story. As well as fostering innovation, patents can protect a monopoly in a context in which competition and free markets are normally relied upon to ensure efficiency in the delivery of products to consumers. Just as patents might be reasonable because of the innovation they facilitate, so monopolies are to be avoided and regulated so as to ensure efficiency. A recent example of this tension was the case of HIV/AIDS medicines, which because of their prohibitive costs coupled with patent protection were unattainable by the sufferers in Africa and elsewhere. Responding to pressure the WTO provided for an exception to its standard treaty regulation of patents in medicines.

Different ethical questions

The discussion of property and its modern version of intellectual property relies on a distinction between two kinds of questions. One set of questions asks about what it is permissible, obligatory or forbidden to do. We recognize this as belonging to the ethics of action. And so as we have seen Aquinas has several questions of his *Summa* addressing the issue of theft, the unlawful taking of what is the property of another. The other set of questions asks about the rules that should be applied to regulate an area of human activity, in these examples the administration of property. This latter discussion is inappropriate in the former context, which of its nature must accept that certain norms are valid. The relationship between the two levels is complex. But there is no simple deduction from the first level to the second, from an affirmation of a moral norm to an incorporation of that norm in a legal code. What is also relevant is a reflection on the requirements of the common good, or of public order.[16]

Conclusion

The market with its norms facilitates the interdependency and co-operation of large numbers of people who do not know one another, and yet can deal fairly and honestly with one another. In examining this phenomenon, it is not appropriate to raise questions and apply the criteria which belong to the morality of personal action. We have looked at the distinction between Aquinas's question about theft and his question about the appropriate arrangement in a society for the holding and management of property. There was no automatic deduction from the norms governing theft or the obligation to share, to the

determination of the best system for the allocation of ownership. Parallel to Aquinas's distinction, there is another to be
drawn between the individual's motivation in action, whether
greed or generosity, and the considerations which a society can
have for regulating forms of interaction between people who
are strangers to one another and nonetheless are interdependent
in forms of collaboration which threaten to be exploitative. The
latter concern for regulation is for the sake of the benefits that
can accrue to society and humankind as a whole. These benefits
are not only the realizations of the enormous range of the
human good, as suggested above, but also the advantages for
social order in terms of avoidance of conflict, harmony of
people with disparate roles and responsibilities and the facilita-
tion of innovation and the achievement of the creative human
spirit. That a scruple about greed or self-interest persists may be
due to a neglect of this perspective which can look at the system
of co-ordination of human activity, and it may also be
explained by a disregard for the richness and complexity of the
good because of a moralistic focus on rules or virtues. But might
it not also be the case that those who raise these questions find
themselves at home in the moral syndrome associated with
taking, and therefore spontaneously tend in the direction of
asceticism, defensiveness of what is already held and advocacy
of sharing among those who already belong? The alternative
moral syndrome sketched by Jacobs, that associated with
trading, is not their natural environment, and so its virtues and
characteristic ideals, in particular the injunctions to be open to
inventiveness and novelty and to promote comfort and con-
venience appear more as vices.[17]

Notes

1 Jane Jacobs, *Systems of Survival: A Dialogue on the Moral
Foundations of Commerce and Politics*, New York, Vintage Books,
1994.
2 My colleague at Heythrop College and the Heythrop Institute for
Religion, Ethics and Public Life, Dr Catherine Cowley, is working on the
adequacy of this analysis of greed or covetousness in relation to virtues

and vices. Her paper on this topic 'Wealth Creation, Holiness and Virtues' is forthcoming in *Louvain Studies*. See also her book *The Value of Money: Ethics and the World of Finance*, Edinburgh, T & T Clark, 2006. Chapter 3, 'Ethical Insufficiency of the Model', is relevant.

3 Clive Wright, *The Business of Virtue*, London, SPCK, 2004.

4 Alasdair MacIntyre, *Three Rival Versions of Moral Enquiry*, London, Duckworth, 1990, is the third book in a trilogy, the earlier being *After Virtue*, second edition, Notre Dame, Indiana, University of Notre Dame Press, 1984, and *Whose Justice? Which Rationality?*, London, Duckworth, 1988.

5 MacIntyre, *After Virtue*, p. 255. *Whose Justice* analyses the contribution of the Scottish Enlightenment and in particular David Hume to shaping this economic order, p. 313.

6 Daniel M. Hausman, *The Inexact and Separate Science of Economics*, Cambridge, Cambridge University Press, 1992.

7 Hausman, *Science of Economics*, p. 30.

8 Hausman, *Science of Economics*, p. 32.

9 Hausman, *Science of Economics*, p. 273.

10 Karl Homann, *Vorteile und Anreize: zur Grundlegung einer Ethik der Zukunft*, edited by Christoph Lütge, Tübingen, Mohr Siebeck, 2002. See also Christoph Lütge, 'Karl Homanns Ordnungsethik', *Information Philosophie*, 5 (2005), pp. 82–5.

11 R. Axelrod, *The Complexity of Cooperation*, Princeton, NJ, Princeton University Press, 1997; Richard Dawkins, *The Selfish Gene*, Oxford, Oxford University Press, 1989; R. Hardin, *Collective Action*, Baltimore, MD, Johns Hopkins University Press, 1982.

12 Thomas Aquinas, *Summa Theologiae*, 2a2ae q66 a2.

13 Cf. Donal Dorr, *Option for the Poor: A Hundred Years of Vatican Social Teaching*, revised edition, Dublin, Gill & Macmillan, 1992, pp. 54f.

14 Herbert McCabe, OP, *The Good Life: Ethics and the Pursuit of Happiness*, edited by Brian Davies, London, Continuum, 2005, pp. 36–7.

15 Cf. Timothy Chappell, *Understanding Human Goods*, Edinburgh, Edinburgh University Press, 1998.

16 I have written on this elsewhere, 'Rights Talk in Political Debate', *Studies*, Dublin, 78:309 (1989) pp. 48–57, and in *A Politics of the Common Good*, Dublin, Institute of Public Administration, 1996.

17 Jacobs, *Systems of Survival*, p. 215.

3. Christian Ethics and Economics after Liberalism

MALCOLM BROWN

It is surprising how much Christian engagement with economic issues – academic and ecclesial – criticizes the global market for its manifest failings yet fails to engage with the moral arguments that have underpinned market economics for decades. If the market apologist can turn around to the Christian moralist and argue that market structures are not only the least bad system around but are also morally superior in significant respects to the alternatives, then those of us who seek a better economic order had better have our responses ready. Too often Christian commentary on economics has seemed to inhabit a world that economists and market enthusiasts are not allowed to enter to state their case.

I want here to address one moral claim made on behalf of market economics and to explore what a workable Christian response might look like. The claim is this: that we no longer inhabit a world where a single moral narrative informs everybody's judgements about value and justice (if, indeed, we ever did). In this plural world, one person's idea of what justice demands may be contradicted by another's: so how to adjudicate between them? One way is to allow those who are powerful, or who shape opinion, to decree what justice means, and any who disagree must fall into line and be forced to live with what they would regard as unjust structures or outcomes. But (it is argued) the market mechanism allows us to get around this unsatisfactory situation. Market outcomes are the result of millions of discrete human decisions, each 'player' in the market acting according to his or her own moral compass. Markets are intrinsically complex and their outcomes are not predictable; no one willed the results and no one was coerced into acting against their will. The market, as Jeremy Bentham noted, is the proper mechanism for addressing questions of value and the distribution of goods in a 'society of strangers'. In a world woven together by instantaneous communication, yet still living by numerous different moral codes and narratives of identity and belief, such a mechanism for settling vexed issues of distributional justice would seem more appropriate than ever.

The market, then, is the quintessential liberal institution – designed to embrace human difference and to secure agreement, not about ends but about means, on grounds independent of the particularities of faith or tradition.

So far, so familiar, perhaps, to those who have listened to the market apologists. What is surprising is that so few Christian commentators have seriously engaged with that element in the argument for market economics. Again and again, in the relatively small literature of theology and economics, the word 'justice' is asserted as if its content was clear and uncontroversial. Over and over, a thoughtful Christian approach to distributional justice is put forward with no account of how it might relate to those whose morality leads them to other conclusions. That overworked word 'community' is frequently appealed to as the arbiter of human justice, but the diversity and contradictory desires of the many communities around the globe (let alone the numerous overlapping communities to which many contemporary individuals belong) are not sufficiently explored. In the absence of a programme for democratic persuasion, one must assume that Christian thinkers have no problem with the coercion that markets claim to avoid or with the implicit elitism of rule by only one narrative of justice. It seems as if we can have social plurality and markets, or strong communities and authoritarianism – but not both.

On liberalism

This dilemma is especially piquant because it seems to create an insoluble contradiction for those who think of themselves as liberals – at least as that word is used in the churches. Liberalism, of course, has many manifestations. Economic liberalism, drawing upon the argument about plurality and justice, emphasizes the market because it appears to make no distinction between persons or communities, yet apparently has no problem with the widening material inequality that seems to be an intrinsic consequence of unfettered markets. Those who are often termed social liberals also stress the diversity of human lives but conclude from this that there is a considerable moral equivalence between persons which can be damaged by too great a material inequality.

Theological liberalism is different again – in the well-known triangulation of scripture, reason and tradition, the liberal will tend to stress reason most highly and to read the Scriptures, and evaluate the Church's traditions, through the prism of human reason. One could express that the other way around to say that the theological liberal gives less critical attention to the nature of reason than to the Scriptures or the traditional teachings of the Church. In consequence, theological liberals may argue that, where there are gaps of perception or practice between the Church and society, it is the Church which should change to accommodate 'social realities'. More theologically, this tendency takes the form of starting, rather uncritically, with human experience and arguing from this to religious truth, rather than starting with given religious truths and using them to critique the way people evaluate their experience.

What these versions of liberalism share is that they find common roots in the Enlightenment's 'project' of transcending the narrow particularities of discrete human communities, each formed through the stories which give each its distinctive ethic. With growing communication between peoples, each forming their notions of justice, value and so on through incommensurate traditions, mercantilism required some commonly acceptable way of settling precisely those ethical qualities. Not surprisingly, attention turned to that which all human beings held in common – *homo sapiens* is, by definition, capable of reason. Reason became the foundation of ethics as if, confronted by the same concrete situation, all people could reason from what is the case to what ought to be the case, and reach identical conclusions.

Liberalism's ideal, then, was to transcend the particularity of local difference. But, as Alasdair MacIntyre has shown so clearly in his *After Virtue* project,[1] rationality cannot be separated from particularity in this way. Reason itself is as much constituted by tradition as religious belief. And so (to cut a rather long argument very short) liberal societies tend to be characterized by considerable difference but no real consensus about how difference is to be explained and understood or how conflicting viewpoints may be reconciled.

And so, although theological liberals are frequently critical of the market as an institution, not least for its claim to remove questions of distributional justice from the realm of moral decisions, there are difficulties in generating a robust critique of the market from within the liberal tradition. Thus the Roman Catholic apologist for markets, Michael Novak, is as clearly a theological liberal as was the democratic socialist Ronald Preston.[2] Both argue from human experience to conclusions about the nature of God. Both accept plurality and difference but look for commonalities from which shared agreements might follow rather than focusing on local communities or the particularities of faiths. Yet politically, Novak is an economic liberal in tune with the policies of the political right, while Preston would seek the moderating influence of the state in ways that place him well to the left. Preston's difficulty is that he has an essentially 'thin' view of plurality – for him, difference is rarely insurmountable although consensus-building is time-consuming and costly. '[M]en and women who are wise', he says, 'will think rather of their resemblances to their fellow human beings than of their differences from them'.[3] But what if that focus on commonality is not enough? If reason itself is culturally formed the exercise of reason alone will not procure ethical agreement.

Theology's turn away from liberalism

In the end, the liberal tradition in theology has difficulty constructing an effective critique of market economics because it shares too many of the same assumptions. Moreover, as it becomes evident that liberal assumptions have not ushered in an era of global harmony, and consciousness of local difference becomes more acute, the trend in Christian thinking is to seek distinctiveness rather than conformity with the prevailing culture. Theology, therefore, has taken a decisive turn away from liberalism's concern to be relevant to culture – away from the privileging of human experience – and looks increasingly to ground its deliberations in revealed truth and in the distinctive lived practices of Christian communities.

Few of these confessional theologians have made any sustained engagement with economic issues. Contemporary exponents of Barthian neo-orthodoxy such as Michael Banner have placed the ethical focus squarely on the beginning and end of life and the nature of the person. Radical Orthodoxy, perhaps because it has tended to align itself with the kind of Christian Socialism once espoused by the Christendom movement, seems to offer a more suggestive theological starting point for thinking about economic justice. In the work of D. Stephen Long, Radical Orthodoxy has seen a serious engagement between confessional theology and economic structures and, not surprisingly, Long is a trenchant critic of the market. But his economics is essentially concerned to make the turn away from liberal attempts to seek understandings of value and justice that are communicable between diverse communities and to articulate instead a distinctive Christian economics which has the capacity to shape the practice of the churches' members.[4] In other words, the problem of negotiating between radically different conceptions of justice is avoided by sidestepping the necessity for such trans-traditional encounter. Yet this is to see theology's task as concerned only with shaping ideals and not with the ethical spadework of addressing the complex confusions of a world in which, despite the inauguration of the Kingdom of God, the impact of the Fall continues to undo the best intentions of human endeavour. Even in closed Christian communities such as the Amish of Pennsylvania, the necessity of engagement with the wider economy is inescapable.[5]

Nevertheless, neo- and radical orthodoxies pose a crucial challenge to liberal theologies at a time when the liberal project is notoriously perplexed by the persistence of plurality and social atomization. What difference does it make to believe in God?

The economy subject to a *status confessionis*

One answer comes from another strand of confessional theology which, although barely recognized as such by radical and neo-orthodoxy, has been influential in some spheres of Church life, notably the World Council of Churches. Exemplified in the work of Ulrich Duchrow, it turns on the idea that a Christian's understanding of justice does not need to be relativized in encounter with others and imposes moral absolutes which must then be enacted as thoroughly as possible in a contingent world. Thus Duchrow (and the WCC) calls for the churches to declare a *status confessionis* on the workings of the global economy, declaring its operations and outcomes to be so immoral that it becomes a matter of Christian integrity to oppose it and to make the public witness of declaring it immoral.[6]

But it is not clear that the global economy exhibits the kind of morally absolute issues that can be appropriately dealt with by a *status confessionis*. It is not clear, for example, how questions of distributional justice, this side of the *eschaton* where the material world is constrained by finitude and (hence) scarcity, can be treated as confessional issues since distributional justice always involves either compromise between competing claims or resolution by the enforcement of one authoritative tradition. To hold before the world a vision of God's Kingdom is a worthy vocation for the Church, but that is not the same as offering an ethic that might enable Christians to approach Kingdom values more closely in the finite, fallen and compromised world as it is. Moreover, Duchrow offers no mechanism whereby the Christian version of justice, as he outlines it, can encounter different understandings of justice formed, no less authentically, within other traditions. There is an uneasy suggestion here of a covert authoritarianism: in a world ordered on Duchrow's principles, the lot of non-Christians and those who reject the 'orthodox' Christian version of justice would seem highly precarious. Confessional approaches to economic justice too often lay themselves open to the charge from market apologists that their ideals could only be enacted with heavy doses of social coercion.

Indeed, if churches are prepared to declare certain human behaviour and human structures to be, of their very nature, incompatible with Christian faith, there is no escape from the obligation to devise an alternative way of living which combines Christian virtues with practical possibility. It has been said that market economics takes an overly pessimistic view of human sinfulness, but any alternative has to offer a better account of the balance between grace and fallenness. Neither theologians in general, nor Duchrow in particular, have put forward any economic model that improves on the market's failings without introducing new – often potentially fatal – consequences.

Difficulties with anti-liberal ideas

Neither the liberal theological tradition, nor Duchrow's approach to confessional theology, offers a convincing account of how Christian objections to market economics get around the problems posed by profound and self-conscious plurality except through an implicitly coercive approach to difference. Is there no alternative, then, to adopting market mechanisms whose acknowledged advantages are severely qualified by particularly baleful consequences?

Liberalism's ambition to transcend the particularities of religion, tradition and locality has manifestly failed. This failure has led, on the one hand, to the idea that difference can be managed and, on the other, to the view that difference is non-problematical. The first response has bequeathed us the poverty of managerialism with its pretension to impartiality cloaking a highly ideological logic of its own.[7] The second implies a hubristic trust in the rightness of a single tradition and the community that embodies it, and acquiescence in the possibly violent consequences of encountering rival traditions with no method of mediation. As Jeffrey Stout puts it, our present condition amid the failures of the liberal project may be, in MacIntyre's terms, 'civil war by other means' but it remains preferable to the bloody civil wars and crusades of pre-modern times.[8] Liberalism arose partly through revulsion against demonizing 'the other', and the current rejection of liberalism as a 'failed project' has not always shown much inclination to avoid the ills that liberalism eclipsed.

Returning to the opening question, can the issue of moral agreement in a plural context be resolved – and thereby undermine one of the philosophical props on which market economics rests – without tumbling the other way into an unacceptable social authoritarianism? Can Christian theology give an account of how authentic Christian ethics can be in dialogue with positions rooted in other traditions so as to offer a consensus on what economic justice might entail? Is it possible to move beyond the failures of the liberal project without rejecting its aspiration to speak to a world beyond any one discrete tradition?

An approach to post-liberalism

The position sketched below is one that I term 'post-liberal' with a very careful definition of terms. In theology, voices such as those of George Lindbeck and Stanley Hauerwas have claimed to be post-liberal in the sense that they regard the liberal project as not only weak but effectively vanquished and no longer worthy of serious Christian consideration. I use the term differently. To accept the weaknesses of a position need not imply its total rejection. My contention is that aspects of the liberal tradition in theology embody important theological truths that ought not to be ignored, even if the overall project has ceased to be coherent. In more personal terms, I am trying to represent the position of people like me whose theological formation was within that liberal tradition, who have come to appreciate its weakness and frequent hubris, but who are reluctant to adopt the convert's demonization of their former position.

The main problem with liberalism is that its claim to transcend the particularity of tradition is patently ill-founded. Economic liberalism offers us the market as the mechanism that, in itself, transcends the multiplicity of ends which human morality seeks to serve. But it is unclear why agreement about means should be easier to achieve than agreement about ends and, as a matter of observable fact, commitment to moral ends frequently leads people to reject the means that the market represents. For instance, the apparent triumph of the global market is often being achieved by the very coercive methods that the market purports to circumvent. Theological liberalism, in its focus on universal truths, frequently fails to give an account of the distinctive and authentic perspective on ethics that stems from faith and, consequently, risks making the very concept of God redundant.

Why, then, should we value liberalism at all? Many positions embodying liberal virtues are not, of any necessity, wedded to the problematic aspects of liberalism. Indeed, if we could speak of liberalism as a tradition among others, rather than concentrating on its claim to transcend the particularity of traditions, then the perceived threat that liberalism seems to pose to tradition-in-general vanishes, making possible a different kind of dialogue in which the destruction of liberalism is not the prerequisite for traditions to flourish.

Liberal virtues

The virtues of such a non-exclusive liberal theological tradition would include: tolerance of difference; belief in objective truth and a commitment to dialogue as a way of pursuing truth; the belief in an active God still revealing God-self to the world in new ways; commitment to making this world a better place and not merely acquiescing in its condition until some future eschaton, and a focus on the incarnation with its promise that the material world can be hallowed.

These are counted as liberal virtues because they all reach beyond the state of the Christian tradition at any one time to seek the God who is not yet fully known but is believed to be revealed in the whole of creation as well as in the texts and traditions of the faith. These, then, are virtues that cannot be lived out within any closed community but require trans-traditional conversation. To that extent they cohere with liberalism's desire to emphasize the commonalities of human experience rather than the differences between traditions. But they do not entail the superseding of tradition-specific insight – indeed they cannot since they are themselves virtues with their own historical, geographical and cultural roots and, as I want to suggest, they have a genealogy through which their roots in Christian theology can be traced. The point is not that Christian virtues should be distinctive in the sense that no one outside the faith can embody them. Rather, the test is whether such virtues are authentically derived from specific Christian themes and doctrines – then one may ask whether similar virtues may also be derived from other traditions and narratives. Thus, in a dialogic encounter with others, Christians may seek moral agreements which extend beyond their own faith community but which do not compromise their authentic theological out-look. And, to return to questions of morals and markets, if sub-stantial moral agreement turns out to be possible, the premise that concepts like distributional justice necessarily entail coer-cion in a plural context cease to carry weight, and the rationale for markets must be made on other grounds (which may in turn be challenged!). Because Christian activists, apologists and theologians have given insufficient attention to the 'markets vs coercion' argument, much Christian challenge to the global economy has been too easily dismissed for being caught on the horns of that dilemma. Post-liberal approaches, rejecting the attempt to transcend tradition while continuing to espouse 'liberal' virtues, help to reveal the dilemma as a false one.

An important way into a post-liberal theological position is through what the sociologist Richard Sennett calls 'the dangerous pronoun' – we. As he puts it, 'a place becomes a community when people use the pronoun "we"'.[9] This is not the facile communitarian 'we' defined by utter agreement on fundamental narratives of identity, but more like MacIntyre's notion of a 'tradition in good order' which consists in an ongoing argument about what it might mean to belong in that tradition. In other words, as Sennett notes, conflict, in which people are forced to listen to each other and struggle towards resolution, is a stronger form of bonding than consensus. The point is that liberal normlessness and confessionalism's indifference to the 'other' both miss this insight, by seeing conflict either as deviant or as irrelevant to primary questions of identity. There is an important theological angle to this, brought out by Peter Selby when he dissects Bonhoeffer's question 'Who is Jesus Christ for us today?' into three component parts: Who am I? (the question of identity), Who is 'us'? (the question of solidarity) and Whose tomorrow will it be? (the question of discernment).[10] Thus, Selby gives us a theological tool for expressing human solidarities through the concept of 'us' in a way that is wider than both atomized individualism and the communitarian unity that relies upon the absence of significant difference, and yet, because governed by the doctrine of a God who takes sides, is tighter than liberalism's universalism. Underpinning this solidarity is the understanding of mutual need, which Sennett sees as severely eroded by the patterns of contemporary capitalism and which MacIntyre calls 'the virtue of acknowledged dependence'.[11] In other words, post-liberalism's attempt to maintain the possibility that moral dialogue can lead to limited moral agreements is both challenging to the market norm and yet well grounded in a philosophical, sociological and, ultimately, theological understanding of what it means to be human.

Virtues grounded in theology

But the case that the liberal virtues are authentically derived from basic Christian narratives still needs strengthening. The case for tolerance is especially pressing as the rise of fundamentalism and intolerance within world faiths conveys the impression that religions are at their most authentic when at their least tolerant. Ian Markham has offered a number of theological arguments in support of tolerance, of which the most striking is the proposition that, because the world appears to have been deliberately made ambiguous and contingent, God actively desires freedom and dialogue. Markham also argues that, as human sinfulness affects the Church, we should not too quickly conflate the Church as it is with the Church as it is called to be (a tendency in Radical Orthodoxy), and that since God alone saves, humanity must tolerate difference rather than presume to identify the saved and the damned. While some of Markham's arguments for tolerance can be juxtaposed with others, also from sound Christian sources, pointing in the other direction, he at least establishes that toleration has as much claim to be an authentic Christian virtue as exclusivism.[12]

The historical reluctance of the churches to engage critically with structures of governance and economics is hard to justify in the light of the Old Testament's continual concern for right social ordering and the New Testament's stress on the relief of suffering. To those who justify Christ's acts of healing only as signs of the coming Kingdom rather than social amelioration, one must ask why structural change in governance and economics in pursuit of greater justice cannot also be portents of God's post-eschaton intentions. The onus is on those who dispute the Christian vocation to social improvement to justify their position theologically when the 'plain meaning of scripture' points so consistently in the other direction.

Some 'liberal' virtues, however, must be kept in tension with other strands in classic Christian theology if they are not to become unbalanced. The focus on the incarnation, for instance, highlights an important truth – that the Christ, who 'did not abhor the Virgin's womb', hallowed the material world by his presence within it. But push that doctrine too far and it risks obscuring the fallen nature of the created order which Christ came to redeem. Here, the 'both–and' nature of classic Christian doctrine becomes very clear. The world is good in God's eyes, but not (yet) the embodiment of God's goodness in its complete-ness. The Kingdom of Heaven is inaugurated among us in Christ, yet not to be seen in its fullness until the eschaton. Christians are called to be citizens of the finite material world, and yet citizens also of the Kingdom that awaits them. However, in retreating from what it perceives as degenerate liberalism, Christian theology in the West has tended to neglect this 'both–and' principle. This aspect of classic Christian doctrine is itself a powerful argument for toleration and dialogue across differences, for an emphasis on one strand of doctrine can obscure another equally authentic theme. Thus, one might argue, the stress on incarnational theology over-reached itself and required the corrective emphasis on atonement and salvation; but that trend may itself have gone too far, requiring a re-examination of the claims of the incarnation in forming our understanding of God's relationship with the finite material world.

More problematical, perhaps, is the commitment to absolute truth which, in a relativistic age, seems strangely elusive. With-out some foundational belief in objective truth, dialogue becomes extraordinarily difficult since the claims of evidence collapse and there are no criteria to distinguish 'your' truth from 'mine'. One might see the current strife in the USA between Darwinism and Creationism as a case study in the difficulty of finding moral agreement where trust in objective truth and evidence-based argument has evaporated.[13] For believers in God, the question revolves around the concept of natural theo-logy – can humanity gain understandings of God through the common experience of being human and not solely through faith-specific scriptures and traditions? The arguments for (and against) natural theology require more space than is available here, but there is a serious case to be made that Christian orthodoxy points in that direction. As Alan Suggate points out, the Bible endorses natural morality on four grounds: the image of God in humanity persists after the Fall; the Gentiles know certain moral norms through the exercise of conscience; St John argues that judgement falls upon those who flout the moral order which God has set up for the world; and redeemed humanity is transformed and renewed rather than totally remade.[14] All these themes point to the idea that God's truth – which, of course, is absolute truth – is approachable by all human beings, and this provides common ground on which the specific self-revelation of God in Christ can work its salvific effects. More than that, Suggate's arguments also make a powerful case in support of the possibility of moral agreement, since they suggest that Christians should be looking for their God to be discovered in other people.

Choosing dialogue partners

So it is possible to justify key liberal virtues on the basis of authentic Christian doctrines without succumbing to the hubristic claim that the particularity of traditions is thereby transcended. That opens the way to the search for moral agreement about issues like economic justice without implying Christian authoritarianism or neglecting Christian doctrines in favour of secular reason alone. But one final point deserves consideration: in the dialogic search for moral agreement, who are the potential dialogue partners? One of the greatest problems of the liberal tradition has been that its desire to embrace everyone has prevented it from giving a convincing account of why some beliefs and practices (fascism, racism, sexism, apartheid) are beyond the liberal pale. Does the pursuit of liberal virtue, even when detached from the aspiration to transcend tradition, in fact degenerate into a value-free zone of facile tolerance and relativism?

Once one treats liberalism as one tradition among others, however, it is absolved from its requirement to be in dialogue with all comers, no matter how illiberal they may be. A tradition may legitimately develop criteria for deciding with whom, and on what terms, it is prepared to enter dialogue. Possible criteria for dialogue might be: a commitment to objective truth at some level; commitment to the possibility of new knowledge rather than treating any particular state of human understanding as complete for all time, and commitment to seek improvement in the world's affairs. The Christian may, like Selby, draw on the idea that God takes sides about whose the future may be, and then get down to the hard graft of seeking to discern who, among potential dialogue partners, has God so favoured.

All these criteria have, as I have tried to show, authentic roots in Christian doctrine, but they can, potentially, be shared equally authentically by some who start from beliefs and narratives rooted elsewhere. That is not to present the tautologous argument that dialogue in search of moral agreement can only take place between those who already agree. Dialogue partners may share basic criteria for dialogue but for different reasons, grounded in very different traditions. Moral agreements achieved on these grounds are far from negligible.

What, then, is the significance of the post-liberal approach for the churches' engagement with economic issues? First, it challenges us to move beyond the discredited and hubristic manifestations of liberalism while avoiding the problems of confessional authoritarianism. It leads us into a process of moral dialogue which is robustly justified in terms of Christian doctrine and yet emphasizes the doctrinal case for seeking agreement beyond the household of faith. In so far as the search for moral agreement on economic justice bears fruit, it undermines one of the key 'moral' arguments for the market economy and frees us from the dilemma of either conceding the necessity and ubiquity of markets or appealing to covertly coercive politics.

Post-liberal approaches to theology thus free the Church to make a genuinely theological – and potentially effective –

engagement with a global market economy which presents itself as the only show in town. Where liberalism shared too many common assumptions to damage that claim, and confessional theologies often fail to address the ills that markets seek to ameliorate, post-liberal thinking, which detaches liberal virtues from the discredited claim to universality and treats liberalism as one tradition among many, opens the way to wide agreement about the nature and shape of real human prosperity, and the purposes to which prosperity may be turned.

Notes

1 The project is worked out in MacIntyre's three books: *After Virtue: A Study in Moral Theory*, London, Duckworth, 2nd edn, 1985; *Whose Justice? Which Rationality?*, London, Duckworth, 1988; and *Three Rival Versions of Moral Enquiry: Encyclopaedia, Genealogy, Tradition*, London, Duckworth, 1990.

2 See: Michael Novak, *The Spirit of Democratic Capitalism*, London, Institute of Economic Affairs Health and Welfare Unit, 1991, and Ronald Preston, *Religion and the Ambiguities of Capitalism*, London, SCM Press, 1991.

3 Ronald Preston, *Church and Society in the Late Twentieth Century: The Economic and Political Task*, London, SCM Press, 1983, p. 47.

4 D. Stephen Long, *Divine Economy: Theology and the Market*, London and New York, Routledge, 2000.

5 Donald B. Kraybill, 'Amish economics: the interface of religious values and economic interests', in Donald A. Hay and Alan Kreider (eds), *Christianity and the Culture of Economics*, Cardiff, University of Wales Press, 2001, pp. 76–90.

6 Ulrich Duchrow, *Global Economy: A Confessional Issue for the Churches*, Geneva, WCC, 1987.

7 This is not to decry the need for human affairs to be well managed. However, the growth of managerialism as a belief in the ubiquity of certain techniques (such as the recruitment of managers and techniques from private-sector commerce to run not-for-profit organizations like the National Health Service or education) has done much to obscure the particular wisdom and virtues inherent in structures which exist for very different ends.

8 Jeffrey Stout, *Ethics After Babel: The Language of Morals and Their Discontents*, Boston, Beacon, 1988.

9 Richard Sennett, *The Corrosion of Character: The Personal Consequences of Work in the New Capitalism*, New York & London, W. W. Norton, 1998, p. 137.

10 Peter Selby, *Grace and Mortgage: The Language of Faith and the Debt of the World*, London, Darton, Longman and Todd, 1997.

11 Sennett, *The Corrosion of Character*, p. 139f.; Alasdair MacIntyre, *Dependent, Rational Animals*, London, Duckworth, 1999.

12 Ian Markham, *Plurality and Christian Ethics*, Cambridge, Cambridge University Press, 1994, pp. 178–183.

13 Nevertheless, the semi-covert presentation of creationist arguments under the guise of 'Intelligent Design' suggests that evidence-based theories of knowledge are too entrenched to be confronted head-on by those who understand truth to be culturally – and religiously – particular.

14 Alan Suggate, *William Temple and Christian Social Ethics Today*, Edinburgh, T & T Clark, 1987, pp. 218–19.

4. On Not Traducing Economics

IAN STEEDMAN

In recent works John Atherton (1992, 2003) has encouraged those of goodwill not to be unduly hostile towards the workings of the economy, or indeed towards economics; and he has urged them to adopt a non-grudging acceptance of the positive arguments for the market economy. His pleas are not otiose since there is a long tradition, among those with warm hearts, of suspicion or downright hostility towards the market and all its works. Such hostility is not shared by the contributors to *Prosperity with a Purpose: Exploring the Ethics of Affluence* (CTBI, 2005), who adopt a generally positive, if questioning, stance with respect to the market economy and to the reasonings of economists, as does Rabbi Sacks in *The Dignity of Difference* (2005) and as do Edmund Newell and Sabina Alkire in their recent essay (2006). There is still far to go, however, before such a stance becomes general among those of goodwill and many misunderstandings, overt or (more dangerously) unspoken, of the economy and of economics continue to be widespread. The present essay seeks to continue the work of Atherton, the contributors to *Prosperity with a Purpose*, Rabbi Sacks, Newell and Alkire and others, by facing head-on certain common misunderstandings/misrepresentations of mainstream *micro*-economic theory, which deals with the fundamental theory of the economic actions of individuals and which is often traduced, wittingly or unwittingly, by non-economists. It is important to remove such misunderstandings from well-meaning commentary on economic affairs, both because understanding and truth are intrinsically better than misunderstanding and falsity and, more instrumentally, because the elimination of misguided criticism clears the way for the creation and successful communication of justified criticism. It will certainly not be implied by what follows that micro-economic theory is immune to criticism – it is not. The point is, rather, that incompetent criticism is, at best, a sheer waste of everyone's time. (Note that we focus on criticism/misunderstanding of economic theory, not on that of actual economies – and that we offer no support to any who misuse economic theory in promoting particular political or social agendas.)

Selfish? Hedonist? Asocial?

Ill-informed objections to economic reasoning strongly suggest, over and over again, that such reasoning is based on the assumption(s) that individual agents are necessarily completely selfish; and/or that they are pure hedonists; and/or that they care only about physical goods and services; and/or that they are completely asocial atoms devoid of any social relations or awareness. All such suggestions are, quite simply, *false*.

That falsity was demonstrated – clearly and at length – in 1910 when P. H. Wicksteed published his *Common Sense of Political Economy*. As Lionel (later Lord) Robbins put it in his introduction to the 1933 reprint of that work:

> Before Wicksteed wrote, it was still possible for intelligent men to give countenance to the belief that the whole structure of Economics depends upon the assumption of a world of economic men, each actuated by egocentric or hedonistic motives. For anyone who has read the *Common Sense*, the expression of such a view is no longer consistent with intellectual honesty. Wicksteed shattered this misconception once and for all. (p. xxi)

Quite so. (Readers are encouraged to discover for themselves, by studying the *Common Sense*, how Wicksteed carried out that 'shattering' by a brilliant combination of abstract reasoning and numerous, vivid concrete examples.)

When discussing consumer demand, the conventional economic theorist does assume that, at any given time, the individual consumer can say of any two bundles of goods and services that they are equally acceptable to the consumer in question or that, say, the first bundle would be preferred to the second. Pointed questions can indeed be asked about this assumption but it *cannot* be responsibly said that it presupposes selfishness on the part of the consumer. The bundles of commodities involved may very well include food for the consumer's children, gifts for the consumer's parents, the water supply in a particular African village, . . . The consumer's preferences as between bundles of consumption commodities may well embody views and attitudes relating to the kinds of work that have to be done to produce them, or relating to the implications of their current production for future resource and environmental conditions and hence the wellbeing of future generations. Does the presence of such concerns for distant workers, children, parents, friends, great grandchildren . . . necessarily cause problems for the economists' assumption that the consumer has 'preferences' over alternative bundles of commodities? Not in the least. Any claim to the effect that basic economic theory has to presuppose universal selfishness is just ignorant.

The above reference to bundles of goods and services might appear, at first glance, to concede that consumers are assumed at least to be materialistic, even if not only on their own behalf. Any such appearance would be deceptive. No physical good is wanted *for itself*. An analgesic may be wanted in order to procure the absence of a headache, a book may be wanted to make possible the pleasure of reading, a particular foodstuff may be wanted to enhance a child's health, a fur coat may be wanted to send a social message, etc., but it is not the analgesic, the book, the foodstuff or the fur coat that is wanted per se. They are all simply *means* to more subtle ends, perhaps cultural and/or social in nature. Consumer preferences need no more be assumed to be essentially materialistic than they need to be taken to be inherently selfish.

Does the economic theorist have to assume that the individual consumer is an asocial, isolated atom, a feral creature? Not in the least – or perhaps one should say, 'quite to the contrary'. A feral creature might prefer food to no food, or water to thirst, of course – but a P. D. James novel to an Agatha Christie? A fine wine to a bottle of plonk (or vice versa)? A Premium Bond to a private health insurance policy? Many preferences of consumers are *inherently* socially-informed preferences, preferences the consumer could not have, or even conceive of, outside some social framework. And this (banal) truth need never be denied by the economist's basic assumptions.

There are only two possible bases for asserting that micro-economic theory *has* to assume agents to be selfish/hedonistic/materialistic/asocial – they are dishonesty and (more common no doubt) ignorance. Neither basis is respectable. (Economic theorizing is sometimes based on the assumption of, say, selfishness; the point made is only that it does not have to be.)

Explaining preferences?

While the above mentioned criticisms of micro-economic theory can – and should – be dismissed out of hand, some other objections to the economic theorist's treatment of preferences merit a more measured response. Critics often object that economists simply take consumer's preferences to be given (at any particular time) whereas those preferences ought to be treated as endogenous and ought to be explained.

Now economic theorists do not always take preferences to be exogenous. There are specialized bodies of economic literature within which an individual's preferences are taken to depend explicitly on the consumption levels of other agents; or within which an individual's preferences now are taken to depend on *that* individual's past consumption levels. To that extent, the criticism that economic theory always presupposes exogenous preferences is simply ill-informed. Yet it cannot just be ignored, in so far as the specialized studies referred to here form the exception rather than the rule; it is certainly quite common for theorists to take preferences as exogenous.

Some economists have indeed defended such an approach, claiming that whatever psychology, anthropology, sociology, sociobiology, etc. may have to say about why agents' preferences are what they are, those preferences can properly be regarded as exogenous by the economist, since they are not affected by the workings of the economy. That is, of course, a substantive claim, open to rejection. Other economists would be more cautious, accepting that economic activities and outcomes may influence preferences but claiming that, in general, it is simply not possible to say anything at all definite about *how* preferences depend on the workings of the economy. Their defence of the given preferences assumption would thus be only the weak one that they do not know how to replace it with something better.

Well-intentioned critics of economic theory may not be too impressed by the hardline defence of the exogenous preferences assumption. The softer, 'it's the best we can do' defence, however, might give them pause for thought, since the only worthwhile way of rejecting it would be to show how something better can be done. 'Show' in some detail and with some precision, that is; vague phrase-mongering would not constitute a meaningful rejection of the soft defence. If some way forward can be demonstrated, however, that will be a significant contribution to economic reasoning and ought to be welcomed by economic theorists; constructive critics please step forward.

(A general and explicit account of how the workings of the economy influence what people want might well embarrass that part of economic theorizing that takes people's given preferences as the criteria in terms of which the performance of the economy is assessed. But we cannot pursue this delicate matter here.)

The zero-sum fallacy

A fundamental failure to understand economic theory is manifested each time it is suggested – or taken for granted – that in an economic exchange one person's gain must necessarily be the other person's loss. It is quite true, of course, that if some vicious, razor-wielding footpad relieves you of your wallet then her gain is indeed your loss. That transaction is, however, involuntary on your part, whereas one of the characteristic, defining features of an economic exchange is that both parties enter into it voluntarily. (See further below.) Both the buyer and the seller *choose* to engage in the exchange despite being free to refrain from doing so – and why would the agents freely choose to engage in an exchange if they did not each consider it to be advantageous? When agents freely choose to exchange (buy and sell) they *both* gain. The idea that one must be gaining at the other's expense is just plain silly when the supposed loser is free not to engage in the transaction at all; the putative loser would simply walk away and refuse the transaction. (Of course, the *extent* to which each party gains will naturally depend on the price at which the transaction is carried out. But that does nothing to alter the fact that if they transact at an agreed price then they have both gained.)

A common reason for failing to acknowledge that both parties gain from an exchange freely entered into, takes the form of pretending that one party is not in fact exchanging voluntarily but is forced by circumstances to make the exchange. It is certainly true that the worse are, for example, my general circumstances then the more ready I may be to sell my house for a price lower than any I would accept if better placed; or to sell my labour time for a wage lower than any I would accept if I were more wealthy, more healthy, better trained, etc. But this truth does nothing to alter the fact that if I agree, for example, to sell my house cheaply because I need to move quickly, I am still choosing to sell it, rather than not do so, because I gain by so doing. It may sometimes be right to protest about the circumstances within which certain agents make their choices;

it is idle, even disingenuous, to pretend that they are not choosing.

Lending and borrowing at interest

One particular – and common – form of the zero-sum fallacy, of the idea that one person's gain must always be another's loss, is found in the idea that if money is lent at a positive (real) rate of interest, then the lenders must be gaining and the borrowers losing; that the lenders are gaining at the expense of the borrowers. The rebuttal of this (pervasive) misunderstanding is essentially the same as that in the previous section. If borrowers would, in their judgement(s) be better off not borrowing, why do they borrow? No one is forcing them to do so. They borrow, rather than not, because they consider that they gain by doing so. (Just as lenders lend, rather than not, because they consider that they gain by doing so.)

Yet it may still be felt (wrongly) that there is some intrinsic difference between the lending/borrowing case and the buying/selling case. More specifically, it may be felt (wrongly) that the lender of, say, £1,000 today who gets back £1,050 in one year's time has gained £50 (5 per cent) in return for doing nothing for/giving nothing to the borrower. To see why any such feeling is misguided, it is helpful to begin by noting that few people want money for its own sake; it is merely a means of purchasing food, clothing, avant-garde literature, etc. It is therefore better not to think in terms of money but, rather, in terms of lending and borrowing, say, tons of rice.

Suppose, then, that I lend you today 100 tons of rice on condition that in one year's time you will give me 105 tons of rice (of the same quality). Why might you choose to engage in such an (inter-temporal) exchange? It could be that, in the absence of this exchange, you would have at your disposal, for example, *no* tons of rice now and 200 tons in one year's time. If you enter the exchange you will have 100 tons available now and 95 (200 – 105) tons available a year hence. And it is entirely plausible that you will *prefer* the time sequence (100 tons, 95 tons), in the presence of the exchange, to the sequence (0 tons, 200 tons), in its absence. You are thus made better off by borrowing from me at 5 per cent. I have *not* gained at your expense; the exchange benefits both of us. (It is true that the *extent* to which each of us gains depends on the rate of interest but we do both gain – otherwise the transaction would not take place.)

More fundamentally, the reason why lending and borrowing occurs at a positive (real) rate of interest is that, in general, individuals do not, today, place an equal value upon an extra unit of rice, say, today and an extra unit of rice one year hence. Hence it is an illusion to suppose that borrowers must be losing if they pay 1.05 units a year hence in order to have 1 unit at their disposal now. Quite to the contrary, in fact, if they place the same value on 1 unit now and, say, 1.08 units a year hence.

It is simply an error to suppose that lenders must be gaining at the expense of borrowers.

Costs and choices

To the warm-hearted but ill-informed it often seems that economists mechanically reduce everything to a matter of money costs, showing no appreciation of values or of inviolable ethical principles. The truth is quite different. Like anyone else, economists may find it a useful shorthand to refer to the cost of something as £X billion, or as £7.49; but for them this is *only* shorthand and, fundamentally, their concept of cost has nothing whatever to do with money. Everyday language gives voice to that concept in such statements as 'The battle was won – but only at the cost of 7,000 lives', or 'She obtained her external B.A. degree in Sanskrit – but only at a considerable cost to her social life.' For the economist, the cost of obtaining some desired thing is another desired thing that must be given up, must be sacrificed in order to obtain that first thing. This has nothing to do with money in any significant sense. It has to do with making choices, hard choices, among valued alternatives. (Here, of course, we link back to preferences, which express the agent's comparative valuation of alternatives.)

On Not Traducing Economics

Once properly understood, the economists' concept of cost is seen to be of fundamental importance. It involves the clear-sighted recognition that, as Isaiah Berlin emphasized, good things can come into conflict and hard choices sometimes have to be made. Any refusal to face this unpleasant truth is not an index of superior virtue but an indicator of intellectual and moral irresponsibility. And it must be said, unfortunately, that the dislike of economic reasoning on the part of the warm-hearted sometimes springs from a reluctance to face up to this truth. It is easy to claim that curing some particular disease is more important than saving money; it is much harder to insist that effecting that cure is more important than eradicating some other disease, or than extending adult education, or than relieving poverty. It is a simple fact that resources of various kinds are limited and that, with the best will in the world, we cannot do everything worth doing. Economics is sometimes disliked for the simple reason that it will not brush these things under the carpet, will not let people get away with easy talk, with naïve slogans.

It is ironic that the traducing of the economic concept of cost, as being merely concerned with money, is often associated with suggesting that economic reasoning is inherently inimical to ethical concerns. In truth, the economic concept of cost, with its built-in recognition that good things can come into conflict and that painful choices sometimes have to be made, can play a perfectly proper – indeed necessary – role within ethical reasoning. It is not the practice of thinking in terms of real cost that is dangerous for ethical thought; it is the practice of descending to such slogans as 'this end must be pursued irrespective of money cost.' (The fact that the results of a careful cost-benefit analysis are sometimes expressed, in summary form, as, say, £Z billion is to be regretted, since it may provoke – albeit without justifying – such slogans.)

Production and distribution

The warm-hearted are ready to speak eloquently of the distribution and the redistribution of income – yet are often strangely reticent about the creation of that which is to be (re-)distributed. They thereby both adopt an irresponsible position and wilfully shut their eyes to some elementary lessons from economic reasoning. For income is not just 'there', like manna from heaven, awaiting its distribution; income is only output, or production under another name – and that which has not been produced cannot be distributed. That is merely definitional (albeit not to be forgotten). The income distribution/output linkage lies deeper, however. Production is carried out in part because agents have an economic incentive to carry it out, an incentive that depends on what they receive, on what is distributed to them. Hence what is produced, what is available for distribution, is not independent of distribution. Which is why it is so irresponsible to speak only of distribution and re-distribution, as if production (output) could simply be taken for granted. It cannot.

In drawing attention to the fact that agents may respond to material incentives, economic theory does not imply that nothing else motivates them, or even that such other motivations are of secondary importance; it asserts only that material incentives can have an effect and cannot intelligently be ignored. Why is it that the well-meaning sometimes appear to denigrate material incentives or responses to them? Do they believe (wrongly) that a response to a material incentive can only come from an agent with crudely materialist goals and purposes? Do they imagine (wrongly) that to recognize the role of such incentives is, *ipso facto,* to be unaware of other motivations?

Competition and co-operation

It is not uncommon for critics of the market and/or of economic theory to extol the virtues of co-operation and to decry the vices of competition. In seeking to assess such emphases, one may note, first, that the implied antithesis is partly spurious. Just as the members of a sports team (are supposed to) co-operate with one another for the precise purpose of competing with other teams, so the partners, or managers, or other employees in a business firm (are supposed to) co-operate for the very purpose of competing against other firms. (Reality can be more complicated, of course, with some employees being driven largely by the desire to sabotage any proposal made by certain of their colleagues – just like some Anglican clergy.) Thus co-operation and competition are not simple contradictories; the latter can even presuppose elements of the former.

Would it nevertheless be plausible to suggest that, in economic life at least, there should *only* be co-operation and no competition? Even if one sets aside plausible ethical arguments to the effect that competition is an inevitable expression of the *desirable* features of freedom, initiative and creativity, the answer is negative. Whatever may be the shortcomings of market processes, it remains true that I can go to a shop at almost any time and purchase, say, half a kilo of long-grain rice. The people who grew that rice, or produced the rice-grower's fertilizer, or made the equipment to produce that fertilizer, . . . were not merely unaware that I would decide to purchase long-grain rice at the precise time and place in question. None of them even knew that I exist. Nevertheless, competitive activity led to the rice being available to me. This example, which can be paralleled many millions of times over every day, is of course trivial; but the point it makes is not. Market processes effect a solution to the truly enormous co-ordination problem of co-ordinating the production and consumption activities of billions of individuals who, with few exceptions, know nothing of each other. It must now be asked: What system of pure worldwide co-operation would be able to co-ordinate billions of people and their myriad economic activities better than (or even as well as) the market? Pointing to the market's shortcomings would do *nothing* towards answering that vital question, it need hardly be said. Those who would eliminate economic competition have the duty to show, concretely and in detail, what would be its superior (or even equally good) replacement. To extol co-operation and denounce competition in general whilst not carrying out that duty is to engage in empty, morally reprehensible posturing. (There is, of course, nothing wrong in the modest activity of asking pointed questions about the effects of competition.)

As noted above, co-operation and competition are not in fact entirely antithetical – and co-operation is not what economists usually counterpose to competition. In the early 1970s the world economy was thrown into turmoil and millions of people suffered disruption to their employment and/or the value of their savings. Why? Because a number of petroleum exporting countries agreed to stop competing with each other and to *start co-operating*. It was this shift from competition *to* co-operation that caused the suffering. In economic life, co-operation can only too often spell monopoly, the co-operation in question being designed to benefit the co-operators at the expense of everybody else. For economists, the opposite of competition is monopoly – whether in the strict sense of a single seller, or in the looser one of a group of sellers with market power. It would be completely naïve (irresponsible) to suppose that whenever agents co-operate it will necessarily be of benefit to all – it may very well benefit only those co-operating and harm all others. If economic theory tends to favour competition, that is because the alternatives may often be *worse* for most people. (Recognized exceptions, such as the natural monopoly case, cannot be entered into here, for lack of space.) Those who advocate co-operation not competition must explain how the dangers of monopoly would be avoided, as well as showing how the co-ordination problem would be solved. Or rather – since they will not in fact be able to do that – they should devote their efforts to showing how a strongly competitive system can be led to work without producing its least acceptable effects.

The environment

It needs no emphasis these days that the market process does not automatically handle well all issues relating to the environment. If it costs a firm nothing to release its noxious smoke into the air and, equally, if it costs a household nothing to dump its old refrigerator in the nearby river, then neither the firm nor the household has a direct economic incentive to refrain from such polluting activities. They may of course have other motives for so refraining but these motives will not be generated by, or even supported by, market incentives. These issues have long been recognized within conventional micro-economic theory, as has the topic of non-renewable resources.

That the market may not deal well with, say, pollution does not mean that economic theory has nothing to suggest concerning the treatment of environmental problems. Such policy matters as car fuel pricing and taxing, aviation fuel pricing and taxing, taxes encouraging the use of cleaner fuels, carbon emission taxing and permit trading, etc., are all influenced by ideas from economic theory. Environmentalists may insist that such economics-inspired policy measures, even in conjunction with market generated pressures to innovate and to reduce the use of increasingly scarce and thus expensive resources, will not be *sufficient* to safeguard the environment. They may therefore urge that political and communal action is needed to change people's values, preferences and goals, to increase their awareness of a joint responsibility to care for the environment. Be that as it may, there is no good reason to dismiss, or even to play down, the contributions that can be made by economics and economic policy. Perhaps green campaigning alone would not be sufficient either.

Free trade

Since current concerns about and demands for fair trade (ill-defined as that often is) sometimes appear to imply that free trade is *ipso facto* unfair trade, it may be helpful to recall briefly what economists claim – and do *not* claim – about free trade.

It may be noted first that if some politicians assert noisily that other countries must open up their markets to free trade and then, the very next day, proclaim vociferously that their own country must impose tariffs to protect employment in a certain domestic industry, then they are not speaking as economist free traders; they are simply charlatans who employ the rhetoric of free trade when it suits them and immediately forget it when it would not. Their speeches do not show what economists mean by free trade.

By universal free trade the economist means a trading system in which *no* country imposes any tariffs, quotas or other restrictions on trade that would result in discrimination between domestic and foreign suppliers of any good or service. Subject to certain clearly recognized exceptions, it is claimed that such universal free trade is potentially beneficial to all. The word 'potentially' is crucial here; merely removing all tariffs, for example, will lead to some people losing their current employment, which hardly makes them better off. The benefits from free trade, then, are only potential benefits: in less abstract terms, the claim is that universal free trade *combined with* suitable other policies can be beneficial *for everyone*.

This is not the place to explain and justify such a bold claim – that would take far too much space – but it may have been useful to state clearly that the economic theorist's case for free trade is a case concerned for the welfare of all – and that it has nothing to do with cheap debating tricks employed in political rhetoric. Those who campaign for fair trade (however defined) should therefore take care not to make ill-informed attacks on free trade reasoning. (They are naturally welcome to make reasoned and well-informed criticism thereof.)

Concluding remarks

It perhaps bears repetition that nothing said here implies that micro-economic theory is beyond criticism; to reject unsound criticism is not to reject all criticism. Rejection of misunderstanding and/or misrepresentation is important, however, as a complement to the (qualified) positive case for the market being put forward by Atherton, Sacks and others. When the well-intentioned criticize market processes or economic reasoning and suggest improvements/alternatives to them, they must not handicap themselves by wilful ignorance, which can only weaken their case. Thus we have a collective responsibility to expose mis-guided criticism.

Acknowledgements

I wish to thank Stan Metcalfe, Paul Steedman, Hillel Steiner and participants at the Cardiff consultation for comments and encouragement.

Further reading

Atherton, J., *Christianity and the Market*, London, SPCK, 1992.
Atherton, J., *Marginalization*, London, SCM Press, 2003.
CTBI, *Prosperity with a Purpose*, London, CTBI, 2005.
Newell, E. and Alkire, S., 'Capitalism and the Gospel for the Rich', in M. Brierly (ed.), *Public Life and the Place of the Church*, Aldershot, Ashgate, 2006, pp. 113–25.
Sacks, J., *The Dignity of Difference*, London and New York, Continuum, 2005[2002].
Wicksteed, P. H., *The Common Sense of Political Economy*, London, Routledge and Sons, 1933 [1910].

5. Exploring the Paradox of Prosperity: Developing Agendas for Christian Social Ethics and Political Economy

JOHN ATHERTON

At no other time has the keen search for common humanity and a practice that follows. . . . been as imperative and urgent as it is now.[1]

The glory of God is the person fully alive (Irenaeus, AD c.130–c.200).[2]

The paradox of prosperity in global localities: locating the problematic

Globalization, particularly as driven by an emerging global economy, occupies a major if contested part in the debates over likely and preferred directions for political economy in the early twenty-first century. It is an easy bandwagon to jump on or off. What is less obvious, and of greater importance for the future, is the dramatic shift in the relative economic influence of the 'first' and 'third' worlds in 2005. The latter, as the foremost 27 *emerging* economies, were recorded as generating slightly more than half world output (measured at purchasing power parity). It reflects the 'biggest shift in economic strength since the emergence of the US more than a century ago.' In this, it begins to represent a momentous historic swing from the Western

82

world's domination of the nineteenth and twentieth centuries, based on political economy foundations, to a more multipolar world, but equally, to a world in greater continuity with its past. For this rebalancing is 'returning the world to the sort of state that endured throughout most of its history. People forget that, until the late nineteenth century, China and India were the world's two biggest economies and today's "emerging economies" accounted for the bulk of world production.'[3] This locating of current globalization in wider non-Western contemporary and historic contexts is also a reminder, theologically, that recent Western secularization processes' attempts to drive religion from the public square are not shared by the rest of today's world[4] or historically.[5] The current resurgence of what Forrester has described as furious religion outside the West,[6] but increasingly impacting on it, reminds us to take both the changing nature of global economics and religion as key parts of our project. The rise of emerging economies, for example, requires the extending of current dialogues between the Abrahamic faiths of Christianity and Islam over economic affairs to include Hinduism, Sikhism, Buddhism, Confucianism and Shintoism. Max Weber's historic explorations of the relationships between religions and economics interestingly included India and China as well as Protestant Europe. The historic debate, so associated with Weber's *Protestant Ethic and the Spirit of Capitalism*, is necessarily now located in much wider frameworks, including South and East Asia in terms of the great non-Christian religions, but also Latin America and the rise of Pentecostalism, all as a recurrence of the argument linking religion and capitalism.[7]

It is against these wider backcloths that I wish to gradually narrow down to a rather focused enquiry. It is at an early stage of formulation, and so rather speculative but based on the emerging findings of my current research project's study of the relationship between religion and capitalism in today's global context. To do this accurately I need to continue a little further this process of elaborating contemporary contextual complexities. For example, the dramatic increase of global wealth since 1945 was powerfully driven by the West, but the rise of the emerging economies is ensuring that they both increasingly contribute to and share in that production of global wealth. This then raises a profound question for these emerging economies, recently formulated in developed economies, namely the paradox of prosperity – that is, above certain levels of per capita income, increasing prosperity does not result in a commensurate increase in happiness. In other words, it is a question which is now beginning to affect emerging as well as emerged economies, and therefore more and more global localities. It is this thesis which was addressed by the ecumenical report, *Prosperity with a Purpose*, a springboard for this book. Equally important for Christian social ethics and its promotion of human fulfilment is that the pursuit of greater global prosperity has been rightly accompanied by major developments in global poverty reduction. Again, the performance of the emerging economies has been central to this achievement: income poverty in China reduced from 33 per cent of the population (1978) to 7 per cent (1994), and in India from 54 per cent (1978) to 39 per cent (1994).[8] This takes my previous work on marginalization into a new set of questions highlighted by this chapter's pursuit of the paradox of prosperity, itself confirmed and complemented by the requirement to reduce poverty as an essential part of the task of promoting greater human fulfilment. These questions are also located in my current research programme on the relationship between religion and capitalism in our contemporary global context.

It is in the light of these series of overlapping contextual complexities that my particular thesis emerges – essentially an archaeological trench dug in and through these contextual layers, but into a specific problematic: what can we learn from the paradox of prosperity for what it means to pursue human fulfilment? By the paradox of prosperity I refer to the challenge for ethics of increasing prosperity's failure to deliver a commensurate increase either in happiness or a reduction of the poverty of inequality. By problematic, I mean that such a research question is:

- Multifaceted – including the different and varied matters which are suggested by researchers, policy makers and the poor as essential for human flourishing. For example, this includes recognition of the different needs of women in terms of what Sen refers to as capabilities.[9]
- Multidimensional – covering the personal, local, national and international levels, allowing for interpersonal and national comparisons. It is as though we now talk of global individuals in global localities.
- Multicausal – of the matters essential for human flourishing, including their absence, and therefore including explanations of poverty as well as prosperity.
- Multidisciplinary: although my focus will be on Christian social ethics and political economy, I have become increasingly aware, from my own research project, of the relevance to such tasks as addressing human fulfilment and poverty, and so why some are rich and some are poor, of a variety of other disciplines including psychology, physiology, genetics, anthropology, evolutionary biology and history.

Explorations in Christian anthropology: a faithful pursuit of human flourishing

The problematic

This exploration of human flourishing is informed by the entry point of work on happiness as the paradox of prosperity. It is therefore a strong multi- and interdisciplinary exercise, both of which will feature in the rest of this chapter. For example, as the multidisciplinary task, a variety of disciplines are addressing this research including Layard's (LSE) and Oswald's (Warwick) material on happiness relating to economics, Halpern (Cambridge) on life satisfaction to sociology (with Veenhoven, Rotterdam), and affluence and wellbeing to economic history (Offer, Oxford). I will then link these to Sen (economics), Nusssbaum (philosophy), Finnis (jurisprudence) and Alkire (theology).[10] Towards the end of this section and conclusion, the nature and implications of the interdisciplinary task in the sense of the interaction of disciplines, and the nature and role of theology in it, will figure prominently.

Against such a complex backcloth I will explore the research question: what can we learn from the paradox of prosperity for what it means to pursue human fulfilment? It is a topic central to Christian belief with its commitment to human flourishing in all its fullness – what I have described as the human and divine imperative inspired and required by the Christ-like God who 'came that they may have life and have it more abundantly' (John 10.10). Given such a commitment, my argument develops through three stages: first, a brief study of happiness as the paradox of prosperity including its connection with poverty reduction; second, a brief multidisciplinary exploration of human flourishing as it emerges from the paradox of prosperity; and third, a reflection on the nature and role of the theological task in the development of an interdisciplinary promotion of human flourishing.

1 From happiness to human flourishing. A study in overlapping consensuses

For the economist Layard,[11] the task is to maximize the sum of human wellbeing through promoting happiness – essentially defined as a continuum from feeling good in contrast to feeling bad. I will use the continuum tool later in my reformulation of Christian social ethics. His research on happiness suggests:

- Since the 1970s in the US and UK, happiness figures indicate barely no change in happiness despite a doubling of living standards.[12]
- Yet 'at any time within any community there is a clear relation between happiness and income.'[13]

This suggests that above a certain level of income, any increase in prosperity is unlikely to generate an equivalent increase in happiness: 'That is the challenge and the paradox.'[14]

This conclusion is confirmed and elaborated by international comparisons, and by my observation that the income of $15,000–18,000 per annum takes us across the related fields of happiness and poverty reduction. For example:

- Layard concludes that once a nation's per capita income is over $15,000, then the level of happiness is independent of rising income – in other words, the paradox of prosperity kicks in. However, and here we link to the poverty reduction challenge, below that level there is a clear impact of income on happiness: 'When you are near the bread-line, income really does matter.'[15]
- Above $15,000, the pursuit of happiness no longer links closely to income enhancement, but other factors (already present) become more influential. These will be examined later.
- An adequate happiness income of $15,000 is essential, but below this, for the poor, income becomes even more important, as Maslow and Herzberg in organization and development theory (O & D) and behavioural psychology reminded us years ago. I will briefly elaborate this connection, both because I am interested in the creative potential of identifying and encouraging such connections, and because, nearly 40 years ago, I came across this O & D theory work in my industrial chaplaincy work with ICI plants in Manchester, as part of their attempts to reformulate their business activities in more ethically productive directions. Interestingly, this has strong links to Peter Heslam's chapter on the transformational potential of business, and reinforces the importance of the business organization, as institutional capital, for economic and human wellbeing. When considering such O & D work, it is particularly informative to observe how Maslow, for example, argued for a hierarchy of needs, from (1) physiological and (2) safety, to (3) belongingness, (4) aesthetics, (5) learning and discovery, (6) esteem, (7) self-actualization and (8) transcendence. Like Herzberg, he is clear that before social interactions and personal development can occur

effectively, people must first satisfy the more basic requirements of safety and security, particularly in terms of basic
fair incomes, what Herzberg refers to as 'hygiene factors'. So
Herzberg argues that these 'lower' activities (say a basic fair
wage) demotivate by their absence rather that motivate by
their presence. So increasing financial rewards above that
level may not increase motivation. As we will soon see, this
earlier work strongly connects to the current happiness and
life satisfaction research.[16]

So pursuing the connection between the $15,000 income
in the happiness research, and the occurrence of such a figure
in the poverty research, and using approximate figures only,
I have observed that:

1 In developed economies, I note how the base line of
   $15,000 for experiencing the paradox of prosperity *also*
   links to recognized official relative poverty levels in the
   USA (Federal Poverty level for family of four) of $18,400,
   and in the UK, $17,500.[17]
2 In the poorest economies, absolute poverty is estimated
   at $1 per day, or $365 per annum. 1.3 billion globally
   currently live at this level. This indicates the sheer size of
   the task facing poverty reduction, and the distance to go
   before the paradox of prosperity problematic kicks in for a
   third of the world's population.
3 Importantly, the UN Development Programme's Human
   Development Index (HDI), much influenced by Sen's work
   on human capabilities, addresses both the pursuit of human
   flourishing and the reduction of poverty, and usefully,
   therefore, works across emerged, emerging and poorest
   economies. This index focuses on income/work, health
   (longevity) and years in education. Again, this links to the
   discussion above on Maslow, etc. and the following
   reflection on the features of happiness and human flourishing.

2 What is a multidiscplinary human flourishing?

Having recognized the paradoxical problem of increasing prosperity yet not increasing happiness, we can identify features of what it means to pursue human fulfilment drawing from a series of overlapping fields, disciplines and contributions – and in particular, the work of Layard on happiness; Halpern on life satisfaction; and Sen, Nussbaum and Alkire (and Finnis) on human capabilities, as shown in Table 1.

In the first column are the elements essential for the pursuit of happiness as human flourishing today, drawn from Layard (*Happiness*) and the World Values Survey of Life Satisfaction. The second column uses Finnis's list of capabilities for human flourishing (1994), as developed by Alkire (*Valuing Freedoms*) comparing Sen's list as the base with Nussbaum's, as part of a series of comparative tables drawn from 39 different tables, including Narayan's survey across continents, based on the voices of the poor, *Can anyone hear us?* Interestingly, S. Huntington's features of national identity is also remarkably similar.[18]

It is the overlap between the different arenas in Table 1 which suggests the basis for the possibility of a shared view of human fulfilment or flourishing (in conjunction, for example, with O & D and identity lists).

3 What is the nature and role of Christian social ethics in the development of an interdisciplinary promotion of human flourishing?

The overlapping consensus developed above as multidisciplinary understandings of human flourishing also confirms theology's relevance to and importance for that task. Alkire's theology, and Finnis's jurisprudence and Roman Catholic moral theology as a reformulated natural law, provides a rich source of material for developing the theological contribution to such an interdisciplinary task. More importantly, the two human profiles in the happiness and capabilities research

Table 1. Happiness and human values

Layard	*Finnis*
Income (basic minimum) Health	Bodily life (health, vigour, safety)
Work (as against unemployment)	Skilful performance in work and play
Private life (including family, marriage, friends and neighbours)	Friendship or sociability (between persons in various forms and strength, including marriage and neighbours)
Freedom, political, personal, economic	Knowledge (of reality, including aesthetic). Practical reasonableness (harmony between one's feelings and judgements)
Philosophy of life (including religion: 'people who believe in God are happier'[19])	Transcendence, religion/ harmony with the widest reaches and most 'ultimate source of all reality including meaning and value.' Alkire, *Valuing Freedoms*, p. 48.

elaborated above *both* recognize the importance of a philosophy of life, including a religious recognition of transcendence, for human fulfilment. Faithful living can therefore be seen to contribute significantly to life satisfaction. Yet that potential for interdisciplinary commitment does not *in itself* exhaust the rich texture of the theological contribution to human flourishing in terms of the integrity and distinctive character of a relatively autonomous discipline. An elaboration of this is now essential, not least because of the requirements imposed by the contextual complexities noted at the beginning of this chapter. By this I mean that an adequate consideration of the religious contribution to human fulfilment today has to be located in the global debates about furious religion, and the British and American debates about the contribution of faith communities to social capital. The latter includes the increasing research pressure from the William Temple Foundation's current research to recognize *religious* capital as a distinct and unique entity.[20] It is the elaboration in brief outline of this corpus of knowledge of what theology contributes to human flourishing that needs attempting now, and in two stages: the contribution to human flourishing in Christian tradition, and a model able to incorporate both what this tradition shares with others and what is unique to it.

First, the foundational importance of the human in biblical and Christian tradition is centred on the belief in the image of God in human beings. For Irenaeus, of seminal formative importance in the early tradition, 'The glory of God is the person fully alive', for 'this Word was manifested when the Word of God was made man, assimilating himself to man and man to himself, that by means of his resemblance to the Son, man might become precious to the Father.'[21] That commitment to the human is developed in a variety of Christian traditions from Orthodoxy to Anglicanism. For example, the latter affirms the foundational importance for Christian belief of a participating God[22] so that Christ's participation in the human through the incarnation invites and resources (through the Spirit) the human's participation in the Godhead. It is a belief also rooted in Anglican liturgy, in the collect for the first Sunday after Christmas: 'Almighty God, who wonderfully created us in your own image and yet more wonderfully restored us through your son Jesus Christ: grant that, as he came to share in our humanity, so we may share the life of his divinity . . .' Yet, in terms of developing tradition, for David Jenkins, Director of the Humanum Research Project of the World Council of Churches in 1970 and then of the William Temple Foundation, these seminal faith reflections on what God has done through Christ in and for and with the human, are 'ultimately concerned not with the Christian doctrine of man but with the fulfilment of all men in the love of God and of one another.'[23] In other words, here lies *both* the nature and justification of Christian participation in the wider multidisciplinary developments noted above of what it means to pursue human flourishing (as the role of faith in the interdisciplinary task) *and also* the recognition that theological integrity includes and contributes a distinctive or unique, certainly very different from the secular, understanding of and commitment to what Christian human flourishing means. For example, the distinction between what Christians share with others and what they hold which is different, can be briefly elaborated with regard to an important theme in contemporary economic philosophy. Interestingly, both Milton Friedman and Amartya Sen, Nobel Prizewinners in Economics, focus on the importance of freedom for human wellbeing. This also links to the presence of freedom in Layard's list of features necessary for the effective pursuit of happiness. For Friedman, in his *Free to Choose*,[24] the freedom to choose provided by the mechanism of the free market is in stark opposition to government-state controls in the economy (leading therefore, for Hayek to the thesis of *The Road to Selfdom*).[25] The free market is therefore integral to human development. For Sen's *Development as Freedom*, freedom is the goal of development, requiring the provision and encouragement of basic capabilities, like the HDI's health, education and income, for human functioning in terms of enabling people to pursue their self-chosen purposes. Yet for Christian belief, these necessary features of what it means to be human, to pursue human fulfilment effectively, although rightly related intrinsically to the pursuit of freedom, are located intrinsically and inextricably to the pursuit of the good in God. It is recognition of the importance of a teleological view of ethics in critical conversation with a deontological view. Importantly, this both connects with the neo-Thomist understandings in Finnis's reformulation of natural law and Nussbaum's Artistotelianism and her links with Sen, but also with the Radical Orthodoxy interpretation of economics by Long.[26] It is this understanding of freedom which therefore attains its fulfilment in the worship and service of God. In itself, it is both gift and obligation, a paradox captured beautifully in the second collect for peace, in Anglican Morning Prayer, which prays that God 'who art the author of peace and lover of concord, in knowledge of whom standeth our eternal life, whose *service is perfect freedom* . . . ' It maybe takes such a faith paradox to engage that paradox of prosperity which is so intimately rooted in economic processes. This is not least of course, because the Christian commitment to human flourishing also recognizes the question of finitude and sin,[27] of the limits placed on human endeavour, of the profound dependency of the human as well as its glorious ability to strive to transcend its limits. This then leads into the central role of redemption in human flourishing, and what I will later argue for in terms of the Christian understanding of transformation, but especially as transfiguration. It becomes both affirmation of the liberal tradition's commitment to the interdisciplinary pursuit of human flourishing, and a recognition that we also now inhabit a post-liberal tradition with its increasing engagement with the realities of human frailty and its location within the wider reality of divine redemption.

When we examine this *added value* of theology's contribution to the interdisciplinary task of promoting human flourishing, this richer fullness must be both recognized and properly accounted for. In other words, in Christian tradition (as past and present) the task becomes how can we best interact theology and overlapping disciplines for the human flourishing task in ways which respect *both* the interdisciplinary requirements *and* the distinctive theological identity?

Second, therefore, I have begun to explore a model for doing this, drawn from the tradition of contemporary Christian social ethics, which is described in the literature as *Christ and culture in synthesis* (one of five historic models for relating *Christ and Culture*,[28] in Niebuhr's classic text of that name). For Niebuhr, this model has particular value and relevance for our task of developing a theological contribution to human flourishing which is both interdisciplinary and distinctive. A brief exposition of this model, using Niebuhr, illustrates these claims:

1 Christ is 'the fulfilment of cultural aspirations and the restorer of the institutions of a true society' (p. 42). So, given the end in God, Aquinas, best exemplar of this model, can 'reconcile the efforts of men direct in their practical life and noncontemplative societies toward the attainment of ordinary ends, such as health, justice, knowledge of temporal realities, economic goods.' (p. 132) This justifies Christian co-operation with other disciplines in the human fulfilment task.

2 Yet in Christ, there is also that 'something that neither arises out of culture nor contributes directly to it. He is discontinuous with social life and its culture' (p. 42). Therefore, as we seek the end of human flourishing, this lies beyond the gifts of culture, and 'in eternity, for which all striving is an inadequate preparation. The attainment of that ultimate happiness is not within the range of human possibilities, but is freely bestowed on men by God through Jesus Christ' (pp. 132–3).

3 Christ and culture in synthesis is therefore the recognition of *both* the overlapping and the unique in Christianity: 'The synthesist alone seems to provide for willing and intelligent cooperation of Christians with non-believers in carrying on the work of the world, while yet maintaining the distinctiveness of Christian faith and life . . . There is always the *more* and the *other*; there is always "all this and heaven too", and for the true synthesist the *more* is not an afterthought, as it so often seems to be to the cultural Christian' (pp. 143–4) (what Wogaman has described as the dominant mainstream liberal tradition of Christian social ethics[29]).

It is this model which I now find particularly appropriate for the task of Christian social ethics in this project, because:

1 like Aquinas, it is essential for faith to engage constructively with contemporary philosophy – in Aquinas's case, Aristotelianism (transmitted through Islam); in my case, with Layard, Sen and Nussbaum as key contemporary contributors to the multidisciplinary engagement with human flourishing.
2 like Alkire, there is likely to be some value in considering Finnis's work on jurisprudence, and as moral theologian, in reformulating natural law (note the link with Jewish and Muslim legal traditions in theology, particularly important for addressing economics from a faith's perspective), in conversation with Nussbaum and Sen (again, note the Aristotelian link).
3 It recognizes the importance of the interdisciplinary but also of the distinctive added value of Christianity by locating human flourishing teleologically in God through Christ (the basis of the 'more' and 'the other' of faith as uniqueness and its implications for the human engagement in the worship and service of God).

Equally clearly, however, the model itself needs to be reformulated in relationship to contemporary understandings and needs, including facing up to its substantial limitations. For example, the relationship in faith between overlapping and unique needs to be a profoundly interactive one, as a dynamic continuing process, and not as generating a once-for-all synthesis, itself so often in history productive of static and hierarchical orderings. Similarly, Radical Orthodoxy needs correcting, as a contemporary furious Western theology using neo-Thomism in Long's work on economics, because it replaces the interaction of interdisciplinary and unique with the uniqueness of out-narrating the other narratives. Other related implications for Christian social ethics of this reformulated model are examined next.

On pursuing more ethically sustainable economics: concluding note

Much of what emerges from this study confirms what other contributors to this book have discovered. For example, the nature and significance of the multidisciplinary and interdisciplinary task is becoming more central to our theological work, as is the growing prominence of global localities. Yet this exploration of the paradox of prosperity has also generated particular implications for Christian social ethics and political economy.

The key such finding is that Christian social ethics, a Cinderella discipline in theology, is justifiably given a new lease of life by, for and in the contemporary context. When addressing any global problematic, including the paradox of prosperity and its relationship to poverty reduction, the most profound ethical questions are raised and will be increasingly central to the development of adequate solutions. Layard therefore argues for ethics to occupy a prominent place in the education process to support this. Sen's promotion of ethical economics is also strongly substantiated by this conclusion. The contribution of Christian social ethics to these wider tasks is therefore of some importance, which is why the following findings may be of some interest.

First is the potential value of the reformulation of a 'Christ and culture in synthesis' model in the discipline of Christian social ethics for particularly addressing problematics in such contemporary complexities as we now inhabit. Its appropriateness is confirmed by its commitment to working with overlaps between Christian and secular, but also with the distinctively different of faith, connecting both with the partnership skills required by global problematics and with the global reformulation of religion. It can play, among other things, a bridge-building role. Second, this model has an important additional value in connecting Christian social ethics (as faith tradition) with ecclesiology (as faith community) – that is they together provide ways of being and doing Church in today's public arena. It is a linkage between doing ethics and being Church, central to Roman Catholic and Anglican moral theology[30] (and to Islamic theology). In reflecting on this wider task of ways of relating faith communities (as churches) and their traditions to economic affairs, I have begun to work with a *continuum* or spectrum of Christian involvements in the public arena in contemporary contexts. This encompasses:

- *From overlapping consensuses*: that is, Christians co-operating with others (faiths, government, business, civil society) in the promotion of policies that Christian beliefs can justify. For example, Christian support for pro-poor economic growth policies locally, nationally and internationally, reflects the connection in Christian tradition between ethics and ecclesiology focused, for example, on St Paul's arguments for the body of Christ as model for the Church, and by implication for society. The contribution of the equally valued different parts to the whole, and therefore, particularly the weakest, provides an enduring paradigm for a bias to inclusivity, and its assertion that a commitment to the common good of all inevitably requires a commitment to ensuring the marginalized are empowered to participate fully in the whole.[31]
- *To promoting practices that are distinctively different from mainstream consensuses*, and embody unique Christian/ religious understandings in contemporary contexts as both *critiques* of and *alternatives* to mainstream consensuses (including in economics and its domination by the neoclassical tradition). For example, the arguments of Jubilee 2000 for debt forgiveness, and of Radical Orthodoxy and Islam for interest-free financial systems, relates also to the local church and mosque and their involvement in developing alternative political economies, for example as elaborated in Chris Baker's chapter. Another Manchester example is provided by an extended conversation between Christians and Muslims and a professional economist, resulting in an agreed statement on *Faiths and Finance: A Place for Faith-Based Economics*.

Now the development of a reformulated Christ and culture in synthesis model suggests adding to that spectrum another type standing between, and more importantly *interacting* with, the overlapping and distinctively different types. It recognizes that an adequate church type must now be engaged *both* in faith-based overlapping *and* the distinctively different. Essentially, it is therefore a *hybrid* type (see Chris Baker's chapter) and, in terms of my current research programme lends itself particularly to my thesis of the transfiguration of capitalism. (By this I mean taking seriously the contemporary materiality of capitalism in terms of its strengths, but because of its limitations, moving beyond it into a reformulated and more ethically sustainable political economy, but never also losing a purchase on its existing realities. It is therefore a continuing process of moving through and beyond, through and beyond. And this model is deeply rooted in Gospel accounts of Jesus' transfiguration (particularly in Mark 9.2–8), itself foretaste of his great redemptive acts, and therefore providing a key model for the theory and practice of contemporary Christian social ethics.)

This hybrid model is strongly post-liberal and post-modern, yet critically engages with changing global religious contexts in terms of the interactions between international furious religion and national religious capital. It is also particularly useful because the important collaboration of Christians and Muslims (as Abrahamic faiths) on distinctively religious economics is now embraced by the hybrid type, which however, also allows for that essential dialogue to be complemented by engaging with non-Abrahamic faiths rooted in India, China and the other Asian emerging economies with which this chapter began. This is a strong embodiment of developing Christian social ethics as an *ecumenical* discipline in the tradition of *Prosperity with a Purpose*, but now also evolving into interfaith social ethics. This development becomes essential in a global context, and for the agenda of Christian social ethics. For example, in the Manchester project on Islamic and Christian perspectives on finance, this required recognizing and promoting what the two

Abrahamic faiths share, but also where they differ, in theory and practice, including local finance schemes for the poor.

In terms of contributing to political economy, this essay on the paradox of prosperity clearly locates conversations with economics as central to the interdisciplinary task. Yet this is not to *restrict* that task, not least because other disciplines have been engaged in the study, but also because this contribution of economics has revealed its breadth and diversity. So Layard and Sen work in relation to the mainstream tradition of neo-classical economics, but engage *critically* with it because of the requirements of a problematic like human flourishing. For this clearly raises issues relating to the breadth of human motivation and choices essentially leading to a search for a wider rationality including more empirically based. Interestingly, Layard's Lionel Robbins Memorial Lectures are also a reminder of LSE's contribution to the scientific positive engineering understanding of economics. Both Layard and Sen are part of the important reformulating of the economic task to reincorporate, reaffirm and reformulate the essential role of ethical rationality in the discipline of economics. Yet for Sen, both ethical and engineering rationality are indispensable to the economic task in relation to such problematics as human flourishing: '(t)here is no scope at all . . . for dissociating the study of (technical) economics from that of ethics and philosophy.'[32] That conversation between ethical and engineering regimes should be strongly encouraged by Christian social ethics in the light of this particular study. It is not about choosing between them, as Ian Steedman has rightly reminded us. It is about restoring and maintaining the balance between them, essentially the manifestation in the discipline of economics of the continuously *interacting syntheses* theme of this conclusion (indeed, this concept describes my reformulation of the Christ and Culture in synthesis model). For when these implications for political economy are increasingly connected to those for Christian social ethics, then it is their cumulative effect which suggests the shared task of promoting more ethically sustainable economies for the twenty-first century.

Notes

1 Z. Bauman, *Community*, Cambridge, Polity, 2001, p. 140.

2 R. Greenwood and H. Burgess, *Power*, London, SPCK, 2005, p. 71.

3 *The Economist*, 21 January 2006.

4 G. Davie, *Europe: the Exceptional Case. Parameters of Faith in the Modern World*, London, Darton, Longman and Todd, 2002.

5 A. Macfarlane, *The Riddle of the Modern World. Of Liberty, Wealth and Equality*, Basingstoke, Palgrave, 2000.

6 D. Forrester, 'The Scope of Public Theology', p. 19, in E. Graham and E. Reed (eds), *The Future of Christian Social Ethics: Essays on the work of Ronald H. Preston, 1913–2001*, London, Continuum, 2004.

7 M. Weber, *The Protestant Ethic and the Spirit of Capitalism*, London, Unwin, 1970. M. Weber, *General Economic History*, London, Macmillan, 1961.

8 J. Atherton, *Marginalization*, London, SCM Press, 2003, p. 75.

9 A. Sen, *Development as Freedom*, Oxford, Oxford University Press, 2001.

10 See R. Layard, *Happiness: Lessons from a New Science*, London, Allen Lane, 2005 (including references to Halpern, Veenhoven, Sen and Nussbaum). J. Finnis, *Natural Law and Natural Rights*, Oxford, Oxford University Press, 2002. S. Alkire, *Valuing Freedoms: Sen's Capability Approach and Poverty Reduction*, Oxford, Oxford University Press, 2002. A. Offer, *The Challenge of Affluence: Self-Control and well-being in the United States and Britain since 1950*, Oxford, Oxford University Press, 2006.

11 R. Layard, Lionel Robbins Memorial Lectures, 2002–03:
- Lecture 1. 'What is Happiness? Are we getting happier?'
- Lecture 2. 'Income and Happiness: rethinking economic policy.'
- Lecture 3. 'How can we make a happier society?'
Available online at <http://cep.lse.ac.uk/events/lectures/layard/RL030303.pdf>

12 R. Layard, *Happiness*, pp. 30–1.

13 Layard, Lecture 1, p. 15.

14 Layard, Lecture 2, p. 3.

15 Layard, Lecture 1, p. 17.

16 See, A. H. Maslow, *Motivation and Personality*, New York, Harper and Row, 1954; F. Herzberg, B. Mausner and B. Snyderman, *The Motivation to Work*, New York, Wiley, 1959; D. McGregor, *The Human Side of Enterprise*, New York, McGraw-Hill, 1960. Also Greenwood and Burgess, *Power*, p. 44 (useful reintroduction for me).

17 *The Economist*, 10 December 2005.

18 Layard, *Happiness*, p. 71; J. Finnis, 'Liberation and Natural Law

Theory', *Mercer Law Review* 45 (1994), pp. 595–604, quoted in Alkire, *Valuing Freedoms*, p. 48; Alkire, *Valuing Freedoms*, p. 110f.; D. Narayan, *Voices of the Poor: Can Anyone Hear Us?* New York, Oxford University Press, 2000; S. Huntington, *Who Are We? America's Great Debate*, London, Simon & Schuster, 2004.

19 Layard, Lecture 3, p. 12.

20 C. Baker and H. Skinner, *Faith in Action: The Dynamic Connection between Spiritual and Religious Capital*, Manchester, William Temple Foundation, 2006.

21 D. Cairns, *The Image of God in Man*, London, Collins, 1973, p. 82.

22 See D. Allchin, *Participation in God: A Forgotten Thread in Anglican Tradition*, London, Darton, Longman and Todd, 1988.

23 D. Jenkins in Cairns, *Image of God in Man*, p. 23.

24 M. & R. Friedman, *Free to Choose*, Harmondsworth, Penguin, 1980.

25 F. Hayek, *The Road to Serfdom*, London, Routledge and Kegan Paul, 1996.

26 D. Long, *Divine Economy: Theology and the Market*, London, Routledge, 2000.

27 C. Insole, *The Politics of Human Frailty*, London, SCM Press, 2004.

28 R. Niebuhr, *Christ and Culture*, New York, Harper and Row, 1951.

29 J. P. Wogaman, *Christian Perspectives on Politics*, London, SCM Press, 1988. J. Atherton, *Social Christianity: A Reader,* London, SPCK, 1994, Introduction.

30 See *Crucible*, October–December 2006, 'Ecumenical Social Ethics'.

31 J. Atherton, *Marginalisation*, pp. 117–22.

32 A. Sen, *On Ethics and Economics*, Oxford, Blackwell, 1987, p. 3.

6. Contours of an Islamic Political Economy

ZAHID HUSSAIN

Introduction

And [remember:] whatever you may give out in riba[1] so that it might increase through [other] people's possessions will bring (you) no increase in the sight of God – whereas all that you give in charity, seeking God's countenance, (will be blessed by Him): for it is they, they (who thus seek His countenance) that shall have their recompense multiplied. (Qur'an 30.39)

We have entered a troubling period in history following the tragic events of September 11 in New York. Since then we have witnessed forced regime change – in Afghanistan and in Iraq – and Muslims have warned of increasing Islamophobia. Despite the increased pressures and heat in the global crucible, many aspects of Islamic thinking have found a new home within the framework of the more liberal West. Among them is the Islamic economic model. This seems at odds with a religion often decried as locked in its own Dark Ages. The Islamic economic model reflects a deep sense of justice and equality that runs parallel with humanized capitalism.

In this essay, I seek to elucidate the key principles of the Islamic economic system and how its holistic approach has verifiable answers for bridging the chasm between rich and poor, reducing the rising tide of world debt and controlling the excesses of a risk-averse private sector. I shall also attempt to elaborate the current global situation vis-à-vis Islamic banking and finance and delineate the size and hue of the Islamic financial system, which is not merely a theoretical, but a growing reality with an 'annual growth of about 10% per year'.[2] This reality, I believe, can bring more prosperity, stability and equality than the current hotchpotch of financial markets, barely controlled by legislation eked out to protect the consumer, the poor and the dispossessed.

Historical context

A shadow has hung over the Muslim world since 1924. Mustafa Kemal Atatürk formally abolished the Muslim Caliphate, six years after the end of World War One. He brought in sweeping changes, exchanging the Arabian Turkish script for a Romanized one and he began the systematic dismantling of the faith foundation of Turkish society. Those Muslim cultures outside the sphere of the Ottoman Empire were colonized by the British, the French and other ex-colonial powers and are still rebuilding their lands, redetermining their role and collective destinies in the world.

If, for instance, we observe the Pakistani legal system, it is British and Victorian in sense and sensibility. The language of the Pakistani military is English, not Urdu, Sindhi, Pushto, Punjabi, Balauchi or Chitrali or any of the other languages or dialects spoken in Pakistan. Algerians are raised effectively bilingual. In Algeria, one cannot be considered educated unless one speaks 'La langue de l'Hexagon' (The French refer to France as the Hexagon – its shape vaguely resembles one).

So, entering the twenty-first century, many Muslims would acknowledge that no Muslim country has fully implemented a modern Islamic political economy. Saudis claim that their penal system is Shari'a[3] compliant, but many Muslims would argue otherwise.

As Muslim nations stutter into the twenty-first century, it is apparent that many elements of an Islamic political economy are non-existent. However, this has changed markedly over the last decade or so, but the foundations, theoretical and spiritual, remain and Muslims are rapidly reasserting their faith. In 1969, following an arson attack against the Al-Aqsa Mosque, Muslim states established the OIC (the Organization of the Islamic Conference). It took the unprecedented step of setting up the Islamic Development Bank (IDB) in 1973. Since then, Islamic financial institutions have gone from strength to strength.

Theory: foundation of the Islamic economy

Central to framing the contours of an Islamic political economy is the understanding that according to the Qur'an wealth in all its forms is created by God, and therefore ultimately His property. A person's right is a privilege granted by God:

> Give to them from the property of Allah which he has bestowed upon you. (Qur'an 24.33)

Human beings merely invest their labour into the production and distribution processes and God is the lone cause that makes such endeavour productive.

> Have you considered what you till? Is it you yourselves who make it grow, or is it We who make it grow? (Qur'an 56.3)

According to Islam, there lies a covenant between human beings and God. The Qur'an and Hadith[4] describe how Muslims should use wealth. However, even though God is seen as the One who truly owns wealth, the participants in the wealth production process have a right to the fortune they earn, but there are social and spiritual obligations – human beings are forbidden to use wealth to bring disorder and destruction on the earth. This social obligation is underlined by obligatory alms giving – one of Islam's five pillars. Annually, Muslims must donate 2.5 per cent of their accrued wealth (not income) to charity.

Wealth is a grave test in Islam: Muslims strive to pass this test by using it in ways God has permitted. In fact, a rich man need not ride a camel through an eye of a needle to enter Paradise: he may do so if he meets his obligations and a pauper may enter Hell by not meeting his.

> Seek the other world by means of what Allah has bestowed upon you, and do not be negligent about your share in this world. And do good as Allah has done good by you, and do not seek to spread disorder on the earth. (Qur'an 28.77)

This verse underlines the Islamic point of view on wealth: its production, distribution, consumption and disposal:

- All human wealth belongs to God.
- Humanity's objective is to use wealth in such a manner as to seek a greater purpose in the afterlife.
- Human beings should not spread disorder on the earth.

The Qur'an is clear that human beings have no absolute and unconditional right over property, because it is believed this would lead to disorder on the earth. Islam encourages a *via media*, which provides social support as well as personal freedoms and privileges. The rich have duties to the poor and they in turn are bound by contentment and equal respect for others. Private ownership is permitted with conditions. However, Islam also determines that wealth should be distributed to everyone as equally as possible. It ensures this by making it clear that everyone has a right to wealth whether they participated in the production of it or not.

In Islam, there are two kinds of people who have a right to wealth:

1 Those with a primary right – those who have directly participated in the production process.
2 Those who have a secondary right – those who have not directly participated in the production process.

In their wealth there is a known right for those who ask for it and those who have need for it. (Qur'an 70.24–25)

The word 'right' makes it clear that participation in the production process is not the sole source of the right to wealth. Islam proposes that those who have taken a part in production receive the reward for their contribution as well as those who God has stated have a right to that share also. The distribution of wealth is necessary to ensure everyone receives his or her rightful share. Allah has made it obligatory on producers of wealth to distribute a portion of their wealth and the Qur'an makes it explicit that in doing so they would not be obliging the poor and the needy in any way – but discharging their own responsibilities.

The global financial system is not a purely capitalist system, with social security and other humanitarian elements bracing the financial infrastructure. However, in many respects these are tweaks to a complex system that inherently reflects inequalities. For example, although Europe enjoys a superlative social security system in comparison to other world nations, there are massive inequalities in terms of the high tariffs and restrictions enforced on developing countries. The Western world hides the source of its wealth: the continued slavery of much of the world.

The third Pillar of Islam: alms-giving

Narrated Anas bin Malik:
While we were sitting with the Prophet in the mosque, a man came riding on a camel . . . The man . . . said, 'I ask you by Allah. Has Allah ordered you to take Zakat (obligatory charity) from our rich people and distribute it amongst our poor people?' The Prophet replied, 'By Allah, yes.' (Hadith: Sahih Al-Bukhari 1.3.6)

Islam seeks social justice and equality through the provision of the third pillar of Islam, Zakah. The Arabic word Zakah means to purify or cleanse. Zakah is obligatory for all those who are financially able and is a key component of Islam's welfare system which redistributes wealth in order to achieve social justice. Muslims must, as an article of faith, pay Zakah. To refuse to pay Zakah is tantamount to war against the Lord. As instructed in the Qur'an:

> The alms are only for the poor and the needy, for those who collect them, for those whose hearts are to be reconciled, for the freedom of those who are captives and in debt, for the cause of Allah, and for the wayfarers; [it is] a duty imposed by Allah. Allah is the Knower, the Wise. (Qur'an 9.60)

Muslims believe that Zakah leads to many outcomes:

- It purifies the heart against greed, selfishness and coveting the wealth of others.
- It instils brotherhood in society.
- It leads towards the eradication of poverty and its related economic, social, and moral problems.

Zakah is due annually on certain types of property and distributed as specified by the Qur'an to the poor, orphans, travellers, beggars, debtors, slaves and efforts to propagate Islam. Zakah is payable at different rates on crops, harvests, herds, gold, silver and merchandise. Relatives may receive the Zakah if they are poor and need help. However, one cannot donate Zakah to one's immediate family, because it is one's duty to take care of them first.

The payment of Zakah is based on Nisaab, which is the minimum wealth an individual must possess before they are liable to pay Zakah. Whoever reaches Nisaab in excess of their essential needs and remains in possession of it for a year is liable to pay Zakah. The Nisaab amount is equivalent to 85g of pure gold and is currently valued at approximately £840.

The matter of interest

> Those who devour usury will not stand except as stands one
> whom the Evil One by his touch hath driven to madness.
> That is because they say: 'Trade is like usury', but Allah
> hath permitted trade and forbidden usury. Those who after
> receiving direction from their Lord desist shall be pardoned
> for the past; their case is for Allah (to judge); but those who
> repeat (the offence) are companions of the fire: they will
> abide therein (for ever). (Qur'an 2.275)

This Qur'anic injunction is perhaps further reinforced with this:

> If ye do it not take notice of war from Allah and his Apostle:
> but if ye turn back ye shall have your capital sums; deal not
> unjustly and ye shall not be dealt with unjustly. (Qur'an
> 2.279)

For Muslims therefore, the issue of Riba is not contestable. It is
a grievous sin to take it, to deal in it, to prosper from it.
However, Riba cannot easily be translated into English, despite
its common translation as usury.

> Narrated 'Umar bin Al-Khattab: Allah's Apostle said:
> The bartering of gold for silver is Riba, (usury), except if it is
> from hand to hand and equal in amount, and wheat grain for
> wheat grain is usury except if it is from hand to hand and
> equal in amount, and dates for dates is usury except if it is
> from hand to hand and equal in amount, and barley for
> barley is usury except if it is from hand to hand and equal in
> amount. (Hadith: Sahih Al-Bukhari 3.34.344)

This is further elaborated in the following traditions:

> Narrated Abu Salih Az Zaiyat, I heard Abu Said Al-Khudri
> saying:
> The selling of a Dinar for a Dinar, and a Dirham for a Dirham

(is permissible). I said to him, 'Ibn 'Abbas does not say the same.' Abu Said replied, 'I asked Ibn 'Abbas whether he had heard it from the Prophet or seen it in the Holy Book.' Ibn 'Abbas replied, 'I do not claim that, and you know Allah's Apostle better than I, but Usama informed me that the Prophet had said, 'There is no Riba (in money exchange) except when it is not done from hand to hand (i.e. when there is delay in payment).' (Hadith: Sahih Al-Bukhari 3.34.386)

Narrated Abu Said Al Khudri and Abu Huraira, Allah's Apostle employed someone as a governor at Khaibar. When the man came to Medina, he brought with him dates called Janib. The Prophet asked him, 'Are all the dates of Khaibar of this kind?' The man replied, '(No), we exchange two Sa's of bad dates for one Sa of this kind of dates (i.e. Janib), or exchange three Sa's for two.' On that, the Prophet said, 'Don't do so, as it is a kind of usury (Riba) but sell the dates of inferior quality for money, and then buy Janib with the money'. The Prophet said the same thing about dates sold by weight. (Hadith: Sahih Al-Bukhari 3.38.499)

An Islamic political economy

Islam delineates the contours of a political economy by:

- establishing clear boundaries and criteria for the production/distribution of wealth;
- making alms-giving obligatory on Muslims who possess a minimum quantity of wealth;
- establishing a Muslim Treasury (bait-al-maal);
- establishing business transactions based on risk sharing;
- forbidding interest (Rib'a);
- forbidding investments based on speculation, illegal activities, alcohol etc.;
- establishing clear and equitable inheritance rights;
- establishing clear and equitable matrimonial rights (dowry).

Following from the essential factors that lay the foundation of an Islamic economic system any Islamic political economic system must:[5]

- work at a grass-roots level to eradicate poverty;
- provide a guaranteed minimum provision for all;
- eradicate monopolies and regional disparities;
- produce goods in a way that is not harmful to God's earth;
- distribute wealth in a fair and equitable way;
- allow personal freedom, but maintain structures that enforce individual responsibility.

Essentially, such a system would have micro- and macro-economic elements that holistically work towards a rational economic base that produces peace, prosperity and sustainability.

Islam does not condone the concentration of wealth in a few hands. Wealth should be circulated as widely as possible, so that the distinction between the rich and the poor is reduced as far as is natural and practicable. No individual or group should have a monopoly over the primary sources of wealth. As the Qur'an elucidates:

> So that this wealth should not become confined only to the rich amongst you. (Qur'an 59.7)

The Islamic sense of justice ensures that all receive their share according to the labour and resources invested by the individual. Any human intervention required for the production of wealth must be given due consideration:

> We have distributed their livelihood among them in worldly life, and have raised some above others in the matter of social degrees, so that some of them may utilise the services of others in their work. (Qur'an 43.32)

Despite social differences in rank, role and status the Qur'an has clarified that such distinctions be kept within limits as is necessary for the establishment of a practicable economic system so that wealth does not become concentrated in a few hands.

Praxis: The size and shape of Islamic finance

The UK and global economies

The United Kingdom, with its large and relatively integrated Muslim communities, has a pivotal role to play not only in the global geopolitical landscape, but also as a bridge for realigning and reasserting a faith-based political economy. It could be mooted that the British Muslim community is in a unique position – it has access to information, networks and social realities that can benefit not only the Islamic world, but other communities as well.

In recent times, there has been a spurt of interest in Islamic banking. The HSBC Bank has launched an Islamic (Shari'a) compliant mortgage product, Amanah Finance, the Islamic Bank of Britain has been established and there are an increasing number of local Islamic finance institutions such as Greater Manchester's Ansar Finance. However, this little revolution has had an effect in other states. In Sweden, the JAK Bank was established and entirely based on zero-interest banking.[6]

In 2004, a minor event took place in the Middle East. The Saudi government permitted the entry of a second mobile phone company to set up base in the kingdom and a consortium of founders converged to raise $2.35 billion for the Ettihad Etisalat Company. This financing was based entirely on Islamic principles.[7] The Eleventh Annual World Islamic Banking Conference in 2004 hailed this as 'the benchmark for Islamic financing deals into the future.'[8]

On 9 June 2006, 'Deutsche Bank, announced a joint venture with Ithmaar Bank of Bahrain and Abraaj Capital of Dubai to launch a $2bn (£1bn) Sharia-compliant financial fund.'[9] In fact, the BBC reported on the same day that: 'Estimates of the value of Islamic banking internationally range from $200bn to $500bn'. This was echoed by Alexander Theocharides, director of Faisal Finance, the Swiss Islamic bank, who stated: 'The volume of Islamic Finance has now reached approximately $500bn'.

In terms of the UK financial markets, in 2005 Datamonitor reported: 'demand for sharia-compliant mortgages was strong, and could yield up to £4.5bn in advances by 2006.'[10]

To elaborate the British situation further there were, according to the International Association of Islamic Banks (IAIB), by 1998:

176 Islamic banks and financial institutions operating in 38 countries. These institutions had total assets of $148 billion, paid up capital of $7.3 billion, and generated $1.2 billion in aggregate net profits in the latest year of operation.

Sir Howard Davies, chairman of the Financial Services Authorities in the UK, said 'there was a gap in the market for retail sector Islamic banking products, which would cater to nearly two million UK Muslims'.

There are approximately 3 million Muslims permanently resident in the UK (i.e. 50% of all UK ethnic minorities) with estimated savings of around £1 billion, while over half a million Muslims visited Britain in 2001, spending nearly £600 million. The 5,000 richest Muslims in the UK have liquid assets of over £3.6 billion, according to wealth analysts' data monitor HSBC, the UK-listed bank, which has £2 billion assets under management and three Islamic funds, is predicting growth of assets under management of up to 40 per cent for year 2002.[11]

However, despite the massive growth in Islamic banking, academics have voiced caution:

The Islamic Banking system is still very new. Its impact, though, has been dramatic. Since its implementation, it is the only system in two major Muslim countries. It can be noted that it has been successful in a number of ways yet has its downfalls especially in terms of the finance area. We feel that with a few minor changes, the system will be able to work very efficiently and effectively. While the idea of interest-free banking may be taboo for Westerners, it fits in well with the religious beliefs held by these Islamic countries. In sum, the story of Islamic finance is a vastly complicated one, and cannot be captured without a full understanding of religion and finance, but also of history, politics, economics, business and culture.[12]

Definitions and technical aspects of Islamic finance

The main categories within Islamic finance are, among many others, *Ijarah*, *Ijarah-wa-iqtina*, *Mudaraba*, *Murabaha* and *Musharaka*.

Ijarah is an agreement lease of an asset to a customer – specified by the customer – for an agreed period against agreed instalments of rental.

An *Ijarah Muntahia Bittamleek* (or *Ijarah-wa-iqtina*) is a form of lease that offers the lessee the option to own the asset at the end of the lease period.

A *Mudaraba* is a contract between the capital provider and an entrepreneur whereby the capital provider contributes capital to an enterprise or activity, which is to be managed by the entrepreneur as the *Mudarib* (or labour provider). Profits are shared in accordance with the terms of the *Mudaraba* agreement. Losses are to borne solely by the capital provider unless the losses are due to the *Mudarib*'s misconduct, negligence or breach.

A *Murabaha* is a sales contract whereby the financial institution agrees to sell an asset to a customer at an agreed profit margin plus cost.

A *Musharaka* is a contract between the financier and a customer to contribute capital to an enterprise, whether existing or new, or to ownership of a real estate or moveable asset on a temporary or permanent basis. Profits generated are shared in accordance with the terms of the *Musharakah* agreement while losses are shared in proportion to each partner's share of capital.

Diminishing Musharaka is a partnership in which one of the partners promises gradually to buy the equity share of the other partner until the title to the equity is completely transferred to the buying partner. The transaction starts with the formation of a partnership after which buying and selling of the equity takes place. The sale/purchase is independent of the partnership contract and should not be stipulated in the contract since the buying partner is only allowed to give a promise to buy.

An example of a British Islamic mortgage

The Ansar Finance Group is an Islamic financial institution based in Manchester. It was established in 1994 to provide and to promote the awareness of Halal financial borrowings and investments among the Muslim community of the UK. It provides an Islamic finance facility, operating within the principles of Islamic Law (Shari'a). Ansar is a membership organization and currently has approximately 1,000 members.

One of its many products includes a mortgage package. This is how it works:

> After a successful application for home finance, the client is authorised to locate and negotiate the purchase of the house that he or she desires. The institution pays cash for the house and obtains legal title in its name and the client contributes his portion of the purchase price under the contract so as to become a partner of Ansar.
>
> The partnership then *leases* the house to the client at an *agreed fixed rental rate* throughout the period of the lease. The individual can *increase his ownership* of the house over a

period of time by purchasing shares in the house from the institution at future times.

During the term of this partnership the individual pays rent for living in the house in proportion to his/her share ownership of the house. The institution's share of the rent goes to the institution and the individual keeps his own.

Ansar Finance stipulates the following:

- Only members of Ansar Personal Loans Ltd may apply.
- Members need to provide at least 20% towards purchase price.
- House ownership shared by member and AHL.
- Contract terms between five and 15 years.
- Residential properties only (no commercial properties).
- AHL finances freeholds and leaseholds.[13]

This can be illustrated as the following:

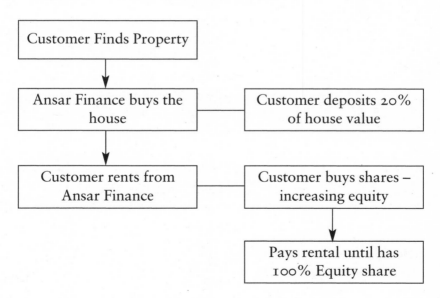

This process is a very commonly used Islamic mortgage product and often cited as an *Ijarah*-based mortgage. *Ijarah* is proving to be the most popular method of Islamic house finance.[14]

The future

We are in the wake of a new Babylon: globalization, multi-faceted, unstoppable, perhaps its essence conveyed most powerfully with one word: internet. There are no boarders in this brave new world, a world that has witnessed the whimpering demise of communism and the lonely figure of the United States straddling the summit of a mountain that reads like a figure of God admonishing the world. Yet, this is not a Babylon, nor will the Burj Tower slowly rising above the skyline of Dubai be Babylon: our world is becoming less multifaceted, cosseted in insularities, its shades of grey diminishing, it is becoming a world of us and them, black and white.

It is paradoxical that despite the ocean of data, communication and information, there appears to be less diversity, less distinction and few alternatives to capitalism. Socialism is considered by many (in the West) to have failed, the communist five-year plans dumped in the scrap heap of history. But there is a viable alternative.

In this essay, I have elucidated the theoretical foundations of an Islamic political economy and sketched the outline of its current size and shape. Islamic finance is a growing phenomenon, not just a reality within Muslim nations, but here in the heart of England. I firmly believe that with Islam's sense of equality, justice and order, it is a tool that can be used by all people, whether they be of faith or not, and help reduce the gaping chasm between rich and poor and increase the accountability of banks.

We live in a world today which holds over 6 billion souls. There are more poor people alive today than ever before, more people will die due to malnutrition than ever before, never before have so few owned so much wealth that so many others lacked – and what is worse, and perhaps intolerable, is that we know. We actually know. But we also have the opportunity to actually choose the world we want to live in.

Let us hope that we can make the right choice.

Notes

1 Riba = Arabic : interest (there is no English equivalent to the word Riba, but it is often, erroneously, translated as usury). Most Muslims believe that all interest is forbidden.

2 Alexander Theocharides, director of Faisal Finance, the first Swiss Islamic bank.

3 Shari'a = Arabic = Divine/Spiritual Law.

4 Hadith = Arabic. Traditions relating to the words and deeds of the Prophet Muhammad (Peace be upon him).

5 M. A. Mannan, *Economic Development and Social Peace in Islam*, London, Ta-Ha Publishers Ltd, 1990.

6 'The case of JAK Bank': <http://www.feasta.org/documents/review2/carrie2.htm>

7 Etihad Etisalat Official Web Site: <http://www.etihadetisalat.com.sa/events.html>

8 Eleventh World Islamic Banking Conference: <http://www.megaevents.net/wibcold/2004/executive_summary.htm>

9 BBC News: <http://news.bbc.co.uk/1/hi/world/middle_east/5064058.stm>

10 BBC News: <http://news.bbc.co.uk/1/hi/business/3548656.stm>

11 Robin Matthews, Issam Tlemsani and Aftab Siddiqui, *Islamic Finance*, Centre for International Business Policy, Kingston Business School, 2002, p. 4.

12 Alyson Schmitz, Troy Stansberry and Leanne Schumacher, *Islamic Banking*, The Creighton University College of Business Administration, 2002.

13 Ansar Finance.

14 Robin Matthews, Issam Tlemsani and Aftab Siddiqui, *Islamic Finance*, Centre for International Business Policy, Kingston Business School, 2002, p. 4.

Further reading

Mohamed Ariff, *Islamic Banking*, Asian-Pacific Economic Literature, 1998.

Abdul Gafoor, *Islamic Banking and Interest-Free Islamic Banking*, 1995.

Abdul Gafoor, *Islamic Banking and Finance: Another Approach*, 1999.

Abdul Azim Islahi, *Economic Concepts of Ibn Taymiyyah*, Leicester, The Islamic Foundation, 1990.

M. A. Mannan, *Economic Development and Social Peace in Islam*, London, Ta-Ha Publishers Ltd, 1990.

Ibrahim Warde, *Islamic Finance in the Global Economy*, Edinburgh, Edinburgh University Press, 2000.

Websites

Islamic Bank of Britain:	<http://www.islamic-bank.com
HSBC Amanah:	<http://www.amanahfinance.hsbc.com/ hsbc/amanah
Ansar Finance Group:	<http://www.ansarfinance.com/
Islamic Development Bank:	<http://www.isdb.org/
Idafa:	<http://www.idafa.com/
Deutsche Bank:	<http://www.db.com/index_e.htm
Abraaj Capital:	<http://www.abraaj.com/english/
Ithmaar Bank:	<http://www.ithmaarbank.com/
Islamic Finance:	<http://www.islamic-finance.com/ indexnew.htm
International Islamic Finance Forum:	<http://www.iiff.net/
Islamic Economics:	<http://islamic-world.net/economics/ index.htm
Islam On-Line:	<http://www.islamonline.net/ english/index.shtml
Muslim Investor:	<http://muslim-investor.com/mi/wealth-in-islam.phtml
Islam's View of Wealth:	<http://www.heramb.org/daniel/ school/islam/wealth.html
IQRA Objects of Wealth Distribution:	<http://ccminc.faithweb.com/iqra/ articles/distrw/04objects.html
BBC News:	<http://news.bbc.co.uk/1/hi/world/ middle_east/5064058.stm

Section 2

The Importance of Difference: Recognizing the Divisions over the Capitalist Market Economy

7. Purposeful Wealth Creation: Eradicating Poverty through Enterprise

PETER S. HESLAM

In 2005, the year that saw the publication *Prosperity with Purpose*, a huge conglomeration of NGOs, campaign groups, trade unions, celebrities, churches and faith groups mobilized under the banner 'Make Poverty History'. While poverty has always been with us, it has never been as high on the agenda of the rich countries as it is today, and much of this is due to the concerted efforts of this movement. For all its strengths, however, the campaign, and the popular sentiments it has engendered, underestimate the potential of business to help in the fight.

After 50 years and more than a trillion dollars spent on international development, between a third and a half of the world's population lives on less than US$2 per day. Yet a flourishing and responsible business sector can deliver the kind of economic growth that lifts people out of poverty.

Business alone is not enough, of course. The campaign rightly stresses the importance of well-targeted aid, debt cancellation and reform of global trading rules. Also needed are the social institutions that characterize free societies, such as property rights and the rule of law, and the cultivation and exercise of virtue beyond the requirements of the law. All these have strong biblical foundations, and provide the context in which business can flourish. But these basic conditions aside, poverty will only be banished long-term through the vigorous growth of enterprise. This has been true for every rich country, and it is true for every poor one now.

Why then is this so often ignored or denied? One reason is the generally suspicious or hostile attitude towards business that is found among the churches, which have played a key role in highlighting the plight of the world's poor. Against this background, this chapter calls for the development of a theology of business that is based on the paradigm of *transformation* rather than on the one that has been used extensively ever since the advent of liberation theology in the 1960s – *liberation*.

Christian attitudes to business

To set this task in a theological framework this chapter will use Richard Niebuhr's characterization, or typology, of Christian perspectives on contemporary culture in his book *Christ and Culture*.[1] Although this typology involves inevitable simplification, it remains a useful analytical tool. For this reason, the Church of England Bishop of Lincoln John Saxbee has referred to Niebuhr's book as 'the key text for studies in religion and culture during the second half of the 20th century'.[2] Stanley Hauerwas, similarly, writes:

> Reinhold Niebuhr may remain better known than H. Richard Niebuhr, but it is arguable that H. Richard Niebuhr's work has had a more lasting impact on contemporary theology. . . . H. Richard Niebuhr published 'only' six books, but his influence on American theology was immense. He became the teacher of teachers who would determine the main directions in theology and ethics in the second half of the twentieth century.[3]

When Niebuhr's typology is applied to attitudes towards business, the following types emerge:

Type One – Christ against business
Type Two – Christ subsumed by business
Type Three – Christ subsumes business
Type Four – Christ and business in paradox
Type Five – Christ transforms business

While there is merit and deficiency in all five of these perspectives, this chapter allows space only for a discussion of the first and last of these types.[4]

Christ against business

With this type, the impact of sin and evil in business is stressed to such an extent that Christ is seen in opposition to business. The only option for Christians is to dissociate themselves as much as possible from the corrupting effects of the business world and focus instead on the new order established by Christ. This attitude has a long history, going back to the Fathers of the early Church and their cultural context.[5] Today it pervades theological reflection, which has been profoundly influenced by liberation theology.[6]

Christ transforming business

With this final type, business is affirmed as an arena of Christ's transformative work. Because it is flawed (along with all other spheres of human society) it is vulnerable to error, perversion and evil. But because it is under God's sovereign rule, human beings have both the capacity and the calling to embody within their work the creative ordering of God. As corrupted good, rather than evil, business needs conversion rather than replacement.

Because of the pervasiveness of Type One in the Church, which coexists with a general antipathy towards business in contemporary culture, it is important that the weaknesses of this type are exposed. Two of these will be given attention before turning to two features that recommend Type Five.

Why Type One will not do

Focus on distribution

In recent years most mainstream churches have produced statements on the economy. While these documents are commend-
able in their solidarity with those in poverty, they generally fail
to give adequate recognition to the fact that, as business is the
means of wealth creation, the market has a key role in the
alleviation of poverty.

Three documents stand out as exceptions to this trend. The
first is one which, though without official ecclesiastical status,
involved crucial input from economists and business leaders as
well as theologians and ethicists: the *Oxford Declaration on
Christian Faith and Economics*. One of its passages reads:

> We recognize that poverty results from and is sustained by
> both constraints on the production of wealth and on the
> inequitable distribution of wealth and income. We acknow-
> ledge the tendency we have had to reduce the causes of
> poverty to one at the expense of the other. We affirm the need
> to analyse and explain the conditions that promote the
> creation of wealth, as well as those that determine the distri-
> bution of wealth.[7]

A second notable exception is the papal encyclical *Centesimus
Annus*, issued in 1991. In it, Pope John Paul II is forthright in
advocating 'a society of free work, of enterprise and of participation' and insists on 'the positive value of the market and
enterprise'.[8] He is even prepared to highlight the advantages
of the free market and provides a qualified endorsement of
capitalism, if by that term is meant 'an economic system
which recognizes the fundamental and positive role of business,
the market, private property and the resulting responsibility
for the means of production, as well as free human creativity
in the economic sector.'[9] In John Paul II's estimation, it is
when poor countries are able to produce goods and services

for the global market that they have the best chance of escaping poverty:

> Even in recent years it was thought that the poorest countries would develop by isolating themselves from the world market and by depending only on their own resources. Recent experience has shown that countries which did this have suffered stagnation and recession, while the countries which experienced development were those which succeeded in taking part in the general interrelated economic activities at the international level. . . . It would appear that, on the level of individual nations and of international relations, the *free market* is the most efficient instrument for utilizing resources and effectively responding to needs.[10]

A third exception is the document in whose wake the current volume has emerged, *Prosperity with a Purpose*. As with the two documents just mentioned, there are plenty of qualifications; its endorsement of the market is by no means absolute. What is significant is that any such endorsement exists in an official Church publication. It clearly wishes to distance itself from the censorious attitudes associated with such statements:

> A purely negative appraisal of economic activity is unacceptable and an injustice to those engaged in it. Economic activity is instead something to celebrate. When it raises the standard of living of the population while relieving the lot of the poor, it is part of God's will for humanity. There is a need to redress a perceived imbalance in the way Christians have regarded the creation of wealth by economic activity. They should recognize that it is one of the chief engines of progress and greater well-being in the modern age, both directly and indirectly; and thank God for it.[11]

Exceptions aside, the general assumption made in Church statements is that the creation of wealth and the mechanisms of production are of little moral importance compared to the inequities of distribution. The ethical demands of distribution cannot, however, be considered in isolation from the ethical demands of production, not least because distribution is dependent on production. Contemporary theologies and spiritualities that seek to identify with the poor and read the gospel through their eyes need to be careful, therefore, not to misunderstand the interests of those in poverty, which include benefiting from the wealth-creating processes of production and not just from more equitable distribution. It is perhaps significant in this regard that a major survey of attitudes to globalization across the world found that support for free markets is higher in many African countries than in the developed world as a whole.[12]

It is remarkable, therefore, how little has changed since the fall of communism; most theology still tends to regard capitalism as a system built on greed, acquisitiveness, materialism, consumerism, economic rationality and individualism. Within this critique, there is little constructive discussion of how theology might apply to the role of business. Developed as it is in isolation from business, most contemporary theology fails to resonate with either business people or people in poverty.

Business theology stifled

Second, the mistrust that inevitably accompanies Type One serves to stifle a full-orbed theology of business. Such mistrust goes back to the early centuries of the Christian Church, but in British society it became a predominant feature of the higher social classes between the two world wars of the twentieth century.[13] To British intellectuals of this period, a career in business was a dull and contemptible way of life. 'Successful business is devastatingly uninteresting' is the way one of C. P. Snow's characters puts it,[14] and C. S. Lewis expressed utter disdain for William Morris (Viscount Nuffield), who as the founding director of the Morris Car Company was Oxford's biggest employer at the time and one of the university's most generous benefactors. In a similar vein, J. B. Priestley and H. G. Wells reproached joint-stock companies, industrialists and financiers.[15] Even children's literature was influenced by this phenomenon.[16]

Against this background it is not surprising that the universities produced no more than a handful of business departments, depriving British companies of relevant expertise. Among those graduating from Cambridge in 1937–8, fewer sons followed their fathers into business than into any other vocation.[17] Business was left to recruit people who had failed to make it into university.[18]

Negative attitudes to business that were shaped between the wars have manifested a die-hard quality. The obituary columns of newspapers have shown a relative disinterest in lives spent in business.[19] When historians refer to William Morris it is generally to the Victorian designer and commentator on art and society, who targeted the rich, rather than his namesake and fellow Oxfordian who sought to make cars for all.[20] Likewise, entries for business people in the monumental 61-volume *Oxford Dictionary of National Biography* are disproportionately fewer than for other major professions.[21]

Few periods have witnessed as much opprobrium towards business, however, as the current one, largely directed at multinationals. National elites have seen these as threats to their rightful authority; conservative populists have condemned them as agents of cosmopolitanism; socialists and anti-globalization protestors have anathematized them as 'the highest stage of capitalism', accusing them of wanton destruction of cultures and ecosystems; extremes on both left and right have blamed them for the loss of Western jobs.[22]

In response, big corporations and business journalists have sought to show how multinationals adapt their products to local taste and how their chief thrust on world markets is for ideas rather than cheap labour. Their concern, they have insisted, is to combine global scale with local knowledge. They have also pointed out that multinationals are considerably less powerful and more socially and environmentally responsible than is maintained by their critics and that they have helped to increase productivity, thereby raising living standards for ordinary people; they should, therefore, despite certain problems related to size, be regarded as a force for good in the world.[23]

It is within this polarized debate that a theology of business has so much to offer, not least because of its potential to affirm what is good and challenge what is bad about business on the grounds of the basic goodness, fallenness and redemption of the created order, as we shall see. Without this double-edged approach, the moral vocation of the business sphere, as distinct from those of the family, education and the state, will not be adequately addressed. This would be a significant failure for the Church, whose mission must include helping the institutions of contemporary life, including business, to find and fulfil their various callings and charisms. As long as it maintains an attitude of contempt or suspicion, the Church will be unable to articulate what it expects of these institutions. It will be left with a mode of theological and ethical discourse of little contemporary relevance.

Why Type Five will do

Whereas Type One will not do, Type Five will do. The choice of words is deliberate. It is not that Type One has to be dismissed entirely. There will always be situations in business in which Christ's 'no!' to sin should be clearly heard. Likewise, 'transformation' is not so all-encompassing that Type Five is the only paradigm with which business can be adequately addressed. It is, rather, one that is badly needed if the Church is to develop a theology of business that makes sense to those in poverty and to those in business. There are two key reasons why this is so.

It takes account of the impact of business

The Latin roots of the word 'company' lie in the two words *cum* and *panis*, which when compounded mean 'breaking bread together'. The word 'corporation', moreover, comes from the Latin *corpus*, which means 'body', and the original meaning of 'commerce' suggested intimacy in communication and relationship, reflected in Shakespeare's use of the term to denote sexual intercourse. These meanings are deeply suggestive of the way in which contemporary business can be a transforming agent in society, helping to build credible, meaningful and inclusive patterns of community. They even suggest that in doing so they manifest a form of sacramentality. This certainly seems in keeping with Pope John Paul II's teaching that the purpose of a business lies in its existence as a 'community of persons' which seeks to serve not only its own needs but those of society.[24] It also corresponds with the experience of many Christian business people, who find that their workplaces provide a relational context for ministry that is deeper and more inclusive than that provided by their local church.

A single example from the past is sufficient to highlight the transformative potential of an inclusive approach to business. Liberation theology assumes that social revolution is the preserve of the economically excluded. And yet the early history of Marks & Spencer suggests that business can be a vehicle of such revolution by way of its inclusiveness. By the mid 1920s, the four brothers-in-law who ran the company had turned it into a major chain of variety stores. At this point they could have retired to a life of leisure. Instead, after visits made by Simon Marks to US retailers in 1924, they decided to re-think the purpose and mission of their business in terms of 'social revolution'. The company would seek to subvert the class structure of Victorian England by making goods of upper-class quality available to the working and lower middle classes, at prices they could easily afford. The focus would be on clothing as, in the England of that time, what people wore was the most visible of class distinctions.

Instead, therefore, of seeing business as the power from which we must be liberated, we could come to hold business in a similar regard to the way we hold our churches, neighbourhoods, voluntary organizations, schools and hospitals. We may even grow to love business, though to do so we would need to take time to understand it and become better acquainted with its opportunities and constraints; it was Augustine of Hippo who wrote: 'You cannot love what you do not know.' To have such love for business would still allow us to find plenty wrong with it. But the attitude of trust that would spring from such love would mean that any judgements and moral demands we were to make would be more likely to be heeded by those in business. Otherwise, as Ronald Cole-Turner writes:

> It is altogether too likely that the church will marginalize itself in the role of chaplain, picking up the pieces, caring for the bruised, mopping up the damage, but never engaging the engines of transformation themselves, steering, persuading and transforming the transformers.[25]

Without developing a transformative theology of business, it is doubtful whether the Church will be able to construct a viable vision for social transformation, as business has become the chief agent of such transformations. It is also the social form distinctive of an increasing amount of co-operative activity outside the family, government and personal friendships. While nation-states have been on the defensive and churches and trade unions have been in decline, business has been gaining in strength. Most people in the West now work in business and business supplies most of the world's products and services.[26] Areas of social life that were once assumed to be public are increasingly regarded as the preserve of business. Given such seismic change, it could be argued that anyone intent on maximizing their social impact would be better pursuing a career in business than running for political office, joining the armed forces or becoming a cleric!

Business is a social institution to which the world is becoming increasingly committed. The biblical message needs, therefore, to be dynamically reconceived in a socio-economic context far removed from those of biblical times – a task that is at least as important to the future of humanity as today's theologies of sexuality and biomedical ethics.[27]

It takes account of the biblical story

A second key advantage of a transformative perspective is that it takes account of the biblical story of creation, fall, redemption and consummation. It is thereby able to avoid extreme positions that either denounce business as irretrievably corrupt or embrace it as synonymous with God's Kingdom. Unlike a liberational perspective, a transformational one advocates the reform, rather than the displacement, of the means of production. The market economy, existing as it does under the sovereignty of God, is fundamentally good rather than bad, and Christians are called to participate in it, to mitigate the effects of the fall, further the effects of redemption and anticipate the coming new order.

A transformative paradigm allows business to be seen, therefore, as one of the foundational spheres of human life that provide the moral and practical framework for human flourishing. This sphere is constituted and shaped, at least in the current era, by market-orientated institutions and practices – in a similar way to which, in the political sphere, at least in high-income countries, democratically oriented institutions and practices are predominant. It should, therefore, be accorded the kind of qualified ethical affirmation given to it in the papal encyclical *Centesimus Annus*, noted earlier in this chapter. This is important because of the potential of business to help extend the Kingdom of God, which is breaking into the created and fallen world through the redeeming work of Christ.

Christian mission and development agencies are slowly waking up to this potential, and some are beginning to encourage business professionals to bring both spiritual and material uplift to needy countries through commercial business activity. This new model of mission reflects the fact that, under the impact of globalization, there has never been a time when so many people in the world have belonged to the same community of work. Business is thereby becoming a transcendent global culture. Through their involvement in it, business missionaries are finding that otherwise impenetrable societies are opening up to the gospel and experiencing increasing prosperity.

Again, this global business culture has great potential for ill as well as for good. It can be used to dominate, exploit and demean, as neo-Marxist post-colonial intellectuals are often swift to point out.[28] The principle of reciprocity must always be maintained, therefore, as a safeguard against abuse. In other words, the transformers need the consent of those whose lives they propose to transform. It is arguable, however, that markets based on free exchange provide a rudimentary form of reciprocity. Many people in poor countries are finding, moreover, that business, though having the potential to exploit, can be a vehicle of social justice, dignity and freedom from oppression. The critical question before us is not, therefore, whether globalization is good or bad but what *kind* of globalization is good? Whether it turns out in practice to be largely good or largely bad depends, at least to some extent, on how radically and creatively business people follow Christ into the global marketplace, seeking to pervade every area of business with his truth, liberty and justice.

For the call to seek first the Kingdom of God (Matthew 6.33) is not just for ministers and professional missionaries, leaving business people merely to support them financially. Rather, in the twenty-first century, business holds a vital key to unlock societies to the freedom and joy of the Kingdom of God. Countries that have closed the door to traditional missionaries are competing with each other to attract professional entrepreneurs who can help grow their economies. Taking the opportunities for mission that are naturally available in commerce is a vital and strategic means of co-operating in God's mission to the world.

This mission involves bringing salvation, healing and *shalom* to every sphere of society. The impact of the Fall is waiting to be undone. Because of the cross and resurrection, evil can be overturned and the scourge of poverty can be addressed. History is replete with examples of how Christians have picked up this challenge – through the political framework of the Roman

Empire, through the invention of the printing press, through even the colonial apparatus, and, most recently, through global business enterprise.

Christian business people working in the global economy are uniquely placed to bring transformation to the circumstances of the world's poor. As they do so, they are ensuring that globalization works as a blessing, rather than as a curse. They are helping to realize globalization's potential to bring social uplift, serve the common good, and even help protect the environment. The economic dogmatisms of liberation theology and of other Type One attitudes have to be set aside for the sake of a rigorous and theologically balanced engagement with the transformative role of business in today's world. Without this, it is not obvious that the Church will have a sufficiently compelling vision to allow it to make a difference in contemporary culture. For a reconstruction of its theology will require a major shift in orientation and tone. But such a reconstruction is an important first step in making poverty history.

Notes

1 Richard Niebuhr, *Christ and Culture*, New York: HarperCollins, 2002 [1951].

2 *Church Times*, 28 May 2004.

3 Stanley Hauerwas, 'H. Richard Niebuhr' in David F. Ford with Rachel Muers (eds), *The Modern Theologians: An Introduction to Christian Theology Since 1918*, 3rd edn, Oxford, Blackwell, 2005, pp. 194–203 (pp. 194–5). For a more detailed account of Niebuhr's impact, see William Werpehowski, *American Protestant Ethics and the Legacy of H. Richard Niebuhr*, Washington, Georgetown University Press, 2003. Notable critiques of Niebuhr's scheme include Peter R. Gathje, 'A Contested Classic: Critics Ask: Whose Christ? Which Culture? – Christ and Culture', in *Christian Century*, 19 June 2002, available online at <www.findarticles.com>; George Marsden, 'Christianity and Cultures: Transforming Niebuhr's Categories' in *Insights: The Faculty Journal of Austin Seminary*, Fall 1999, available at <www.religion-online.org>; John Howard Yoder, 'How H Richard Niebuhr Reasoned: A Critique of Christ and Culture', in Glen H. Stassen, D. M. Yeager and John Howard Yoder (eds), *Authentic Transformation: A New Vision of Christ and Culture*, Nashville, Abingdon, 1996, pp. 31–89.

4 For fuller applications of Niebuhr's scheme to economic institutions, see Ronald Preston, *Religion and the Persistence of Capitalism*, London, SCM Press, 1979, pp. 7–9; David Krueger, *The Business Corporation and Productive Justice*, Nashville, Abingdon Press, 1997, pp. 30–4; Louke van Wensveen Siker, 'Christ and Business: A Typology for Christian Business Ethics', *Journal of Business Ethics* 8 (1989), pp. 883–8.

5 For an exposition and evaluation of the key teachings on wealth and poverty of the patristic period, see Peter S. Heslam, 'Can Christianity Give a Positive Value to Wealth? An Engagement with the Early Church Fathers' at <www.transformingbusiness.net>.

6 See, for example, Timothy Gorringe, 'The Principalities and Powers: A Framework for Thinking about Globalization' in Peter S. Heslam (ed.), *Globalization and the Good*, London, SPCK, 2004, pp. 79–91. Many theologians influenced by feminist and Radical Orthodox theology conform to this type. See, for instance, Cynthia Moe-Lobeda, 'Offering Resistance to Globalization: Insights from Luther' in *Globalization and the Good*, pp. 95–104.

7 The declaration was first published in *Transformation* (April/June 1990), pp. 1–8. It was later published, with analysis and comment, in Herbert Schlossberg, Vinay Samuel and Ronald J. Sider (eds), *Christianity and Economics in the Post-Cold War Era: The Oxford Declaration and Beyond*, Grand Rapids, Eerdmans, 1994 and in Max L. Stackhouse, Dennis P. McCann and Shirley J. Roels (eds), *On Moral Business: Classical and Contemporary Resources for Ethics in Economic Life*, Grand Rapids, Eerdmans, 1995, pp. 472–82. The citation is from section 36.

8 *Centesimus Annus*, sections 43 and 35.

9 *Centesimus Annus*, sections 40 and 42.

10 *Centesimus Annus*, sections 33 and 34. It is important to re-emphasize that John Paul II's endorsement of the free market is not unqualified and he reserves a strong role for the state in regulating the economy.

11 *Prosperity with a Purpose: Christians and the Ethics of Affluence*, London, CTBI, 2005, pp. 15–16.

12 Taking all the countries surveyed, support for free-market economic systems is greater in high-income rather than low-income countries, but only marginally so (66% compared to 63%). Nigeria (80%) and the Ivory Coast (79%) were the developing countries showing the greatest support in Africa. Vietnam (90%) showed the greatest support overall. See The Pew Global Attitudes Project, *Views of a Changing Word*, 2003, pp. 103–5 (<www.people-press.org>).

13 Precedents can, however, be found in the Victorian novel. See, for

instance, the prejudice expressed towards those involved in trade in Elizabeth Gaskell's novel *North and South* 2 vols, London, Chapman & Hall, 1855. The heroine, Margaret Hale, attempts to defend John Thornton, a wealthy manufacturer, against the snobbery of her mother but unwittingly her words are full of irony: 'And as for Mr Thornton being in trade, why he can't help that now, poor fellow. I don't suppose his education would fit him for much else' (I, 114 – in Chapter IX). See also George Eliot's Mr Bulstrode, the 'evangelical' though hypocritical banker in *Middlemarch* (1871–73).

14 See C. P. Snow's *The Masters*, London, Macmillan, 1951, p. 93. This novel is part of Snow's *Strangers and Brothers* series which was published between 1940 and 1974 but depicts English life between 1930 and 1960.

15 J. B. Priestley, *English Journey: Being a Rambling but Truthful Account of What One Man Saw and Heard and Felt and Thought During a Journey Through England During the Autumn of the Year 1933*, London, Penguin, 1977 [1934], p. 66; H. G. Wells, *The Work, Wealth and Happiness of Mankind*, London, Heinemann, 1932, p. 318.

16 See, for instance, the attitudes expressed by George Banks, the London banker, in P. L. Travers' *Mary Poppins*, London, Peter Davies, 1934.

17 *University Education and Business: A Report by a Committee Appointed by the Cambridge University Appointments Board*, published in 1946. Cited in Michael Sanderson, *The Universities and British Industry, 1850–1970*, London, Routledge and Kegan Paul, 1972, p. 283.

18 See Martin J. Wiener, *English Culture and the Decline of the Industrial Spirit, 1850–1980*, Cambridge, Cambridge University Press, 1981.

19 Roy Lewis and Rosemary Stewart studied the obituaries in *The Times* for three months in 1957 and noted that out of 203 obituaries only 12 featured businessmen (whereas 34 featured military professionals) and that these 12 were comparatively short. See their book *The Boss: The Life and Times of the British Business Man*, 2nd edition, London, Phoenix, 1961, p. 29.

20 Neil McKendrick, 'General Introduction' to R. J. Overy, *William Morris, Viscount Nuffield*, London: Europa Publications, p. xxxix.

21 Edited by H. C. G. Matthew and Brian Harrison (Oxford, Oxford University Press, 2004).

22 The irrelevance of traditional categories of 'right' and 'left' within this debate is noted in Peter S. Heslam, *Globalization: Unravelling the New Capitalism*, Cambridge, Grove Books, 2002, pp. 4–5.

23 See 'How Big are Multinational Companies?' by Paul de Grauwe

and Filip Camerman at <www.econ.kuleuven.ac.be>. The defensive tone of the argument is reflected in the titles of Johan Norberg's *In Defence of Global Capitalism*, Stockholm, Timbro, 2001 and Jagdish Bhagwati's *In Defence of Globalization*, Oxford, Oxford University Press, 2004. See also Steve Hilton and Giles Gibbons, *Good Business: Your World Needs You*, London, Texere, 2002; John Lloyd, *The Protest Ethic: How the Anti-Globalization Movement Challenges Social Democracy*, London, Demos, 2001; Michael Mosbacher, *Marketing the Revolution: The New Anti-Capitalism and the Attack upon Corporate Brands*, London, The Social Affairs Unit, 2002; Martin Wolf, *Why Globalization Works*, New Haven, Yale University Press, 2004.

24 *Centesimus Annus*, section 35.

25 Ronald Cole-Turner, 'Science, Technology, and the Mission of Theology in a New Century', in Max L. Stackhouse with Don S. Browning (eds), *The Spirit and the Modern Authorities*, Harrisburg, PA, Trinity Press International, 2001, pp. 139–65 (p. 143).

26 According to the National Audit Office, there are around 4 million companies in the UK, 99% of them being relatively small (employing fewer than 50 people).

27 John Micklethwait and Adrian Wooldridge, *The Company: A Short History of a Revolutionary Idea*, London, Weidenfeld & Nicolson, 2003, p. 10; Max L. Stackhouse and Dennis P. McCann, 'Post-Communist Manifesto, Public Theology after the Collapse of Socialism', *Christian Century*, 16 January 1991, pp. 1, 44–7. Reprinted in Stackhouse et al., *On Moral Business*, pp. 949–54.

28 See, for instance, Michael Hardt and Antonio Negri, *Empire*, Cambridge, MA, Harvard University Press, 2000, especially sections 3.4 and 3.6.

8. The Market and the Environment: Greening Ludwig Erhard's Social Market

JOHN KENNEDY

Introduction

On Armistice Day 1918, two German soldiers lay seriously wounded in nearby military hospitals, both the victims of recent British artillery attacks. One was Adolf Hitler. The other was Ludwig Erhard. They are strange, modern archetypes of the Bad German and the Good German.

Hitler was, of course, the instrument of Germany's destruction, and of the rest of Europe. At his command, my family and I were bombed in Clydebank in 1941. He is a global media megastar. The English-speaking media are obsessed with him. He is shown perpetually on cable TV, and frequently in mainstream broadcasting. We are constantly invited to endure serious revisions of his meaning in history. In the English history school curriculum, only Henry VIII rivals him.

Erhard, by contrast, was the single most powerful force in Germany's post-war recovery. He is now almost totally unknown. There is only one current biography in English, and that is American[1] (from which the biographical material below is largely drawn). There has also been an invaluable if partisan contribution from the Ludwig Erhard Foundation, notably by its Director, Horst Friedrich Wünsche.[2]

This chapter wants to argue for the following point of view.

It is that Erhard's version of the social market was central to the extraordinary economic and social progress of Germany. His approach was rather unpopular. Yet the measures currently required to revive the flagging economies of Europe, including that of Germany, are those which Erhard advocated. The political obstacles that inhibited his policies are somewhat the same now as they were then. These rather simple principles largely delivered Europe from its most pressing problem, that of poverty. Something like them must now be applied to deliver the world from its present pressing problem – environmental degradation resulting from expanding prosperity. It, is, therefore, an essay in prosperity with a purpose.

This chapter acknowledges but sidesteps the increasingly valuable theological discussions of political liberalism. A rather disparate group of Anglicans has produced especially valuable work – Robert Song, Peter Sedgwick and Andrew Britton, and most recently Christopher Insole.[3] But it also acknowledges the important work of the Jesuit philosopher Patrick Riordan, who brings a sharp and critical mind to the pieties of Catholic thought about the common good.[4] These works do much to counter the lazy diffidence and self-righteous condemnation that Christian thinkers so frequently adopt when considering the phenomenon of the competitive market. This chapter simply draws attention to the framework whose construction seems necessary to a successful political liberalism. It points up a truth of major importance, arising from the success of Erhard's social market. It is that the success of a vigorously competitive free market depends on the intervention and protection of a strong state. The unfettered market is invariably a monopoly. But that protection always threatens to undermine the efficacy of enterprise, as the protector adopts the role of jailer.

The shilling life

Erhard was a Bavarian, with a Catholic father and Protestant mother, a confessional ambiguity that marked his future. In the event he was raised a Protestant, but never became any more than a conventional churchgoer. His father set up his own clothing business, and Erhard trained in Nuremberg, intending to follow in the family firm. Like every German aged over 50, for two centuries past, Erhard did not die in the same country he was born in. Raised in Wilhelmine Germany, he survived the Third Reich, helped create the Federal Republic and missed the reunification of Germany by only 11 years. By contrast Bavaria has been Germany's largest and longest established state, perhaps the most intensely self-affirming of all the *Länder*.

This, of course, was the Germany created by Bismarck, and only partly destroyed by Wilhelm II. The German state tended to follow the intuitive line that market competition was divisive and destabilizing. There was therefore an inclination of the state to collude with business in permitting it to minimize competition through the construction of price-fixing cartels. Social welfare, on the other hand, was a hugely ambitious and complex ensemble of self-help and employer contribution. This corporatist system was widely admired, not least by David Lloyd George and Winston Churchill.[5]

On the contrary, Erhard's father belonged to the tiny German Liberal People's Party, and held exactly the views that suited his small-business milieu. Wilhelm Erhard was unwilling to work for a cartel that rigged the market, but he thrived by competing against it. Not only did he do this, but argued that this was the way Germany should be run. It is important to emphasize that this notion of progress through market competition was held to be somewhat eccentric throughout continental Europe.

Ludwig Erhard is (perhaps wrongly) credited with the view that World War One was provoked by a hidebound ensemble of empires, armies and cartels, somewhat inevitably destroying itself. But first he had to endure that destruction – first on the Romanian Front, then at Ypres where he was wounded. He was seriously disabled, and left the family firm in order to study economics. It was there that his father's tacit knowledge of the market was formalized. From 1922, he acquired the conviction that the market price is the only just price, that firms exist to make money by taking risks, that cartels are damaging to consumers (whom he took to be the bulk of ordinary people) and that competing innovative technologies should be allowed to shape the market.

He began his working life just as the German currency collapsed in 1923, and served in a number of what we would now call business consultancies. Six years later the world economy collapsed in the Depression, and Erhard continued to press his counter-intuitive ideas, soon to be taken up by Maynard Keynes – that the market should be restored by giving credit to consumers rather than subsidies to industry, which was already over-capitalized. But the rise of Hitler made the Bismarckian model a total way of life, as the armies and the cartels – and the National Socialist Party – became the overwhelmingly dominant institutions.

Erhard refused to join any of these institutions, though he was close to the Gauleiter of the Rhineland-Pfalz, Josef Burckel. It is odd to see Germans going about their business in this cataclysmic time – Bonhoeffer was a Nazi spy, albeit a double agent.[6] By 1943 it was clear to Erhard's circle that the war was lost. It was a matter of high treason to discuss the post-war world, but that is what he and his friends did — among them Walter Eucken, creator of the Freiburg or ordo-liberal school of political economy.[7]

The big idea: the free market and the strong state

The idea that Erhard shared with Eucken was not new, but was of great significance for the future of Germany. Eucken was in favour of a thoroughly competitive market economy, but he differed from the mainstream of classical liberals. He was sure that free markets do not occur spontaneously, but that governments need to nurture them; the free market is not inimical to the strong state, but is dependent upon such a state. This notion is central to what Erhard and Eucken began to call the *social market economy*, as we shall see below. But their original formulation of this term is now misleading; they envisaged

Germany rebuilt by the creation of consumer power in the free market, itself the deliberate construction of the state, rather than through a system of state planning with which the term is now associated.

With the defeat of Germany, the stage became set for the struggle between a teeming mass of ideas and their proponents, as to how Germany would be rebuilt, and whether or not it would prosper. But the winter of 1945–6 was a terrible culmination of all the sufferings that the German people had endured since the beginning of unrestricted bombing. It was a chaos of punitive treatment, generous aid, and military and civil plans for reconstruction. The country, and Berlin itself, was divided between the Soviet Union, the United States, Britain and France, each with its plans for both retribution and renewal.

There was a strong instinct, civil and military, shared by the four powers, even by the United States, for a planned reconstruction that would centre on the rebuilding of heavy industry. The dominant new political parties, the Christian Democratic Union and the Bavarian Christian Social Union, held to that kind of dirigiste, collectivist vision of renewal. Nonetheless, after two years of complex politicking, Erhard acquired the support of market friendly Americans, and was appointed director of the Administration for Economics. He launched a two-pronged campaign. First was the establishment of the *Deutschmark*, on 20 June 1948. At the same time he began the freeing up of prices, banking on the proposition that a consumer market would indeed be the best allocator of desperately scarce resources. So it turned out. When the Federal Republic was established in 1949, all the elements for a new, highly competitive ensemble were in place, and Germany began to be transformed. It is extraordinary that this market-led change could take place in the midst of such terrible privation, in sharp contrast to the collectivist approaches found both desirable and necessary in the rest of Europe.

The Erhard-Adenauer model

All this however, had been achieved under the auspices of a foreign military dictatorship. With the inauguration of the new Federal Republic, everything changed. Its first Chancellor was Konrad Adenauer, a Rhineland Catholic, who had conventional views on the role of the state. His attitudes developed over the decades in which Rome had denounced the evils of market capitalism, while developing its own Christian Democratic view, in competition with what it (often justly) saw as godless socialism.[8] Under Adenauer, Germany reverted somewhat to the intuitive view that markets are to be regarded with some suspicion, and that the most trusted provider must be the state. So the stage was set. It was undergirded by a system of independent economic governance, working through a meticulously constructed set of institutions, which left local initiative to banks, businesses and a wide array of public bodies.[9] There naturally grew an increasing consensus between Social Democrats and Christian Democrats around a state-led version of the social market.

Erhard's views were much too radical to be politically viable. His commitment to an uncompromising ideal of freedom made it unlikely that his convictions could fit into modern German (or perhaps any) acceptable social order.[10] The story seemed to have a happy ending, though not for Erhard: even while Chancellor in succession to Adenauer, he struggled to keep his ideas afloat.

By 1959, the Social Democrats had begun to see the virtue of the Adenauer-Erhard form of market economy, and a historic consensus was reached at Bad Godesberg.[11] By contrast, such a consensus was not reached in France until 1983 with the collapse of the Mitterrand socialist experiment;[12] and not among British Socialists until at least a decade later.[13] It was an oddity of twentieth-century politics that European socialists sought to establish a radically different version of social justice, with the expectation that such an achievement would permanently alter the face of their societies. In fact, even at their most successful, it simply produced a debilitating alternation of public policy.

Ironically, the weaknesses in the German system were beginning to show, as Erhard had foretold. The phenomenal success of the German economy had led to the huge social welfare commitments with which the term social market is now associated. All this more or less made sense in the budgetary context of the day, and even within reasonable future projections. The future, however, is by nature unreasonable. The 1973 oil price increase, and the costs of German unification from 1989, placed unbearable strains on the German economy. Most challenging of all was the politically inevitable union between the Western and Eastern currencies at equal value – a burden for both East and West that none of the new economies in the former Soviet Bloc had to bear. The result has been a permanent level of around 10 per cent unemployment, with levels much higher in the East. The progress achieved post-1945 has not been replicated post-1989.[14] German society is admirable and its economic performance formidable, but there are persistent difficulties in renegotiating its social market settlement.

Visits to Aachen in recent years reveal some of the achievements and the difficulties of the Erhard-Adenauer model. The city engages in serious co-operation with Liège in French-speaking Belgium, and with Maastricht in the Netherlands – using English as the common language. The technical university, established in 1825, bears an enormous, ugly Prussian eagle above its oldest building – visible testimony to the post-Napoleonic settlement that had the Rhineland governed from Potsdam. The new buildings comprise an enormous technology park. The superb modern hospital is a greatly superior version of the Pompidou Centre in Paris, with hundreds of bikes in front and the blades of a wind farm turning in the distance. There simply is not anywhere like this in the United Kingdom. Yet economic development, fed by high quality technical training and served by magnificent health care, is under critical budgetary pressure due to the long term stagnation of the economy. The protector of enterprise has become its jailer.

A comparison between Britain and Germany in this period is instructive. Britain's crisis is arguably different. In the 1970s,

British Conservatives sought to break out of national economic decline by adopting radical market solutions, in a fashion that seems to parallel Erhard's success. Unfortunately, this enterprise proceeded without regard to the kind of social institutions that underpins such success in Germany. Only in 1976 did Keith Joseph begin to offer the German model as more suitable, but by then it was already in crisis.[15]

In the meantime, British social institutions have been under attack by central government in a deeply damaging way, under the banner of reform, at least since Tony Crosland's 'The party's over' speech in 1976. That moment signalled an assault on Britain's welfare institutions, especially in the areas of education and health care, that remains unabated to this day. British performance in these areas has been markedly bad, and increased expenditure through inadequate institutions will not necessarily solve the problems. Levels of competence in vocational training are abysmal, but educational debate continues to rage around other issues, disastrously for the employment prospects of the poorest. In January 2006, German levels of public expenditure declined to meet the rising levels of British spending. The future is not bright, in either case.

Both societies are in different kinds of crisis, but Britain's will be evident only at the next economic downturn. There is a certain paradox in the contrast between Britain and Germany. Britain is supposedly suspicious of state interference, yet the ravages on public institutions inflicted by central government are by now a permanent feature of our polity. By contrast German *Länder*, often with long traditions of autonomy, are constitutionally protected against Federal experiment – even when that autonomy blocks reform whose urgency is widely evident.

This is perhaps the key difficulty faced by modern liberal democracies. Welfare commitments, eminently justifiable at the time, are virtually irreversible, and lead to a belated discovery that the often-despised market has a central role in sustaining the prosperity of the great mass of people. And it is the cultured despisers of the market – theologians, novelists, academics and the like – who are often most elaborately critical. And all such societies are in a special kind of double bind. They depend for their rising prosperity on increased productivity – selling things cheaper. But the goods we most value – those provided by our welfare systems – are not amenable to such cost-cutting. Hence the perpetual struggle to afford systems which, by some malign magic, become harder to afford even as we get richer. That is the strange phenomenon that has given rise to the perpetual crisis in public provision which afflicts nearly all developed societies. Our politicians promise to pay for it all from the proceeds of economic growth, without admitting that it is this very growth that makes public provision harder to afford. This little known phenomenon was remarked upon by Linden and Kennedy in *Prosperity with a Purpose*.[16]

Meanwhile, a global tendency has arisen. Societies have chosen in favour of markets, as the only way of serving the basic needs of burgeoning populations, let alone fulfilling their desires – again dealt with by Linden and Kennedy.[17]

Greening the social market

It is fairly widely acknowledged now that the dominant threat to global society is not poverty, but the environmental consequences of prosperity. Jennifer Potter's chapter in *Prosperity with a Purpose* was devoted to the issue.[18] The rise in sea levels has been an unarguable feature of the complex of events. Yet every assertion of the urgency of the issue is assailed as special pleading instigated by those of an apocalyptic cast of mind. At the risk of appearing frivolous, my own illustration is, I hope tellingly, not drawn at all from the literature of green apocalypse. It involves a photograph in a book celebrating the Royal Air Force, 1946–95. It shows an RAF Nimrod aircraft above two surfaced nuclear submarines, HMS *Trenchant* and USS *Spadefish*, peeking out of the ice at the North Pole. The caption regrets that 'the ice was too thin for the British and American crews to play their usual game of football at the annual rendezvous.' The photograph was taken on 7 May 1992.[19] This anecdote is emblematic of much evidence, civil and military, not necessarily of apocalyptic provenance, which goes to demonstrate the case. So what to do, and what is being done?

I want to argue that the Erhardian social market approach is of vital significance here. It seemed counter-intuitive in 1946 to suggest that competition in the marketplace might be the solution to the terrible problems of poverty in Germany. But, given the right infrastructure of law, education and welfare provision, it proved to be so. It must also be noted that those provisions were somewhat dictated by an occupying military government.

The environmental issue is as chaotically problematic in 2006 as the economic issue was in 1946. Two illustrations will suffice.

First – as you approach the German city of Aachen from Düsseldorf, you see the octagon of the ancient cathedral – the chapel of Charlemagne and arguably the cradle of Western European civilization. Nothing quite so anciently symbolic exists in England. But clearly visible behind the cathedral turn the blades of a wind turbine. Such a dramatic symbol of commitment to the future among the icons of the past would be simply impossible in Britain. But Germany has the most influential Green movement in the world. So the Aachen wind farm is a deeply significant emblem. And, it could be argued, largely futile. For if the required reductions of greenhouse gas emissions are to be achieved, then the chief instruments are likely to be clean coal, conservation, nuclear power and, in distant fourth place, renewable resources. The Intergovernmental Panel on Climate Change has suggested that by 2050, half of all emissions mitigation may be accounted for by carbon capture.[20]

Second is the catastrophic failure of the Green movement in the United States. During the 2000 US election, Al Gore was the vastly more credible environmental candidate. Yet 3 million voters chose the environmentalist Ralph Nader. 400,000 of them were in Florida. If only 1 per cent of them had voted for Gore, then Bush, the relentlessly pro-business candidate, would have been history. History deals ruthlessly at times with the simply well-intentioned.

Jennifer Potter has spelt out the process for CO_2 emission reduction required by the Kyoto Protocol on Climate Change.[21] Yet much more is required than Kyoto if the effects of climate change are to be mitigated. And the whole question of liability for climate change remains contested. Two factors are particularly significant. First, that the United States and its infinitely more amenable northern neighbour, Canada, maintain the scientifically based case that their emissions are absorbed by their extensive forestry. The details appear in an article in *Science* in 2002.[22] The second is that the Protocol has been rigged to favour the European Union. The baseline date of 1990 precedes the period when EU member states largely switched from coal to gas, whereas the United States had a sharply increased level of emission-related consumption after that date. Some other formula, distributing burdens more equitably, is therefore required to draw in those currently outside Kyoto – notably India, China and Australia.

At this early stage, conflict and confusion reigns. First, there is the conflict over *adaptation* to climate change, or *mitigation* of climate change. Among the most influential of the Adaptors has been Bjorn Lomborg.[23] He acknowledges the reality of global warming, but insists that the instinctive, head-on Command and Control approach to the issue is likely to be ineffective. He argues that the simplest way for poor countries to cope with the adverse effects of climate change is – to get rich.

A personal example may illuminate. The Cretan resort of Paleochora is much frequented by the tougher sort of trekker and rock-climber, and is marked by a certain muscular, tanned austerity. But the road to this haven lies through steep mountain passes, which were cut by severe flooding in the winter of 2002. Within months, an EU emergency financial package had been agreed, and the old drainage channels had been replaced by massive stone and concrete storm drains. The tourist season on the remote south-east coast was saved, and the environmentally sensitive could travel by public transport over the rugged mountains without their dolphin-hugging credentials being called into question. The point is that this happened without anybody thinking it was a feature of environmental policy; the vulnerable, in default of significant policy action on the part of the big polluters, must plan on ever greater proportions of their wealth being spent on adaptation to rather than mitigation of global harm.

The challenges that face the Mitigators are ever more uncomfortable. In the European Union, for instance, an important Erhardian victory has been won. The classical European route to emissions reduction is regulation and taxation. Instead, in the area of emission, the EU has opted for the encouragement of emissions trading. This gives an incentive to firms to generate innovation that minimizes emissions, and forces those who continue to pollute to pay for the privilege. This use of the market to manage the problem has, however, come somewhat to grief. Far too many permits to pollute have been issued, and so the market rewards rather than punishes polluters. The *Economist* magazine has reported this debacle rather gently, in view of the fact that its own surprising preference is for a carbon tax. It explains carefully that such an ambitious policy was bound to have teething troubles, and calls for persistence based on a rigorous examination of experience.[24] Yet again, however, something like chaos reigns.

In the same issue, the paper points to the difficulties arising in the case of air travel. That mode of transport suffers from certain rather serious rigidities. Lifting heavy weights off the ground requires a big-punch fuel like paraffin – the fuel of choice not only for jet-setters but for the more fortunate of the world's poor. Argument rages as to whether taxation or carbon trading is the best way to reduce emissions. And a salutary warning is given. Airlines' net losses in the past six years amount to $44 billion.[25] The message is this; business capacity to respond to environmental challenges depends on business success.

The sheer number of enterprises now seeking to make money out of saving the planet is in some ways encouraging. Although dated now, the 1998 Report to the Club of Rome made fascinating reading.[26] It marks a change from the doom-mongering with which that worthy institution is often charged. The Report's pro-market approach was evident in its own design. It moved from the particular to the general, devoting its first third to practical examples of how wealth could be doubled while halving resource use – the 'Factor Four' of its title. Only then do the authors move to the general policy areas. This approach has its limits; green businesses cannot really take off until the policy framework is put in place which punishes the bad and rewards the good.

The main fascination lies in how many of the examples given are the result of American ingenuity. Perhaps most interesting are the admittedly one-off experiments in different forms of air conditioning. US power consumption in this area is phenomenal, and the case studies record equally astonishing reductions in energy consumption. Just as carbon-capture technology provides real possibilities for the actual situation in coal-rich India and China, so cooling technology offers new, hopeful perspectives for the hot, poor parts of the world. All who travel there are struck by the huge benefits enjoyed by the multinational manufacturers of conventional air conditioning equipment. I found this so especially in Sandinista Nicaragua, where offices and homes like concrete blockhouses were making US-style air conditioning a necessity rather than a luxury. Perhaps they do things differently in Cuba. *Factor Four* has begun to offer a different way of doing things, even under present energy regimes.

The churches: a case of criminal negligence?

A brief note is required on the churches' response to the environmental challenge. Having said the wrong things about the market for so long, we continue to get it half wrong when we talk about the environment. There have been many ringing denunciations of the environmental catastrophe to come, usually excoriating the market at the same time. But on enquiry it often appears that the sometimes resplendent premises in which the hot air rises have yet to enjoy a switch to low energy light bulbs in their elaborate chandeliers. Nobody sees this as a problem, and it is felt to be in bad taste to mention it.

The question was raised most sharply by Roger Hutchings in a recent *Methodist Recorder* review of an edition of *Songs of Praise* which dealt with the environment.[27] The programme was imaginatively passionate and outspoken, but Roger felt, with neat understatement, that the tidying up of an Oxford churchyard was not an adequate practical response.

At the time of writing, *Christian Aid* has launched an environmental element to its activities, some years after it had ensured that the issue was kept off the agenda of the enormously influential and misguided *Make Poverty History* campaign.[28] But the antique, anti-capitalist tenor of its approach makes it less valuable than it might be, perhaps worse than useless. We shall see if the big agencies are able to comprehend that the human economy, and its market instruments, are serious and permanent features of the environment.

Some attention has been paid by the churches' central organizations to getting church headquarters to switch to green electricity; so far the United Reformed Church, the Methodist Church and Churches Together in Britain and Ireland have done the deed. Surveying the scene in Hampshire, it is stunning how little, amounting to virtually nothing, is said here – never mind done. All this is despite the efforts of campaigning bodies like *Eco-Congregation* and *Operation Noah,* whom readers can Google for a slightly more encouraging view. As most churches have a perhaps providential east–west orientation, it might be expected that their south-facing roofs would increasingly sport solar panels of some sort. Not yet, though when the price of electricity rises further, and Chinese production of the panels drives the price down, perhaps there will be some response. Again, we shall see.

Where from here?

The future is tantalizingly close and yet distant. Innovation will bring radically new technologies to the market. By the middle of this century, our buying and selling will have a quite different character (on a pessimistic forecast, anticipating global economic collapse, a radically different character). Quite remarkable outcomes have been achieved in other areas. Water was made clean in the middle of the nineteenth century. Air was made clean in the middle of the last century. US energy consumption per unit of production has declined by half since 1973, though overall consumption increased by 2 per cent a year. It seems likely that the upper atmosphere will begin to be cleansed in the middle of this century, but we do not yet know how.

One thing is clear, however; the creation of effective market instruments requires the engagement of strong government. The free market requires a strong state as a necessary but not sufficient condition of success. The further requirement is that governments should give marketplace innovation the incentive to transform our world. There is little sign yet that governments are prepared to reshape market behaviour in the radical ways that would enable humanity to get rich by saving the planet. As always, enterprise is imprisoned by politics rather than nurtured and shaped by them. Ludwig Erhard's insight into that feature of the human condition, in a world differently daunting than our own, calls for a degree of recollection.

Christians have often allowed themselves to be excluded from envisioning the future by their historically rooted prejudice against the market. A whole generation of political theologians harrumphed that capitalism was bad for poor people, when the reverse was ever more clearly the case. The problems created by the rapid expansion of global prosperity seem often to be seized on as the next reason why the market must be overthrown in favour of a new paradigm. Few of us are still holding our breath. In the meantime, the Erhardian vision of a powerfully innovative free market, directed by an increasingly coherent set of global or intergovernmental institutions, seems the last, best hope of earth. And the market, sustained by the right social institutions, seems the best instrument to shape our lives in the unknown that lies ahead. Theologians and others should note an adaptation of L. P. Hartley's phrase: the future is another country – they do things differently there.

Notes

1 Alfred C. Mierzejewski, *Ludwig Erhard*, Chapel Hill, University of North Carolina Press, 2004.

2 H. F. Wuensche, *Standard Texts on the Social Market Economy*, Stuttgart, Gustav Fischer, 1982.

3 Robert Song, *Christianity and Liberal Society*, Oxford, Oxford University Press, 1997; Andrew Britton and Peter Sedgwick, *Economic Theory and Christian Belief*, Oxford, Peter Lang, 2003; Christopher J. Insole, *The Politics of Human Frailty*, London, SCM Press, 2004.

4 Patrick Riordan, *A Politics of the Common Good*, Dublin, Institute of Public Administration, 1996.

5 Steven Ozment, *A Mighty Fortress: A New History of Germany*, London, Routledge 1997, pp. 212–66.

6 Stephen Plant, *Dietrich Bonhoeffer*, London, Continuum, 2004, p. 32.

7 Wuensche, *Social Market Economy*, pp. 115–32.

8 Tom Buchanan and Martin Conway, *Political Catholicism in Europe, 1918–1965*, Oxford, Oxford University Press, 1996, pp. 156–86.

9 Stuart Parkes, *Understanding Contemporary Germany*, London, Routledge, 1997, pp. 25–41.

10 Horst Friedrich Wuensche, 'Economic Policy in Germany: what lessons can be learned from Ludwig Erhard?' in Jörn Leonard and Lothar Funk (eds), *Ten years of German Unification*, Birmingham, University of Birmingham Press, 1996.

11 Parkes, *Understanding Contemporary Germany*, pp. 38–9.

12 Ronald Tiersky, *François Mitterand*, Basingstoke, Palgrave, 2000, pp. 249–58.

13 Paul Anderson and Nita Mann, *Safety First, the Making of New Labour*, Cambridge, Granta, pp. 34–9.

14 Parkes, *Understanding Contemporary Germany*, p. 208.

15 Andrew Denham and Mark Garnett, *Keith Joseph*, London, Acumen, 2001, pp. 241–3.

16 Ian Linden and John Kennedy, 'An Overview', in *Prosperity with a Purpose: Exploring the Ethics of Affluence*, Churches Together in Britain and Ireland, 2005, pp. 27–8.

17 Ian Linden, 'Global Justice', in *Prosperity with a Purpose*, pp. 78–82.

18 Jennifer Potter, 'The Environmental Challenge', in *Prosperity with a Purpose*, pp. 92–95.

19 Roy Nesbit, *RAF in Camera*, London, Sutton Publishing, 1997, p. 124.

20 International Panel on Climate Change, *Special Report on CO$_2$ Capture and Storage*, IPCC, 2005.

21 Potter, 'The Environmental Challenge', pp. 85–7.

22 S. Fan, 'A large Terrestrial Carbon Sink in North America' in *Science* 282 (14 October 2002), p. 442.

23 Bjorn Lomborg, *The Skeptical Environmentalist*, Cambridge, Cambridge University Press, 2001, pp. 159–62.

24 *The Economist* 379 no. 8481 (10 June 2006), p. 83.

25 *The Economist* 379 no. 8481 (10 June 2006), pp. 81–3.

26 Ernst von Weizsäcker, Amory B. Lovins and L. Hunter Lovins, *Factor Four: Doubling Wealth, Halving Resource Use*, London, Earthscan, 1998.

27 Roger Hutchings, 'A Christian Climate', *Methodist Recorder*, 8 June 2006, p. 18.

28 *The Climate of Poverty: Facts Fears and Hope*, London, Christian Aid, 2006.

9. Faith Journey: Radical Political Economy and the Empire of Oil

WILF WILDE

Evangelical engagement and reformulation

When John and Vannie Atherton drop me off at the Reebok Station, by the new Bolton football ground, I am reminded of my faith journey. Coming out of Manchester on the Blackpool train, on what used to be my route to 'Nana's', this is the first time you glimpse a good view of the Pennine Hills. When John Atherton mentioned this series of essays on the dialogue between social ethics and economics, I first thought of my history, which is why this piece is biographical. Rather than writing a theoretical article for the uninitiated reader, it seemed a better idea to explain my calling to engage with the harsh economic and political realities all too evident on the streets of Manchester, in an Ardwick where my dad grew up, or in Miles Platting where my son worked in a homeless hostel or in Fallowfield, where my daughter attends Manchester University.

My subsequent experience in the oil industry and in the City has reconfirmed a quest to engage my faith with a search for a practical radical political economy. In my present work on the global empire of oil I plan to continue as an advocate for justice and for a libertarian Christian socialism. Here all I can leave are some signposts as to why I believe the theoretical reformulation[1] of the dialogue between theology and political economy in the twenty-first century should be threefold:

1 Interdisciplinary, based on classical political economy, but also using the insights of anthropology, history, sociology and politics.
2 Global and comparative, directly addressing the issues of global poverty, injustice and political power.
3 Theologically aware of the biblical and political critique of empire.

In this chapter, I will focus most on the first and third of these issues. Globalization, poverty, debt and trade are covered in more detail in my book on global capitalism.[2] My faith journey has always been linked to economics and to Manchester. Until I was nine, I went to school at Alfred Street Primary in Harpurhey, Manchester, which Chris Baker describes in this book as now being the second most deprived ward in the country.[3] All I remember is the bleak Rochdale Road and parents who were by no means socialists, but much more aspiring working class, in my dad's case, or lower middle in my mum's. Discovering Jesus for the first time at 18, from a unchurched background, in Durham University's strong Christian Union evangelical tradition, my sense of a call to engage with the material and dialectical world of political economy has lasted for 35 years. The formative years of Manchester cotton were perhaps more influential than I realized then. I have discovered a granddad who was a cotton warehouseman in Harpurhey in 1901 and another who was the child of cotton bleachers out on the moors of Newhey. Somehow this early upbringing in Manchester's earthy realities attracted me to a Marxist-influenced political economy. This makes an odd theological bedfellow with what can be the most conservative of Christian traditions (evangelicalism).

Evangelical theology and political economy

My faith journey has evolved into an evangelical perception that 'this Jesus', Peter first proclaimed in Acts (2.36) was rejected by the rulers of empire and their client elites. The vision of the incarnation, the rejection of the cross and the hope of resurrection need to be central to our engagement with the harsh realities of poverty and injustice – the global economy – and the ideological veil with which it is so often obscured – conventional economics – and the spiritual powers of the ruling global elites – empire. It has been a fascinating journey from deciding that my Christian faith and the discipline of political economy were locked in a dialectical relationship. This is the conceptual story of that journey – from the early days of studying economics to my work on the empire of oil and its importance for understanding the political economy of global capitalism.

At 19, I made a vital academic decision. After nearly three years on economics, which I had always intended to study, it did not seem to be able to enlighten me as to why so much of the world was poor and why the USA was fighting it through a war against 'terrorists' in Vietnam. Sacks admits to part of the same problem: even though he had gained academic tenure at Harvard, he had no clue about development economics even as he began to advise the Bolivians on their problems with hyperinflation.[4] Sociology, so derided as an academic lightweight, seemed more promising. Even in the less job-orientated undergraduate world of 1972, I had learnt early to compromise: I would do joint honours in economics and sociology.

When I read the CTBI books of 2005, I was reminded of my criticisms of 30 years earlier. For here the results of global capitalism drop from the skies: 'industrialization, urbanization, and globalization' – even democracy – all, as in neo-classical economics, are exogenous givens. Even the neo-classical view on entrepreneurship as a reward to capital is borrowed, as is the concept of economic capital, so that moral capital is brought in from the outside.[5]

When JustShare asked the *Economist*'s Deputy Editor, Clive Crook, to speak on globalization and I read his piece in September 2001, it brought back the same memories.[6] Such economists would have benefited from some education in good old fashioned sociology; they seemed unaware of the debate that lay at the heart of the discussions on sociological theory.[7] How can we analyse a society – particularly one undergoing an experience like globalization? Sociologists learnt, through the lack of respect for their academic speciality, that it was impossible to say much without knowing about history, culture, politics and ideology – as well as economics. Far too many of the economists, secure in their greater prestige as a hard social science[8], were too busy discussing theoretical models of general or partial equilibriums in micro-economics to take much notice of silly sociological theory. If that was rather obtuse, better still, do macro-economics: cobble together a bit of Keynesianism (do not bother with Keynes himself or 1914–45), add a dash of monetarism and before you knew it, you too might be a Gordon Brown, 20 years later.[9]

Durham had a compulsory course excitingly called 'Econ-omics 3'. This is where globalization was hemmed in with regional policy, monopoly and competition policy and cost benefit analysis. Despite this, I did not have a clue about business or the stock market either – but this was 1974. I am not sure I even knew the *Financial Times* existed, so I was not aware of the 1974 stock market crash.

The wealth of nations

I voted Labour for the first time and studied by candlelight during the miners' strike (which I do not remember ever being mentioned in the economics department). Going into the sociology department was difficult, on the other hand, because one had to decide whether to cross the student pickets, out in sympathy with the miners. I had three Christian friends who had decided on a third-year course in the history of economic thought. How amazing to discover that Adam Smith's *Wealth of Nations* seemed to combine an analysis of why some nations were rich and others poor, with a moral concern[10] and an ability to do micro- and macro-economics and 'Economics 3' all at the same time, and all without drawing supply and demand curves. Remarkably a clergyman, Malthus, and a man made rich by stocks and bonds, Ricardo, seemed to have worked to a similar fashion in this funny subject, then known only in Scottish universities as political economy. (Unless you were at Oxford, where you were sufficiently clever to add another 'P' for philosophy.) Who should we come across but that old bogeyman from sociology, Karl Marx? Despite the fact that we had spent time in sociology discussing Marx, no one had pointed out that Marx had daftly decided to spend 40 years of his life writing three volumes of *Das Kapital* and a few more on the theories of surplus value, partly analysing the fallacies of economists who tried to analyse society with no appreciation of history and politics. They had invented a wonderful Robinson Crusoe world, which had apparently dropped down from the skies, where only individual desires mattered and where usually corrupt governments stopped the wealth of nations from being spread.[11]

Atherton complains that by 1890, Marshall, the academic guru of neo-classical economics at Cambridge, allowed himself to be 'controlled by the discipline'.[12] But this is to ignore what had happened in the intervening 50 years. Marshall came from a tradition of economics, which had deliberately set itself against the Marxist insights and aided the split of the social sciences. Marshall's ethical moralism was subsequently pushed into a corner – rather like religion in today's society – and ignored by the thundering herd of modern positive economics.[13] With the rise of the marginal utility revolution after the 1860s, and with the resurrection of a more militant working class after the defeat of Chartism, the bourgeois economists of Marx's own time were eventually to turn political economy into one box called economics, another called politics and left another set of people to invent an academic subject called sociology. I got rather interested in this ideological shift and thought of a PhD on neo-Ricardian economics to look at it, but decided it was not practical enough.[14] But I had learnt a lot from the history of economic thought; pity most modern economists never take the speciality.

The sociology department, where I was lucky enough to be

taught by Ruth First, specialized on the sociology of development. Building on work like Barrington Moore, we looked at the UK, Germany, Japan and Russia. We then studied China and Latin America. The latter was particularly interesting, given that in the early 1970s not only underdevelopment theory, but also a new liberation theology was emerging from Latin America. How was it that South America – which seemed on the face of it to have as much going for it as the North – was underdeveloped and the United States was developed? The South had massive resources, plenty of immigrants from Italy and Spain, independent governments, lots of capital injected from the West. To answer such questions, I discovered, requires an analysis of history, politics, sociology, culture and ideology, as well as economics. This is what Sacks discovered in his Bolivian experience.

Big Bang and 1979

To analyse properly the wealth and poverty of nations also required an understanding of the global connection between periphery and metropolis, colony and empire. A wider political economy then asks: How is the surplus of any given society created? Who keeps it? And what do 'they' do with it once they have it? Answering these questions with reference to the differences between the USA and the lopsided political economy of Argentina takes a chapter of my book on global capitalism. After a few years teaching the dismal science and business at A level, when I chose to do a PhD, I did so in what I regarded as political economy but Sussex called development studies. In business studies, teaching the importance of what are today called transnational corporations (TNCs)[15] took me on to a thesis on an oil company's (now BP) impact on Trinidad (English-speaking South America). This was a major introduction into the developing global economy despite the TNCs in the 1970s being excluded from most of China, India and Russia, while being nationalized in parts of Latin America and the Middle East. Fascinated in Trinidad by the workings of the oil industry, my hopes to return to be a strategist for what was then BNOC, or for imperial BP or bureaucratic Shell, were to be doomed. Ending up in a US multinational – now Exxon Mobil – my life until 1991 was then dominated by the empire of oil. After three years, a 15 per cent mortgage rate drove me to the City and I began work as an oil specialist salesman in UK equities.

Once into the new Big Bang City culture, there were many strange lessons to learn. Conventional economists used their macro-economics to pretend they were in the Treasury and predicted Thatcherism's next call on interest rates as they celebrated her and Reagan's return to full-blooded capitalism; the welfare variety that had served so well in the post-war boom to the mid 1960s was getting rather costly. When I started to research the oil industry, it was as North Sea production was coming up to full stream, while the Iranian revolution had helped the last great oil price spike of 1979–81. Predicting OPEC pricing policy and strategy became a City game, from 1973 to 1986 when the world economic cycle, the UK exchange rate and bond market and the oil shares all hung on the potential oil price. Apart from a brief time in the first Gulf War, oil prices from then had been in decline to 2004. Yet even at their lowest in 1986 (nominally $13) and 1998 ($12) – the oil price never returned to being as low as those from 1929 to 1973. Yet as we are learning again, oil price spikes – as in 1973, 1979, 1990 and 2004–06 – are just as likely to have political causes as environmental ones and will certainly have political consequences.

Brown and Ballard make 1979 a dividing point in the British Church's economic life.[16] In that pivotal year came the Iranian revolution – the geopolitics of which are still being played out – and the election of a British government based on a strong state and a free market capitalism. I moved South to Sussex in 1979, tried to persuade my father not to vote Tory and yet became a grown up child of Thatcherism. Even then, conventional economics was not the best academic training in the heartlands of global capitalism. After the Iranian revolution, woe betide any global multinational oil company, almost the leaders of the new global breed from the early twentieth century, that invested in the new global markets unaware of the history, culture and politics of where they invested. As with Shell in Nigeria not much has changed on that score since 1979.

The empire of oil

In a final stint in the City at Barings, I soon learnt that investing in emerging markets was an exercise in pricing the risks of political economy. On all conventional market indices Russian and Chinese stocks were cheap and those in Singapore were expensive.

To understand global capitalism then is not only to analyse the dynamics of the system – for which globalization is the propaganda jargon – but to understand that it is made up of a series of capitalisms – each with its own history and political story. One example in this book is John Kennedy's piece on the German social market model.[17] The real practitioners in industry and the City knew with Marx that politics and history and economics were not to be kept in separate boxes; has anyone told the neo-classical economic propagandists out there in academia? Because neo-classical analysis assumes government and societies drop down from the sky, they make poor use of the real laboratory of the social sciences – the history of particular societies. We need instead to ground our theology and political economy in the work of empirical history – as I attempted briefly on El Salvador.[18]

Engaging with political economy should not be confused with a dialogue with neo-classical economic orthodoxy: it becomes impossible even to discuss the role of economics as a justifying ideology.[19] No one in the City questioned the ideology either: capitalist profit accumulation explained all. Propagandists do not really want to know what causes poverty. Fighting wars against terror is a great excuse to rattle all that military hardware, while increasing the powers of an authoritarian centralized state. A visitor from Mars, even marooned in Manchester, could only assume that our global expenditure priorities tell us that the dominant ideology prefers to fight poverty with a sword.[20]

When the USA invaded Iraq in 2003 most of the war's critics argued that this was a war for oil. The argument of my last book was that it was more than this alone – it was a war for empire; not just the US empire, but even more a war for the expansion of global capital.[21] The need to further control oil in the Middle East and potentially then in Central Asia, Africa and Latin America was nevertheless at the heart of the war. For the wars in Afghanistan and Iraq, and the pressures put on rogue states – Iran, Libya and Syria – plus US interventions elsewhere, as in Colombia and Venezuela, for example, tell us a great deal about the new century's imperialist project – to remake the world in the image of, and for, capital. The life blood provided by oil is still a key political resource. Even the reincorporation of Russia and China back into global capitalism has particular interacting consequences for the political economy of oil and the possibilities of development. It is the irony of oil production that while the geopolitical and economic power it bequeaths on the owners of capital is huge, as the global oil companies once again stride the world like the old Seven Sisters, it does provide an opportunity for the poorer nations of the periphery to transform their possibilities.

There is a consistent biblical narrative against empire – starting with the Egypt of the Exodus, the Babylon facing Isaiah, the Seleucid Empire that dominates Daniel and the Roman Empire that crucified Jesus and probably killed Paul. The biblical story deals far more with such hard political, economic and military realities than in abstract theology or in ahistorical political economy. This is one radical way forward for theology in dialogue with political economy. The geopolitical quest in my present work will be to see the empire of oil at work as one of the core components of the empire of capital.

Mark and the oracles of Tyre

A major reason for choosing Mark's Gospel in my book was because it was the first of its genre to subvert the Roman propaganda for empire with a new message about an emperor who died a slave's death on a cross. Coming from a culture of popular protest, with a new model of a popular assembly – ecclesia or church – Mark uses clever symbolic language parables to critique the empire and its client states. The legion of demons, the swine that oppressed Israel, did so with the collusion of the religious mountain on which the Judaean Temple state stood. Both needed to be cast down and out into the sea of chaos from which they came.[22]

This critique is also illuminated, as Richard Higginson points out, through the 'Oracles Against Tyre'. Isaiah 23 and Ezekiel 27—8 stressed the dangers of the hubris of wealth and power.[23] The island and city of Tyre has a downfall akin to that announced in Mark's Gospel for the Judaean state and for the Roman legions; Tyre is to be submerged in 'the heart of the sea' (Ezek. 27.25–7). The condemnation of Tyre is reflected in John's description of Rome as Babylon in Revelation 18. Tyre, Babylon and Rome are all symbolic biblical expressions, of economic, political, social – and indeed spiritual – power. They are all case studies of the dangers of empire.

What Higginson stresses less is the long and largely hostile relationship between Israel and Tyre, which forms the context for Jesus' trenchant dialogue with the woman asking for healing for her daughter in Mark chapter 7. First, we have a story of the abuse of autocratic political power by Israel's monarchy. Kings 9.10–15 tells a story not only of the use of forced labour to fortify Megiddo (9.15), but the ceding of 20 towns in Galilee (9.11). Second, we have military and imperial power: if Israel as a whole suffered from a loss of independence for 600 years before Jesus, being dominated and ruled by imperial outsiders was even worse and lasted longest in Galilee. When the northern kingdom broke away after Solomon, Galilee was often in the path of invading armies. The key link between Tyre and

Galilee was economic. The resentment of Tyre was linked to the poverty of the peasantry, particularly in years of drought, as in the time of Elijah. Galilee was the breadbasket, which provided Tyre with its food. The agrarian Jewish economy was largely a self-sufficient one not geared to the market economy. The pressure of Herod and Rome's taxes often meant that to pay their debts, Galilean wheat would be sold to Tyre while their own children would go hungry.[24] In the biblical critique of Tyre, we have an interlinked warning of the dangers of military, political and economic power, as we can see today in the empire of global capital.

In Mark, the scorched earth policy and the swooping 'birds of the air' from Rome combined with the Herodian state's rents, taxes and tithes were preventing the miracle of the natural productivity of the land and resources.[25] Summing up the experience of the Niger Delta, which has had one of the worst consequent experiences of environmental degradation, James Marriott says: 'This is our Empire. We were born in it, we inherited it, its comforts and cruelties. This is our Empire. Ours to retreat from and ours to dismantle'.[26]

In the empire of oil, what possibilities of resistance and of transformation have been thrown up? What chance is there that popular movements, as Christianity was and is, have any hope of seizing any opportunities thus presented?

Aufhebung: or on a socialist transformation

Peter Heslam and I share a similar call. Where he looks to transform business with its Christian past, present and future vocations, I look to see, with John Atherton, the whole of capitalism potentially transformed or transfigured.[27] There is one piece of jargon which I believe can help here. This is the German word *Aufhebung* which Marx uses in his works on the transition from capitalism to socialism. For *aufhebung* is often translated as abolition, which is only half the story. The other positive half of its meaning is to supersede or to transcend, to move to a higher level, while at the same time preserving the best of the old.[28] We can build on the best of capitalism.

This means not setting the state against the market, but building on the best of a decentralized, open and liberal economy.[29] The problem with capital – and thereby capitalism – is not the market but the unequal ownership structures of capital itself. This is in turn causes unequal control over the mechanisms of production and automatically unequal distribution. The attempt to remedy this through state or Stalinist nationalizations has been a disaster. Likewise, a welfare bureaucratic redistribution has equally failed because you cannot control the distribution of wealth without controlling its production.

In a libertarian socialist alternative therefore I do not reject, to use John Atherton's words, the market, nor even reject capitalism, but I do reject the present fact that capital is owned and controlled by the few not the many. My proposal is to democratize the voting structures of our major corporations:[30] a revolutionary proposal that would strike at the heart of capital's control of our lives. The contradictions of capitalism, its ability to generate prosperity and the commonwealth, can be recognized by radicals, while never forgetting its equal contradictory ability to generate poverty. Capitalism can be built on, the benefits of a true globalization can be welcomed. Empire in the service of unequal global capital is however to be rejected. Christ is against empire: not against culture or business.

Unlike Bolton's football stadium, there is as John Atherton puts it: 'no radical starting again'.[31] We have to build on the capitalism we have. To replace the old Christendom, new democratic assemblies will have to grow around discipleship groups where ordinary people can start to control the politics and economics of their lives. There will still be the space for each to pursue our individual faith journeys, but despite empire, there is also the possibility of transforming our world. This may be as difficult as squeezing a camel through the eye of the needle, but with God all things are possible.

Notes

1 John Atherton has made an eloquent case for a reformulation of Christian political economy. See John Atherton, *Marginalization*, London, SCM Press, 2003, p. 142f.

2 Wilf Wilde, *Crossing the River of Fire: Mark's Gospel and Global Capitalism*, Peterborough, Epworth, 2006.

3 Chris Baker, Chapter 11 in this volume.

4 J. Sacks, *The End of Poverty Economic Possibilities for Our Time*, London, Penguin, 2005, pp. 90–2.

5 Churches Together in Britain and Ireland, *Prosperity with a Purpose: Exploring the Ethics of Affluence*, London, CTBI, 2005.On globalization and democracy, pp. 12, 17–20. On entrepreneurship, p. 11. On economic capital, p. 16.

6 See the *Economist*, 'Globalization and its Critics', 29 September 2001.

7 A. Giddens, *Capitalism and Modern Social Theory: An Analysis of the Writings of Marx, Durkheim and Weber*, Cambridge, Cambridge University Press, 1971.

8 The claim of neo-classical economics to be a hard science of positive economics is accepted far too easily by A. Britton and P. Sedgwick, *Economic Theory and Christian Belief*, Bern, Peter Lang, 2003, pp. 13, 27–33, and even by the far more critical M. D. Meeks, *God the Economist: The Doctrine of God and Political Economy*, Minneapolis, Augsburg Fortress, 1989, p. 2. D. A. Hay, *Christianity and the Culture of Economics*, Cardiff, University of Wales Press, 2001, the academic economist, argues on the other hand that there is no such pure positive economics, p. 167.

9 Despite many speeches on economics and Keynes, Brown trained as a historian. See G. Brown, *Maxton*, Edinburgh, Mainstream Press, 1986.

10 Sacks, *End of Poverty*, comments that going to Bolivia he had to read Smith for the first time in years (p. 105). The CTBI quotes Smith approvingly but only on his moral critique of 'conspiracies against the public' (*Prosperity with a Purpose*, p. 30).

11 I have not seen a Christian critique of Marx which notices that most of his work would be today with what we would call economics. Ronald Preston, *Religion and the Ambiguities of Capitalism,* London, SCM Press, 1991, notes that economics played little part in the Christian–Marxist dialogue of the 1970s (p. 49). If they do deal with Marx's economics, it is usually to dismiss him to economic history or as 'meaningless or wrong' for today's 'professionals'. See Britton and Sedgwick, *Economic Theory and Christian Belief*, pp. 177–8.

12 A. Marshall, *Principles of Economics*, London, Macmillan, 1890. It is ironic that this work drops the concept of political economy when the year of the dock strike marked at the same time the symbolic – and very political – entry of British trade unions and society into the era of monopoly capitalism and imperialism. Also see Atherton, pp. 145–50.

13 The invention of the term positive economics is in M. Friedman, *Essays in Positive Economics,* Chicago, Chicago University Press, 1953. The history of Friedman's influence on policy points to the ideological basis for what passed itself off as a non-ideological economics.

14 For an introduction to the thinking of this time see M. Dobb, *Theories of Value and Distribution since Adam Smith: Ideology and Economic Theory*, Cambridge, Cambridge University Press, 1973.

15 For an excellent summary of the US experience of a Christian critique of the TNCs in the 1970s see R. W. Gillett, *The New Globalization*, Cleveland, Pilgrim Press, 2005, pp. 86–94.

16 Malcolm Brown and Paul Ballard, *The Church and Economic Life: A Documentary Study 1945 to the Present*, Peterborough, Epworth, 2006.

17 See J. Kennedy, Chapter 8, in this volume.

18 See Wilde, *Crossing the River of Fire*, chapter 2 on Argentina and chapter 8 on El Salvador.

19 A. Britton and P. Sedgwick, *Economic Theory and Christian Belief*, p. 26 explicitly rules out discussing the role of economics as an ideology. Despite its claim to engage with the 'philosophical foundations of economic theory', this work only deals with neo-classical theory.

20 The CTBI's *Prosperity with a Purpose* does point to globalization as a form of economic imperialism (pp. 11–12), but sticking to its econ-omistic approach it goes no further. The reference here is to the BBC documentary 'Life on Mars' filmed often in Miles Platting, Manchester.

21 For an excellent summary see E. M. Wood, *The Empire of Capital*, London, Verso, 2003.

22 See Ched Myers, *Binding The Strong Man: A Political Reading Of Mark*, Maryknoll, Orbis, 1988.

23 R. Higginson, 'Oracles about Tyre: Pride before a Fall', *Faith in Business Quarterly* 9:2 (Summer 2005), pp. 3–8.

24 For a fuller exposition and references see Wilde, *Crossing the River of Fire*, chapter 6.

25 W. R. Herzog, *Jesus, Justice and the Reign of God: A Ministry of Liberation,* Louisville, John Knox Press, 2000, pp. 193–5 stresses that the words used to describe the failure of the seed in the Parable of the Sower to grow are violent and lost in some translations: the birds did not come and eat they 'devoured' (Mark 4.4); some plants are 'scorched' (4.6) while others are 'choked' (4.7).

26 See Peter Heslam (Chapter 7), John Atherton's conclusion (Chapter 13) and Ken Leech on Anglican social thought and transformation in Gillett, *The New Globalization*, p xiv. Note also the April 2006 Ridley Hall, Cambridge Conference called 'Past Present and Future: Christian Faith and Business Practice'.

27 J. Marriott, A. Rowell and L. Stockman, *The Next Gulf: London, Washington and the Oil Conflict in Nigeria*, London, Constable, 2005, p. 246.

28 K. Marx, *Early Writings*, 'A Glossary of Terms', London, Penguin and *New Left Review*, 1975, p. 432.

29 I can share Peter Sedgwick's vision here quoting David Marquand in Chapter 12 of this volume.

30 Wilde, *Crossing the River of Fire*, chapter 9.

31 Atherton, *Marginalization*, p. 2.

10. The World Trade Organization, Fair Trade and the Body Politics of Saint Paul

MICHAEL NORTHCOTT

The foot-and-mouth crisis of 2001 ranks as one of the low points in the recent economic and environmental history of Britain. A little known incident made it all much worse. In March 2001 government vets advised the Prime Minister and the Ministry of Agriculture, Fisheries and Food (MAFF) that a policy of vaccination would be much less costly to the country than mass slaughter. Holland had tried it and many other countries around the world used it successfully. Among the principal scientific advocates of this strategy were Dr Simon Barteling, a leading Dutch vet, and Keith Sumption, a veterinary expert from University of Edinburgh who put out a paper, which was passed by Prince Charles to the Prime Minister, showing that vaccination would stop the disease in its tracks.[1] At a meeting at Chequers on 12 April 2001, chaired by Prime Minister Tony Blair, and which included representatives from the food industry, the National Farmers' Union, MAFF, and government vets, the policy of vaccination was announced and 500,000 injections were already distributed to the army and trained civilian volunteers. However there was strong lobbying by Professor Anderson, the government's scientific adviser on this issue, who had long recommended a mass cull. The NFU were also deeply opposed to vaccination despite its success in many other countries, including Holland and Belgium. An anti-vaccination campaign rapidly gathered momentum after the Chequers meeting and Anderson and the NFU recruited food industry representatives, and in particular Peter Blackburn, chief executive of Nestlé, which has a large powdered milk factory in Dalston, Cumbria, which employs 500 people and 75 per cent of whose output goes to developing countries. There powdered milk is sold to mothers who are persuaded by adverts of healthy white babies that it is better for their children than their own breast milk, despite the fact that they very often lack either clean water or the means to sterilize bottles to make the powdered milk safe. Nestlé was concerned that powdered milk from vaccinated herds might be rejected by the domestic or export market. Between the food industry, MAFF and the NFU, the Prime Minister and his advisors were unable to carry the argument and the government abandoned the advice of its own Chief Veterinary Officer and chose instead to cull more than a million animals.[2]

Britain is of course not alone in putting powerful economic interests ahead of the welfare of its animals, farmers and consumers. Indeed the essence of the rules of world trade overseen by the devolved sovereignty of the World Trade Organization (WTO) is that international exchange of goods across borders ought to take priority over parochial interests. The reason for this is no secret: it is the neo-liberal economic assumption that unfettered economic growth is the key to the welfare of all the citizens of the planet.

Despite ecological concerns about economic growth – that a constantly expanding economy runs counter to the limited ability of the planet to resource growth and absorb wastes, and not least carbon dioxide – it must be admitted that in developing countries such as Malaysia, Thailand, Korea and Singapore, economic growth has reduced poverty, and enhanced educational and cultural opportunities for their citizens. However the economic growth that these countries – known as the new industrialized countries – achieved in the 1970s and 1980s was achieved using the same classical economic policies as those which enabled the economies of America and Europe to grow in the late nineteenth century, and throughout most of the twentieth. These policies involved a good deal of protection for nascent industries and farmers, including subsidies, tariffs and price stabilization, and latterly protection of workers' rights and the environment. Thus Malaysia has for many years used tariffs and subsidies to develop indigenous production – for example of the Malaysian car the Proton Saga – by pricing imported goods through tariffs which put them beyond the reach of ordinary consumers. Malaysia is now under pressure to phase out all such tariffs in exchange for its membership of the WTO, and indeed in the area of agricultural tariffs it has so successfully industrialized its agricultural sector that it is one of those countries pushing for greater liberalization in agricultural commodities trading.[3]

Under WTO rules many developing countries are in theory permitted to subsidize their farm outputs to at least the same levels as those which obtain in the United States and Europe. The difficulty is that no developing country is in the position to match the subsidies given to developed country farmers. One reason for this is that they simply do not have sufficient government revenues to achieve this, even if they wanted to. The other is that they are in most cases subject to external economic management regimes imposed by the World Bank and the International Monetary Fund as a consequence of external debt. Apart from agriculture most forms of protection are banned to developing nations but this is not the case for Europe, North America, Japan, Australia and New Zealand. Under the terms of the initial establishment of the WTO these early members of the WTO are exempted from many of the trade liberalization measures that are enforced on new member nations. These exemptions reflect the fact that the rules of the WTO were drawn up by the developed nations, and in their interests, and before most developing countries had been invited to join the new trading regime. The rules as they were originally drawn up reflect the unequal power relations that exist between strong trading blocs like the United States and the European Union and the less developed countries. Although more advanced non-

Western countries like Malaysia have been able to cope with this extremely unjust state of affairs, the poorer developing countries have been, are being, devastated by the new rules of world trade.

Despite the growing advocacy of free trade and deregulation in the 1980s and 1990s as universal economic panaceas, and their imposition on more than 70 developing countries under the regime of conditionality and austerity of the World Bank and the International Monetary Fund, these policies have not produced the results in the poorer developing countries which their advocates promised.[4] On the contrary developing countries subjected to the full gamut of the deregulatory toolkit have seen economic growth shrink and the welfare of their citizens and ecosystems decline dramatically in the period of deregulation. Instead of growing new sustainable industries and strengthening the farming sector, these policies have seen a gradual erosion of even those nascent manufacturing enterprises that were operative in poorer African economies. Food poverty is now a major problem among rural and shanty town dwellers of most sub-Saharan countries, and in many Latin American countries, a state of affairs which was not the case in the 1970s.[5] The extent of debt servicing in many of these countries, combined with high rates of infection with HIV/AIDS, particularly in sub-Saharan Africa, have worsened this state of affairs. But the primary cause of the decline in wellbeing in many developing countries was the enforced imposition of extreme trade deregulation in both agricultural and industrial sectors under the terms of structural adjustment policies imposed on highly indebted developing countries by teams of economists from the World Bank and the International Monetary Fund acting on behalf of the creditors.[6]

Take one example which is widely cited – that of second-hand clothing. Europe and the USA have large internal markets in second-hand clothes, fed in large part by charity shops of one kind and another. These shops collect thousands of tonnes of discarded Western clothes every year, the vast bulk of which they sell on to the rag trade who in turn sift and select much of this product for export to Africa where it turns up in local markets and on street stalls in the cities. As a consequence local textile and clothing producers are put out of business as they are unable to compete.

The dumping of the subsidized produce of American and European farmers on developing countries has had similar effects on food markets. Under WTO rules African countries may put up no trade barriers to imports of either textiles or food, regardless of the conditions under which imported food-stuffs have been procured. Hence, though European or American cereals are heavily subsidized, WTO member nations are not allowed to erect tariff barriers against them. A recent in-depth study sponsored by Christian Aid in Ghana shows how the dumping of cheap subsidized European food is destroying livelihoods and turning smallholders into unemployed shanty dwellers.[7] For example, much European industrially farmed chicken is exported outside Europe. In order to compete, Ghanaian chicken producers have to buy subsidized European animal feed or they cannot sell at a unit cost that can compete with European chicken. The result is that Ghanaian maize farmers face a situation where the market price for their product does not provide their families with a livelihood sufficient to cover the kinds of everyday cash costs that a typical Ghanaian now faces as a consequence of World Bank and IMF intervention in Ghana these last 20 years, including for example user fees for clinics, hospital treatment and schooling.

Underlying the policy shifts in development economics at the World Bank and the IMF, at the Department for International Development in the UK, and also informing advocacy of the WTO trade regime in Western political circles in the 1990s, was the view that underdevelopment in Africa was primarily a consequence of corrupt governance, and of excessive state intervention in rural and urban economies which resulted in hidden transfers of resources out of rural into urban areas. Hence food subsidies and price controls were seen as having a detrimental effect on subsistence farmers and as benefiting urban consumers while their abolition, combined with privatization of state enterprises, was supposed to improve the balance between urban and rural sectors. However, as Stiglitz and Charlton point out, the evidential base for the policy of deregulation was actually very limited and it ignored the fact that industrialized countries at similar stages of development had all used the kinds of industrial support and protection policies that economists now believe are detrimental to growth.[8]

There are few regions in the world where there are absolute shortages of food in physical, material terms. Even if not enough is grown locally, mechanisms exist – either governmental or non-governmental – to supply the population with the staples it needs. However, these mechanisms require access to cash and the rural poor do not have cash, or have less cash than they used to, precisely because the market prices of their own farm surpluses are driven lower and lower by the effects of subsidized food from developed countries. Dreze and Sen have shown famine and hunger are not so much to do with food production as food distribution mechanisms.[9] Food poverty is growing in Africa because the rules of world trade imposed by the WTO as condition for access to international markets, combined with the conditionality and austerity regimes of the World Bank and the IMF, produce a situation where both rural and urban poor are losing the ability to earn enough cash to buy sufficient quality food to provide themselves and their families with a decent diet.

Defenders of the World Trade Organization argue that it does not set the unfair rules of world trade, that these are a historic hangover from the colonial era, and that it is the long-term aim of the WTO to erode and ultimately erase the resultant distortions in international markets. However, it is the case that the WTO continues to enforce trade rules that allow Europe and the United States to continue to impose tariffs on textiles, manufactures as well as food products from Africa and much of Asia and Latin America. And even if all these evident and indefensible injustices were swept away, the fact remains that no industrial country ever industrialized without the benefit of tariff and other kinds of protection for its nascent industries. Even with a level playing field between developed and developing countries the resultant 'free' trade regime would still be unfairly stacked against the poorest countries because already developed and industrialized countries benefit from centuries of history in which they have been allowed to protect and nurture their own nascent industrial and service sectors. Even fully transparent global deregulation of international trade will not advance economic growth and reduce food poverty in Africa. Only conditions that allowed less developed countries to develop their own industries and services and protect them from the invasive effects of world trade, while at the same time developed economies are fully open to competition, would be sufficient to allow these countries even to get back to the more favourable trading and economic conditions they enjoyed in the 1970s, let alone to advance beyond these.

Back of these questions of the fairness of the existing trade rules lie a number of fundamental ecological, moral and spiritual questions. Even if African countries could overcome food poverty by globally trading flowers and mangetout with Europe and America while importing subsidized American maize or European wheat, would this actually be ecologically, morally or spiritually advantageous to African countries? The answer is a resounding no, and the study of Ghanaian farmers in part explains why. This study involved extensive qualitative interviews with farmers, both as individuals and in groups. What the researchers found was that small rural farmers, and the traders who market their produce in towns and cities, are all relatively poor and as a consequence they seek to farm and trade in ways that avoid undue risks. Examples of risk averse behaviour include the use by small farmers of more than one maize variety each year, and the saving of seed, to ensure that adverse climatic conditions do not destroy a whole crop, and to provide for the next year's crop without having to break into the limited supply of household cash available to the farmer. But the deleterious effects of globalization on small farmers have forced many of them to adopt new crops or products – coffee being a prime example – which are supposed to be more valuable in world markets and hence to provide a better source of income. However, as coffee farmers all over the world have found to their cost, it is not possible to eat coffee beans when the price of coffee falls below the cost of production as has happened as a consequence of the IMF and World Bank advising, but also requiring, indebted countries such as Vietnam to grub up indigenous agricultural and timber products and substitute the putatively more valuable coffee plant to earn foreign exchange to pay off their external debt. Since the same policies were foisted on dozens of indebted tropical countries at the same time the world price of coffee has fallen through the floor, something any economics undergraduate could have predicted but which apparently escaped the overseers of what Stiglitz now recognizes as the collective folly of the 'Washington Consensus'.[10] Similarly Africans have found they cannot eat cut flowers, nor do they have a lot of use for exotic foodstuffs such as mangetout, which is not a regular part of their diet, when prices for such crops fall and they have converted their family plots from staple foods to grow these cash crops.

We in Britain know all about risk aversion when it comes to food supplies because it was precisely food scarcity during World War Two that led to the policies of subsidy and over-production in Britain, which have contributed to the vast food surpluses the European Union is now dumping on other parts of the world. Risk averse behaviours are perfectly rational but curiously they play no part in the rational-choice theories of firm and consumer behaviour now in vogue with Western neo-liberal economists. Nor are they allowed for by current world trade rules and debt conditionalities. Local agriculture that supplies local people is by far and away the most secure way of providing people with food in good times and in bad. Not only is it more secure, since it does not leave a populace at the mercy of futures traders in Chicago or London, but it is also more eco-logically benign. It involves fewer food miles, and hence less energy expenditure, and it helps sustain connections between urban and rural communities, and between city dwellers and the cultures of farming. But why, the reader may ask, are such con-nections important?

There is certainly not space here for a history of chemical and industrial agriculture in the last 50 years.[11] Suffice to say that the industrial food economy in the last 50 years has made paupers of small farmers all over the world, has destroyed local food markets and the connections between diet, food growing and nutrition which for thousands of years were the basis of agriculture. At the same time industrial farming has decimated the habitats of the other species – birds, small mammals, insects – with which farmers have traditionally shared their fields. There is also a spatial disconnect between farming and food consumption which has consequences for human food cultures, hence the growth in the diseases of obesity and of malnutrition. The globalization and industrialization of the food economy has brought about an orgy of over-consumption in the West, where many no longer even know how to eat well or to prepare fresh food, let alone understand how food is grown, and in many inner city areas people do not have local access to fresh food. There is, as Graham Harvey puts it, a 'famine at the heart of the feast' that the chemically laden and technologically driven over-production of food has produced in the world these last 50 years.[12] This global 'famine at the heart of the feast' has been powerfully advanced by the Western neo-liberal vision of economic globalization, the theory that the market economy is the best governor of human affairs, that it is best able to deliver human welfare when it is most untrammelled (at least overtly) by government regulation and intervention. And yet as I have albeit briefly tried to show the imposition of this ideology has done anything but advance the welfare of the poorest peoples of the earth, and has been equally harmful to the welfare of non-human species.

In their book *Fair Trade for All* economists Joseph Stiglitz and Andrew Charlton, while critical of such consequences of the present global trade regime, nonetheless suggest that modest reforms to the international regulatory framework will make it possible for just and sustainable outcomes to be achieved. Their foundational assumption is that farmers and traders in developing countries who are given freer access to international markets benefit materially. However the authors also recognize that none of the developed industrial nations achieved their present state of material advancement by granting unfettered access to their markets to foreign producers. But they nonetheless continue to adhere to the neo-liberal claim that provided a global free market is shorn of its colonial biases it will ultimately enhance the wellbeing of both developed and developing countries. They do however point out that the costs of further liberalization will fall not on the rich but on the poorer nations. To address this they argue that the WTO, and in particular negotiations on the next development round, ought to move away from mercantilist priorities where each nation or trading bloc begins from a position of defending its own economic interests and instead embrace a regime in which active assistance to developing countries in adjusting to a new more liberal international trade regime is offered by the developed world.[13]

Most economists favour the abolition of tariffs and subsidies because they hinder efficiency. However, protection can aid nascent industries in developing countries and small farms in developed countries, neither of which, in a global comparison of equivalent producers, could be said to be efficient. The *moral* contest is between efficiency and fairness. But economists do not recognize fairness as an intrinsic element in the mathematical models that guide their policy proposals. And international trade negotiators and lobbyists in Geneva and elsewhere are also not known for their prioritization of fairness. There is nothing intrinsically fair about an international institution such as the WTO where the outcomes of its deliberations are guided by the extent to which member nations can afford to provide trade counsellors and negotiators. Where the United States and the European Union can field hundreds of staff to argue their cause, many developing countries can only afford a contribution to the salary and expenses of one shared regional trade representative. Just as the historical process that led to the creation of the WTO was dominated by the historic colonial trade regime, so the WTO continues in its processes and procedures to offer a playing field that is still weighted toward the rich.

Stiglitz and Charlton argue that a fairer form of free trade can be realized through a reframing of outcomes in trade negotiations in which development for the poorest becomes a priority, and national self-interest takes a back seat to international efforts to improve the welfare of the more than 2 billion people who live on less than two dollars a day. How likely though is this kind of shift in the priorities of developed nation trade counsellors likely to occur? Stiglitz and Charlton are optimistic, though the recent WTO conference in Hong Kong did not provide much evidence of this kind of moral shift. The reality is that what passes for free trade under the policing of the WTO is still rigged in favour of those nations, and especially the United States and the European Union, which can and do continue to protect and subsidize their domestic markets while dumping excess agricultural and other products on the newly liberalized markets of Africa and Latin America with the consequent undermining of indigenous markets and local incomes.

In Latin America, where the problem of these trading imbalances was first exposed by intellectuals who included liberation theologians as well as economists, a small number of politicians have been elected in the last five years who are prepared to renationalize domestic resources and protect domestic markets from the kind of unfair and rigged deregulation which has characterized the international economic regime for the last 30 years. But presidents such as Hugo Chavez of Venezuela and Evo Morales of Bolivia are regarded in the West as threats to democracy, freedom and prosperity, just as were democratically elected leaders in the 1950s in Iran, Guatemala and elsewhere who similarly sought to recover control of their national resources from the foreign companies which remained in control after the granting of titular independence. It may be that Stiglitz and Charlton are right and that there is a new moral dimension to international trade and economic relations which was not present 30 or 40 years ago. But will this moral dimension be enough to prevent Western-orchestrated removals of democratically elected leaders who do not serve Western interests? History will be the judge of that. If Chavez and Lula survive unmolested by CIA-inspired coups, if they are allowed to take back control of their own countries' resources and allow their own citizens to benefit materially from their fair and proper deployment, then the kind of turn towards genuine fairness in international trade negotiations may eventuate. What however is missing from the reformist account is any recognition that this turn does not only depend on adjustments in economic models; it also requires political change in developing countries themselves of the kind that the West has in the past strenuously resisted.

It is because they recognize the need for radical political and economic change if developing countries are to achieve strong and sustainable local economies that critics of the WTO such as Martin Khor of the Penang Consumers' Association and Walden Bellow of the Third World Network argue that what is needed is not reform but abolition of the WTO. And they argue this because, as Bellow points out, world trade expanded seventeen-fold between 1948 and 1997 without the aid of the WTO, under the more flexible arrangements of the GATT, while the real motive for the founding of the WTO was not the further expansion of world trade but the unilateral desire of the United States to reshape global markets, including agricultural markets, in its interests.[14] Neither Europe nor Japan was pressing for the end of the GATT. The WTO was above all the creation of the Clinton administration as it sought to shape the new emergent reality of globalization so that it would continue to favour America's corporate financial interests. The Washington approach to world trade, and the reason it wanted agricultural products as well as manufacturing products included in the purview of the WTO was put quite bluntly by the US Agriculture Secretary John Block at the start of the Uruguay Round negotiations in 1986: '(The) idea that developing countries should feed themselves is an anachronism from a bygone era. They could better ensure their food security by relying on US agricultural products, which are available, in most cases at much lower cost.'[15] As Bello comments 'Washington, of course, did not just have developing country markets in mind, but also

Japan, South Korea, and the European Union.' And he continues:

It was the US that mainly pushed to bring services under WTO coverage, with its assessment that in the new burgeoning area of international services, and particularly in financial services, its corporations had a lead that needed to be preserved. It was also the US that pushed to expand WTO jurisdiction to the so-called 'Trade-Related Investment Measures' (TRIMs) and 'Trade-Related Intellectual Property Rights (TRIPs).' . . . It was not global necessity that gave birth to the WTO in 1995. It was the US's assessment that the interests of its corporations were no longer served by a loose and flexible GATT but needed an all-powerful and wide-ranging WTO. From the free-market paradigm that underpins it, to the rules and regulations set forth in the different agreements that make up the Uruguay Round, to its system of decision-making and accountability, the WTO is a blueprint for the global hegemony of Corporate America. It seeks to institutionalize the accumulated advantages of US corporations.[16]

The first question a moral theologian should ask about the World Trade Organization is what kind of thing it is. Only then can we make a judgement on Bello's contentious claim that abolition would be preferable to reform. Clearly the WTO is a political organization in the classical sense of the word political – it rules, it exercises sovereignty. What kind of sovereignty does it exercise? It is a corporate body and exercises shared sovereignty on behalf of those member nations who sign up to it. It is not only political but judicial – that is, it acts as a court and judges cases between plaintiffs. What kinds of judgement? Well it has no body of case law and seems to follow none. It would appear that its method of judgement is closer to Roman than common law which is to say it makes judgements on the basis of the claims of property, and of conformity or otherwise to the laws of fair exchange as laid down in the founding articles of the WTO, laws written in large part by the United States

Federal Government and the European Commission before the inauguration of the now putatively democratic institutional procedures of the WTO.

Already when we describe the WTO in this way we see how complex a beast it is: in traditional political parlance it is at one and the same time an executive body, a governing body and a legislative body. Now it is both fascinating and strange that the prime mover behind the creation of this body was the United States. The United States has in its own founding articles a division of powers between elected political representatives, executive agents and judicial authority which reflects a particular theological vision of human governance and its attendant difficulties and dangers. The tradition of a balance of powers is intended to ensure that no one arm of government acquires overweening power. This is also enshrined in the federal structure of the American States. Federalism was closely linked in the minds of the founding fathers with Calvinist notions of covenant and community and their theological intertwining in biblical traditions. Combined with the enshrining of the unsustainable economics of neo-liberalism in the foundational procedures of the WTO, these problems in the form of sovereignty exercised by the WTO indicate that the trade regime it oversees ought to be resisted by those who believe in the Christian understanding of justice, and in particular the moral priority of the weak.

The fair trade movement represents the most significant form of resistance to the exploitative and inequitable effects of the international trade regime overseen by the WTO, though Stiglitz and Charlton make no reference to this movement despite using the phrase 'fair trade' for their book title. As defined by the European Fair Trade Association fair trade represents 'a trading partnership, based on dialogue, transparency and respect, which seeks greater equity in international trade.'[17] As Geoff Moore argues, this approach to trade includes a number of goals including the intention to improve the livelihoods of producers by paying a better price and continuity in a trading relationship; the promotion of trading opportunities to disadvantaged groups including indigenous people and women; raising awareness among consumers about the problematic ethics of other forms of international trade and campaigning for fairer rules of international trade.[18] Fair trade also involves the intention to increase in country added value – for example in the case of coffee by the producer country processing and packaging the finished product – to revise the colonial practice of treating colonized terrains as extractive economies of raw materials whose value is added in the colonizing country.

The Fair Trade Mark is now recognized very widely and is being taken up as a model of trade not only by other NGOs but even by large multinationals whose other practices – such as persuading developing country women that baby milk is better than breast milk or selling farmers short and driving local traders out of business – are far from just. However it may well be asked whether the principles of fair trade are honoured when a large corporation which regularly engages in forms of trade that are coercive and exploitative in their effects on the conditions of farmers and other workers also presents a fair trade brand among a range of other products. The difficulty here is an ethical one. Multinationals who follow the letter of the rules of fair trade may not in reality be fairly trading.

It is important at this point to recall the origins of fair trade in Britain. The model was pioneered by a group of Christians in St John's College, Durham in the 1970s who were exercised about the injustice of trading relations between First and Third World and who established the first fair trade co-operative in Britain, dealing initially in tea, coffee and a small range of crafts, to exemplify an alternative model of trade.[19] The organization they established, Traidcraft, has become the largest fair trade organization in Britain and now trades as a PLC. The model of fair trade for those who first established it arose out of an understanding of the ethics of the New Testament and the command of Christ to 'love your neighbour as yourself'. It is highly significant that the word Christ uses in this 'new commandment' is not respect or honour but love. The use of this word love – *agape* – implies something more than a legal relation or a formal duty between neighbours. It commits Christians, as St Paul later recognized, to a law of love whose moral standard is far above any formal and legal ordering of human relationships. In his account of the politics of the body of Christ in 1 Corinthians 12—14 St Paul argues that the law of love commits Christians in their body politics to standards of love for one another that are so radical in terms of the ethic of mutual service and respect for the weak and the vulnerable that they provide the crucial qualitative difference between the sacred politics of Christians and the *saeculum* of the Roman *imperium*.

In seeking to establish a standard of trade that respects the poor, the founders of Traidcraft enacted in the global economic order a Christian alternative which is a witness to the body politics of Paul and to the alternative practices that these politics sustain. The message Traidcraft has advanced in the churches whose members still constitute the majority of its customers and supporters is that it is not possible for Christians to live as anonymous consumers in an international economy. Trading exchanges set persons in moral relationships with those from whom they purchase, even though they may be at great geographical distance from one another. The command to 'love neighbour as self' therefore must find expression in the virtue of justice enacted in the practices of seeking just prices, which reflect just wages and just conditions of work.

There is a long-standing tendency in the history of the Church to turn the spiritual service of Christian community back into the letter of the law, a tendency which Max Weber identified as the routinization of charisma.[20] In a sense this is what the transformation of fair trade into a global trade mark which may be used by Nestlé or Tesco, as well as Traidcraft or Oxfam, does; it routinizes the original charismatic insight of the first Christian fair traders. And with routinization comes the potential for declension from the charisma or original spirit of the founders. It is therefore crucial that it is not forgotten that in Britain the practice of fair trade emerged from the distinctive moral and spiritual vision of members of a Christian community if its contribution to reshaping and resisting neo-liberal approaches to world trade is to be sustained.

The early twentieth-century idea of progress in development involved the claim that through material improvements it is possible for human dignity and spiritual orientation both to be advanced. This idea of human development has close affinities, and ideological roots, in the idea of the guidance of the Spirit in the life of the Church in the development of doctrine and tradition first put forward by John Henry Newman in his seminal *Essay on the Development of Christian Doctrine.*[21] However the connection between material and spiritual development is increasingly lost in the context of the growing dogma of neo-liberalism, and the primacy of the market and money exchanges over real measures of human, and other than human, wellbeing. A Christian approach to development requires continual attendance to the guidance of the Spirit as well as to accounts and theories of economic development. It also requires recognition of the divine origins of justice in the story of God who sets a standard of justice in the world in the rule of Christ and the fellowship of the saints on earth in which the poor are given honour alongside the rich. The early story of Traidcraft is therefore not just an incidental piece of history. On the contrary the story of the founders is intricately connected with the story of the founder. There is no universal logic that can require rational assent to the principles of fair trade. Fair trade is a set of practices that arose as an expression of a distinctively Christian account of justice and fairness. And fair trade will make less impact on the mal-development promoted by neo-liberalism if it neglects the intricate connection between its Christian origins and the distinctiveness of its practices. Equally these practices will only continue to have a *spiritual* as well as a material impact in sustaining a divine standard of justice in the world if they are regularly scrutinized by a higher standard than that of profit and loss, or even of fair trade rules. As St Paul puts it, 'the written code (*gramma*) kills but the Spirit (*pneuma*) gives life' (2 Corinthians 3.6).

The imperial economy being imposed on world agriculture under the auspices of the WTO was designed by the strong to serve the interests of the strong. There could not be a greater contrast than between the monistic monopoly of legislative, economic and political power exercised by the WTO and the devolved local polities of the first Christian communities in which power was shared, and was exercised in such a way as to give priority to the weak. Christians have no reason to expect that this New Testament account of the polity of the body of Christ will come to shape the powers which govern the world. However in Christ Christians believe that the powers have been defeated, even if their defeat has yet to be fully realized on earth. The WTO is a classic instance of one of the fallen powers that continue to resist the lordship of Christ over the earth. The fair trade movement is a hopeful exemplar of an alternative pattern of trading in which the power of greed is dethroned and the human and ecological sacrifices it requires are curtailed. So long as the WTO retains its current in-built biases to its most powerful members, the richest nations on earth, and its unitary constitution, it will continue to stand not only as a direct contradiction to the principles, in part biblical in origin, of fair trade, but also as an institution which rules in direct opposition to the Biblical account of the just and peaceable rule of Christ.

Notes

1 For a published version of Keith Sumption's paper see Paul Sutmoller, Simon S. Barteling, Raul Casas Olaascoaga and Keith J. Sumption, 'Control and eradication of food-and-mouth disease', *Virus Research* 91 (2003), pp. 101–44.

2 John Vidal and Peter Hetherington, 'Food lobby forced PM into u-turn on plan for vaccination', *Guardian,* 8 September 2001. See also 'Brown Blames Foot and Mouth Slaughtermen', *Daily Telegraph,* 27 March 2002. The Royal Society report on the disaster the following year noted that the government had considered but failed to implement a vaccination strategy although it would have prevented millions of animals being culled and recommended that in future vaccination of animals on neighbouring farms to an outbreak should become standard practice rather than mass culling: The Royal Society, *Infectious Diseases in Livestock: Scientific Questions Relating to the Transmission,*

Prevention and Control of Epidemic Outbreaks of Infectious Disease in Livestock in Great Britain, London, Royal Society, 2002.

3 The author lived in Malaysia in the 1980s and describes the challenge the NICs represent to neo-liberalism in Michael Northcott, *Life After Debt: Christianity and Global Justice*, London, SPCK, 1999.

4 For a fuller account of the impact of debt conditionalities on indebted developing countries see Northcott, *Life After Debt*.

5 Stiglitz and Charlton cite the case of Mexico which under the regime of the North America Free Trade Area has seen rural poverty rise drastically: Joseph E. Stiglitz and Andrew Charlton, *Fair Trade for All: How Trade Can Promote Development*, Oxford, Oxford University Press, 2005, pp. 22–4.

6 See Northcott, *Life After Debt* for a fuller account of structural adjustment and its effects on indebted countries.

7 *Talking Trade: Communities Making Trade Policy in Ghana*, London, Christian Aid, 2003 at <http://www.christian-aid.org.uk/indepth/311talkingtrade/talking_trade1103.pdf>.

8 Stiglitz and Charlton, *Fair Trade for All*, p. 34.

9 Jean Dreze and Amartya Sen, *Hunger and Public Action*, Oxford, Clarendon Press, 1989.

10 Joseph E. Stiglitz, *Globalization and its Discontents*, London, Penguin, 2002.

11 For an excellent survey see Colin Tudge, *So Shall We Reap: What's Gone Wrong with the World's Food and How to Fix It*, London, Penguin, 2004.

12 See further '"Behold I have set the land before you" (Deut 1.8): Christian Ethics, GM Foods, and the Culture of Modern Farming', in Celia Deane-Drummond, Bronislaw Szerszynski with Robin Grove-White (eds) *Reordering Nature: Theology, Society and the New Genetics*, London, T. and T. Clark, 2003, pp. 85–106.

13 Stiglitz and Charlton, *Fair Trade for All?*, pp. 66–79.

14 Walden Bello, 'Why reform of the WTO is the wrong agenda' at <http://www.focusweb.org/publications/Books/wto.pdf>.

15 Quoted in Bello, 'Why reform of the WTO is the wrong agenda'.

16 Bello, 'Why reform of the WTO is the wrong agenda', pp. 4–5.

17 European Fair Trade Association (2002) at <http://www.eftaadvocacy.org/definition.asp>.

18 Geoff Moore, 'The Fair Trade Movement: Parameters, Issues, and Future Research', *Journal of Business Ethics* 53 (2004), 73–86.

19 Chris Sugden, *Fair Trade as Christian Mission*, Bramcote, Nottingham, Grove Books, 1999.

20 Max Weber, *The Sociology of Religion*, trans. Ephraim Fischoff, New York, Free Press, 1965.

21 John Henry Newman, *An Essay on the Development of Christian Doctrine*, London, Longmans, Green, and Co., 1909. See also M. P. Cohen and R. W. Shenton, *Doctrines of Development*, London, Routledge, 1995.

Section 3

Affirming Global Localities: The Importance of the Faith Contributions to Political Economy through Individuals and Communities

11. Entry to Enterprise: Constructing Local Political Economies in Manchester

CHRIS BAKER

This chapter examines two contrasting examples of Christian-based local political economy in Manchester (as a case study of a regional UK city undergoing rapid economic and spatial change due to the global competitiveness of the market). The purpose of this praxis-based examination is to see what it reveals about the nature and identity of a Christian political economy for the twenty-first century, and in particular, how it might create more nuanced understandings of traditional concepts such as devolution and the common good. For the purposes of this discussion I am assuming political economy can be defined as the 'interrelationships between political and economic institutions and processes'.[1]

New Manchester – a case study of a global context for a Christian local political economy

Nowhere is the ability of the market to dictate what happens at the local level more obvious than in the speed with which Manchester has been regenerated. In the space of less than 20 years old Manchester has successfully transformed itself from a declining *Cottonopolis* (that is, a city based on textiles and other heavy manufacturing industries) to an *Ideopolis* (a new city region whose capital is now predicated on the ability to create knowledge, ideas and information). Ideopolis is an American theory based on an updated version of the Italian renaissance city-state,[2] which stresses the importance for city-regions of generating the necessary economic conditions to remain globally competitive especially in ideas, research and design. There are key infrastructures needed to encourage this human capital and create a city 'where people want to live, to learn, to generate and exchange ideas and do business'.[3]

The following list of desirable infrastructures was developed by the 'Core Cities Group' (a network of eight former industrialized English cities outside London) as a response to the concept of Ideopolis. They include:

- effective communications and transport infrastructure, including international airport and IT connections;
- a distinctive city centre, including strong architectural heritage and iconic new physical development;
- nationally and internationally recognized facilities;
- facilities for research, development and innovation involving good links between higher education and commercial sector;
- large numbers of highly skilled professionals and a well-educated work force;
- an inclusive and diverse population;
- a reputation for excellence in arts and culture with supporting service sector;
- good local governance and policy/political autonomy;
- commitment to environmental responsibility and investment;
- a good stock of high-quality residential options.

I attempt to capture the urban impact of the shift towards these structures in an article written with other Manchester-based theologians:

(Ideopolis) means bidding farewell to the old industrial Manchester of factories and mills – a city built on manufacturing and production – and ushering in the brave new world of café-bars, nightclubs, huge retailing hubs, cultural and heritage industries, urban lifestyle apartments, university mergers attracting 74,000 fulltime students, cutting edged research and small-business incubators. This is a city making its living through the thriving 'knowledge industries' and a 24/7 party culture, and representing a decisive shift from production to consumption. The attempt to create a city of 'liveability' based on cultural diversity, leisure and high-quality architecture and design thus reflects significant economic and urban shifts. 11 per cent of all jobs in Manchester are now retailing-based with thousands more employed in bars, restaurants, hotels, cultural industries and fitness clubs. Sankey's Soap factory in Ancoats (once Manchester's industrial heartland) is now a state-of-the art dance club . . . some former factories are now desirable apartment blocks for young single professionals, named after that 1960s movie epitomising urban chic, *La Dolce Vita*.[4]

However, there have been high costs to this transformation of New Manchester into an Ideopolis. The fact remains that this major urban investment has failed to shift local unequal income distribution in any progressive way, since the majority of new employment opportunities are low-skill, low-pay and insecure service sector type jobs. According to the Greater Manchester Low Pay Unit research summary for 2004, one third of all jobs advertised in the conurbation were connected with catering, cleaning, care work and shop work – jobs predominantly associated with female employment and low pay. Over 90 per cent of part-time jobs paid less than a couple with two children would receive in Income Support. More than 40 per cent of part-time jobs also paid insufficient to cover access to statutory sick and maternity pay, and did not entitle the worker to a state pension in older age. More than a third of all jobs in Manchester (full-time as well as part-time) paid less than £5.15 per hour.

Equally reduced quality of life indicators reinforce these poor economic indicators. For example, men still die below the age of 70 in the Manchester urban area, over five and a half years younger than the national England and Wales average. The infant mortality rate is nearly double the national average, death rates from heart disease and strokes are 90 per cent higher than national averages and suicide rates 60 per cent higher.

Two case studies of Christian-based local political economy

The following case studies represent the reality of life for many communities caught in the shift to New Manchester's successful reorientation to the global market. They provide the low-cost, low-skill workforce for the service economy and as a result tend to suffer the effects of chronic ill-health, poverty and poor educational attainment, often accompanied by more acute symptoms of crime and social breakdown. However, many living in these globalized localities are resilient and hopeful and have the resources capable of producing viable forms of social and economic capital with encouragement and support.

Eden Harpurhey Youth Project

This project was established in 2001 under the umbrella of the Message Trust, a Christian charity working with disadvantaged young people in the Manchester area. Harpurhey, in the northeast of the city and on the edge of a huge new business park, has been designated the second most deprived neighbourhood in the whole country (see ODPM indices of deprivation). Eden's initial response was to establish partnerships with local institutional churches (an Anglican and United church) to set up a Youth Project. The Project has grown into a multi-service deliverer for young people including:

- Tuesday Youth Club – for 11–16 year olds, providing sport, games, cooking and craft activities;
- Chaos 2 – for 12–16 year olds, providing sports and craft activities;
- Made It – a mentoring scheme partnered with the local secondary school combining creative arts with addressing issues of non-attendance;

- Detached – a street-level outreach programme on Harpurhey's housing estates;
- Groovy Chicks – for girls under 12, offering social activities and a space to discuss informally life issues;
- Monday girls – a similar group for 13–15 year olds;
- football teams and two or three overtly faith-based activities.

All these services are run by a team of three full-time youth workers, supported by 15 volunteers, all of whom live within Harpurhey. Other partners include Greater Manchester Police, local schools and the North Manchester Youth Inclusion project, a statutory agency run by the Youth Justice Board.

Alongside this impressive range of youth projects, other programmes exist which demonstrate a further level of sophistication and innovation.

First, Eden's work emerges from close consultation with the service users (i.e. young people in Harpurhey) but is also reflective of current academic research and government policy. The connections with research-led policy developments are impressive, and their report, *Building a Bridge to Inclusion for the Young People of North East Manchester* (2005), was produced by the Centre for Citizenship Studies at the University of Leicester.

Second, the Project has developed two innovatory pieces of community development and social enterprise that take forward secular-based praxis. First is the *Matrix Mentoring* programme that creates 'multiple mentoring points' for individual young people. This means the current practice of statutory mentoring, usually delivered from one fixed point (a school or youth club), is expanded to provide what Eden call a 'fabric' of support through projects and adults who are connected and regularly communicate with one another. This is possible because of the distinctively Christian nature of the Project's methodology – namely a radical discipleship and incarnational model of community engagement (i.e. all its workers live in Harpurhey). This 'community-within-a-community' model allows a constant low-key presence to be maintained (through the various youth club 'delivery points' mentioned above) which is open-access, informal and non-judgemental but also well-connected to statutory agencies who can provide further support and advice. Thus the Project works as a 'gateway' to other services – for example, help with dyslexia or self-harm behaviour. The Matrix Mentoring programme's strength derives from relationships created with those excluded from accessing other services (perhaps because of a criminal record or exclusion order).

The second concept Eden offers directly addresses the economic deficits a community like Harpurhey experiences in the face of global expansion. The *Entry to Enterprise* programme helps young people develop enterprise skills and set up their own micro-enterprise ventures. Thus 14–19-year-olds using Eden's mentoring schemes are offered opportunities to visit local businesses prior to undergoing placements with them. These opportunities are linked to other strands – building up confidence, addressing communication and presentation skills, CV writing, enhancing emotional intelligence (i.e. addressing issues of anger or low self-esteem). The Entry to Enterprise scheme develops partnerships with a variety of businesses and builds up the competencies of young people to an entry level of emotional and practical competence as potential micro-entrepreneurs. It thus augments the economic and educational capacity of a disadvantaged local community to compete against some of the global forces washing around its borders. It will help attract flows of income into the local community and create opportunities for young people to stay in Harpurhey and invest their human capital there rather than in the city centre and beyond.

Community Pride Initiative

The Community Pride Initiative (CPI) was established in the 1999 under the auspices of a national Christian charity, Church Action on Poverty. It has built up an impressive portfolio of engagements with a variety of partners across Manchester and Salford and currently has a staff of ten. Its mission is to address issues arising from a lack of empowerment due to poverty and exclusion. In CPI's view, this inequality in accessing power is linked to inequality in the distribution of information and lack of public space where that information can be shaped and challenged from the local perspective.

CPI's theological roots lie in a more liberal *kerygma*. Its gospel presentation is based on shared praxis rather than an explicit commitment to share the message of the Good News which lies at the heart of Eden's ethos. It is also more rooted within an overt liberation theology tradition. This means 'engaging critically' in strategies and policy debates that affect the lives of poor communities around the 'core issues of poverty, social exclusion, urban renewal and debate'.[5] It also means implementing development strategies used within the poorer South; a participatory budgeting scheme in Salford borrowed from the Porto Alegre model in Brazil; comic strips to explain regeneration policy to local groups; running schools of participation with leaders from ethnic and other local groups, also based on Latin American models.

Two elements of Community Pride's work are distinctive. First is the unique mixture of skills and approaches held within a single organization. The sheer diversity of groups and networks that Community Pride works with is immense: local community networks, New Deal for Communities programmes, a Gender and Engagement project, tenants' associations, local churches, café projects, leadership programmes for young people, community organizers' programmes, national programmes on active citizenship, establishing disability networks and funding a deaf linkworker, as well as annual conferences on local democracy. To resource a client group as diverse as this requires an extraordinary range of overlapping but also distinctive skills and competencies that have to be well managed and co-ordinated.

This is a powerful example of social entrepreneurship but with added value. That added value is directly linked to what CPI call 'a desire to make real the values of the Christian Gospel'.[6] In other words, the breadth of issues and groups covered by Community Pride's work reflects a belief that every aspect of a person's wellbeing needs to be addressed when talking about civil renewal – political, social and economic. A CPI worker once told me that Community Pride's *raison d'être* was to bring 'life in all its fullness'. In a three-year impact report written by the European Institute for Urban Affairs at Liverpool John Moores University (2005), the following distinctive elements to CPI's *modus operandi* were identified from interviews with both users and partners:

- a firm value base that allowed it to 'go the extra mile';
- a moral force and impact beyond its numbers;
- a sense of sharing that leads to mutual support;
- a belief in partnership;
- a commitment to trailblazing and identifying needs that are not otherwise being met;
- creating self-sustaining structures, not dependency;
- creating a niche market of operating that mixes both analysis and group work skills;
- recognizing the significance of power structures;
- keeping up to date with current policy initiatives;
- translating knowledge and information for those who are affected by the decisions of others;
- feeding intelligence back to the policy makers.[7]

Central to CPI's stated way of working is the commitment to 'participate in learning and exchange with organizations and networks with similar aims and methods across the UK and internationally'.[8] This commitment is a key element in the construction of a local political economy because it helps ensure a freshness and flexibility of approach.

Weaknesses of the local political economy model

By its nature, the approach adopted by these projects falls into a number of traps. Workers from both projects have spoken of the difficulty in finding time to reflect theologically on experience –

a classic dilemma faced by proactive and entrepreneurial groups. Other critiques contained in its report suggested that CPI was good at short-term solutions but raised question marks about longer-term continuity due to being overstretched. Multi-level, multitasking organizations such as CPI run the risk of seeming larger than they really are, with the attendant issues of burn out and over-dependence on a small number of individuals which that perception brings. There is also a temptation to allow principled stands to create over-ambitious goals that override the importance of small steps and incremental processes.[9]

Contours of a twenty-first-century political economy

Emerging from these two contrasting Christian based case studies I propose three emerging contours of a twenty-first-century political economy.

1 The growing impact of religious capital

The first contour is to introduce the concept of religious capital as a way of describing the innovative and impactful contributions of these two projects to the political and economic regeneration of local communities. Although still an evolving idea, the concept of religious capital begins to address the overlapping but distinctive contributions faith communities bring. Much work is being done in the United States on this concept, for example by the Metanexus Institute and the Templeton Foundation, and it is increasing in significance in the UK. William Temple Foundation, after three years' close mapping of nine different churches engaged in regeneration and urban renewal in Manchester, has recently proposed the following definition of religious capital, and its close links to spiritual capital:

> *Religious* capital is the practical contribution to local and national life made by faith groups.

Spiritual capital energizes religious capital by providing a theological identity and worshipping tradition, but also a value system, moral vision and a basis of faith. Spiritual capital is often embedded locally within faith groups but also expressed in the lives of individuals.[10]

From these case studies, we see that religious capital embraces a number of practical responses to the hydra-headed problem of social exclusion, ranging from adult education techniques, mentoring and entrepreneurial development. All this work is underpinned by a moral and spiritual vision of transformation and hope which is applied at individual (micro) as well as strategic (macro) level. Much of this religious and spiritual capital is happy to work within the accepted parameters of mainly secularized discourses on the nature and outcomes of regeneration, for example, creating and hitting key targets on housing, health and education, etc. But it has also stressed the unique Christian base from which its values and motivations spring and this has expressed itself in going beyond the accepted boundaries of secular-based interventions by consciously living out the principles of 'going the extra mile', open acceptance and unconditional love. This has been recognized by secular agencies as a deeper, moral type of engagement that treats people as individuals and is prepared to take risks and push boundaries. It is also prepared to critique accepted norms, values and methodologies if these go against the fundamental value of human dignity and worth made in the image of God.

There is more work to be done in testing out this concept of religious capital within current discourses on other types of capital, for example, social, human and cultural. Work also needs to be done in understanding those forms of religious capital which implacably oppose the mainstream norms and values of the liberal society in which they are placed. But by using the language of religious and spiritual capital a proper debate can take place for the first time about the nature of what inspires and motivates faith communities, including the nature of faith and the significance of theological identity.

2 Recognizing the hybrid church within multilevelled governance

Hybridity is also an increasingly important contour because it is a concept that has been around for over 20 years and is finally making its way into theological circles. It is a key concept for understanding the emergence of diversity and plurality in post-colonial, post-modern cities like Manchester. A key exponent of hybrid theory is Homi Bhabha and his concept of the Third Space.[11] The Third Space is the unstable and constantly evolving area within culture and language that lies between the fixed ends of binary oppositions. He develops his theory to show how colonial assumptions of the superiority of Western culture based on rationality, technology, capitalism and Christianity have collapsed in the post-war period. The West's ability to label and define the East based on crude and imagined binary categories such as the Occident versus the Orient is similar to the way we now understand language has been manipulated. Language almost inevitably represents at any one time the cultural idiom of a prevailing ideology. The Third Space is thus that area which refuses to be bound by the expectations of stereotypes and takes risks to allow new identities and patterns of thought to emerge.

Ecclesiologically, the Third Space is important because it puts a name to the emerging methodologies of church projects like Eden and CPI. It identifies the *methodological* hybridity whereby the Church refuses to occupy spaces at either end of the spectrum, but works from the creative space in the middle. Thus for example, both Eden and CPI achieve results by occupying the creative space *between* a network and an institution. Their approach is network-based but they are supported and work in partnership with institutions of all kinds. They act as a liminal space of interaction and interpretation between different levels of economic and political regeneration at the local level. As we have seen from both projects, a hybrid church is not ideologically wedded to one way of achieving outcomes, but is prepared to learn from a wide variety of models and to be creative in the different people and groups it can gather together. For example, both projects are politically hybrid: prepared to acknowledge the importance of the market in relation to the economic benefits of entrepreneurial activity while simultaneously reserving the right to critique 'the powers' when the benefits that global drivers bring are outweighed by specific instances which politically and economically disenfranchise the local.

These projects also adopt a *hybrid identity* by deploying both explicit and implicit expressions of Christian identity to achieve pragmatic outcomes. Both overtly state their Christian origin at key moments in their reports. CPI refers to the 'values of the Christian gospel', and makes a straightforward reference to it being 'thankful for the ongoing link with Church Action on Poverty and the mainstream Churches by whose inspiration and vision Community Pride was founded'.[12] Eden similarly refers to itself as a 'Christian charity' and draws attention to their 'mainstream Christian ethos'.[13]

Elsewhere, Christian identity is more implicit, and the report reader infers the significance of faith. For example, Eden states that its 'unique operating policy' of locating its staff residentially within the Harpurhey neighbourhood is as a consequence of its 'faith ethos'.[14] Note how Eden uses technical language ('unique operating policy') to soften the impact of its Christian identity. That somewhat bland phrase describes what fellow Christians would recognize as a radical expression of discipleship and incarnational theology (namely living as a community within a community). The use of the adjective 'mainstream' in the above paragraph similarly modifies the explicit use of the word 'Christian'.

Meanwhile, CPI's assertion of its Christian links in their report's introduction is not alluded to again. Instead, later on, key references to the 'moral' impact of its work allow the reader to make the connections between their explicit Christian identity and the implicit outcomes of that identity.

These references lifted from these two reports represent a balancing act between explicit and implicit identity and language that properly recognizes the fluidity and complexity of working in partnership with others as part of both formal and informal systems of governance. This balancing act meshes with the current philosophy behind political governance espoused by New Labour and its policy of new localism or multilevel governance. Managerialism at local authority level is not equated with pure economic efficiency (as under Thatcherism), but with taking on the challenge of working across boundaries between national government and statutory providers, the market and the community/voluntary sector, what Stoker calls 'the goal of holistic working.'[15]

But the medium is also the message. The placement of a few explicit references to Christian identity within an empirical, technical and academic piece of research sends out a message that while Christian identity is important, that identity is also non-threatening to other partners. Not only is it non-threatening, but it is well-informed, technically credible and increasingly indispensable. This raises the question of political efficacy – is the Christian identity reflected within the overall tone and ethos of these reports strong enough to be noticed and respected or is it sufficiently buried so as not to be an offence or concern? This question is difficult to answer because the political economy that prompts it is so fluid and unpredictable.

3   Dynamic and triple devolution

Prosperity with a Purpose correctly reminds us that traditional notions of Christian political economy are constructed around understandings of the *common good* and the principle of *subsidiarity*. The idea of the common good is built on the moral importance of 'commitment to one's neighbour at the level of community as well as the individual'. In practical terms the common good is therefore the 'whole network of social conditions enabling human individuals and groups to flourish and live a genuinely human life'.[16] Integral to the notion of the common good is the idea of subsidiarity, that is, the devolving down of opportunity and autonomy to the most local levels of society. This allows everyone to feel that they have a stake in contributing to the common good. The role of government (so the theory goes) is to provide the maximum opportunity through social and fiscal policy for individuals and communities to contribute some of the individual goods that make up the common good.

We have observed two examples of local political economy emerging from post-modern and post-industrial New Manchester, which allow these ideals of the common good and subsidiarity to come alive in a dynamic and relevant way. By way of conclusion I would like to offer as my third contour the idea of a *dynamic form of devolution* that does not rely on geographical boundaries (for example the difference between Wales and Northern Ireland), but is expressive of *highly localized processes* of political economy that are shaped by both a resistance to, but also working with, the dynamics of the global market.

Unlike traditional assumptions of Christian political economy which envisage a centralized institution such as the Church of England or bodies of churches or faiths addressing the nation through policy documents and the apparatus of synods, the hybridized model of Christian political economy described here recognizes more intentionally the fragmented and pluralized nature of political governance. In other words, it is how faith groups negotiate their religious capital, their skills, gifts and competencies and innovations, at the *local* level which probably has more impact on the ground than adherence to central guidelines, important though these might be.

This form of dynamic devolution, informed by religious capital also becomes a *triple* form of devolution with the inclusion of *spiritual* capital as identified above (namely, the value systems, moral visions and bases of faith that energise religious capital). The reference to *triple* devolution deliberately engages with the concept currently being deployed by New Labour of double devolution. Before that, the buzz phrase was new localism. These rapid shifts in language highlight the importance all political parties attach to trapping that elusive idea or phrase which will once again connect citizens to politics. According to the former Minister of Communities and Local Government, David Miliband, double devolution refers to the passing of 'power from Whitehall to the Town Hall, and from the Town Hall to citizens and local communities'.[17] As part of that devolution of power he warns his government colleagues against micro-managing the third sector. In what could be described as another dimension of double devolution he outlines the importance of developing contracts with the voluntary sector that stress broad *outcomes* that can be achieved rather than detailed outputs, thus allowing what he calls the how as well as the what a chance to breathe. Spiritual and religious capitals take this important discussion of how and what one stage further by talking about the why. Irrespective of whether one defines oneself as religious or even spiritual, the growing significance of the faith sector reminds the public policy world of the importance of not only listening to, but *harnessing the energizing power* of values and motivations when it comes to creating sustainable localism. Stoker articulates the need, in this era of complex multi-governance, 'for a more engaging form of politics and recognition of the importance of issues of empathy and feelings of involvement to enable political mobilisation'.[18]

The idea of spiritual and religious capital helps move us towards this vision of political mobilization by highlighting the importance of the why *as well as* the how and the what – the triple process of devolution. When combined with hybrid ways of being Church, these concepts describe an emerging pattern of Christian political economy which seeks to operate effectively within local communities as a specific response to both the opportunities and challenges of globalization impacting on city/regions such as Manchester.

Notes

1 P Johnson, 'Political economy – a glossary of Political Economy Terms', <http://www.auburn.edu/-johnspm/gloss/political_economy>.

2 See Max Nathan and Andy Westwood, *Manchester: Ideopolis? Developing a Knowledge Capital*, London, The Work Foundation, 2002.

3 Nathan and Westwood, *Ideopolis*, p. 3.

4 John Atherton, Chris Baker and Elaine Graham, 'A Genius of Place?' in Elaine Graham and Anna Rowlands (eds), *Pathways to the Public Square*, Münster, Lit Verlag, 2005, p. 72.

5 European Institute for Urban Affairs *Impact Report 2002–5*, Manchester, Community Pride Initiative, 2005, p. 7.

6 Community Pride Initiative Impact Report, p. 6.

7 Community Pride Initiative Impact Report, p. 8.

8 Community Pride Initiative Impact Report, p. 7.

9 Community Pride Initiative Impact Report, p. 9.

10 Chris Baker and Hannah Skinner, *Faith in Action: The Dynamic Connection between Spiritual and Religious Capital*, Manchester, William Temple Foundation, 2006, p. 9.

11 Homi Bhabha, *The Location of Culture*, London, Routledge, 1994.

12 Community Pride Initiative Impact Report, p. 4.

13 Centre for Citizenship Studies in Education, University of Leicester, *Building a Bridge to Inclusion for the Young People of North East Manchester*, Manchester, Message Trust, 2005, p. 8.

14 *Building a Bridge*, p. 8.

15 Gerry Stoker, *Transforming Local Government: From Thatcherism to New Labour*, Basingstoke, Palgrave Macmillan, 2004, p. 14.

16 Churches Together in Britain and Ireland, *Prosperity with a Purpose: Christians and the Ethics of Affluence*, London, CTBI, 2005, p. 35.

17 David Miliband, 'Empowerment not abandonment', speech delivered to NCVO on 21 February, 2006, <http://www.odpm.gov.uk/index.asp?id=1163772>.

18 Gerry Stoker, 'New Localism: The argument for Decentralisation Gains Ground in England', <www.ipeg.org.uk/docs/Newlocalism>.

12. The Vocation of the Christian in the World of Work: A Theological Basis for Vocation

PETER SEDGWICK

In this chapter I wish to examine the huge changes that have been wrought by the market, and in particular by the culture of modern capitalism, to Western European society in the last two decades. It is increasingly common that people look for a sense of meaning in their work, even if (perhaps especially if) they are not religious. I say especially if, because one option for religious people is to carry on with their daily job, but to find their sense of meaning from an internal, and not always easily observed, spiritual self-discipline, that provides the sense of continuity of the self in a fractured and fast changing world. However, this move to a renewed religious vocation can end in separating the Christian from his or her neighbours at work, so that the non-religious person seeking a sense of meaning in their life at work rejects the religious perspective as being about a set of rules and inner conformity that is of no use to their own dilemma. So it is that paradoxically it can be the non-religious person who looks for a sense of meaning in their work. Religion (in the sense of clear beliefs and standards) is rejected, but a troubling sense that there must be more to work than greater affluence and a faster life style still remains. They have no wish to join what is seen as a religious club of like-minded people, but they do seek some sense of their own gifts being valued, and that work can nurture those gifts, however small and fragile. But where, asks the person at work, can such a sense of meaning be found? Not surely in the allure of advertising, nor in the empty promises of politicians. So where is one to look? Can a religious faith answer the need to provide meaning not away from work, but precisely in the world portrayed by sitcoms such as *The Office* or *Drop The Dead Donkey*?

Is there a way through this problem? I believe an answer can be found in some contemporary theological writing that does not give up on the modern world too soon. That is easier said than done, and as this chapter progresses, the strains in modern work become all too frighteningly apparent. Nevertheless the answer for Christianity is to provide a sense of meaning (spirituality would be another word, or vocation) that honours the secular and the everyday, without being bland and permissive of everything that flourishes in the twenty-first-century world of work. David Ford is a leading Anglican theologian who has written recently on what it means to have an identity, or in Ford's words to be a self.[1] He wrestles with how a Christian may live in the world so that his or her vocation is to be both a Christian and a person at work, live as a person in relationships (friend, family, sexual, collaboration at work, etc.) or perhaps become a person with civic responsibilities. The combinations are endless.

What is striking in Ford's writings is that the 1960s ethic of the Church in the world is here rediscovered but given a new depth. Many theologians have grown weary in the last decade of the apparently undisciplined activism of the 1960s, which is seen as a time guilty of having ignored the riches of the Christian tradition for a life of radical self-expression. Whether in liturgy, church architecture, theology or social responsibility the tide has turned against that era, and a deep conservatism pervades much of Church life and theology, including perhaps most of all the area of theological ethics. However I feel this criticism of 40 years ago is often ill-judged and too sweeping. By an engagement with Ford's theology, and beyond this with a renewed appreciation of Bonhoeffer, I want to rehabilitate the idea that a Christian ethic is found most of all in the living of daily life in the world. I wish to argue (perhaps controversially) that a renewed Christian ethic, or vocation for daily life at work, will not be found in the perfectionism I often see in some young Christians, nor will it be found in theological writing that turns on the liberal West as the source of human dis-ease. That is too focused on an ideal (often non-existent) Christian community. Perfectionism is a term that does not entirely catch what I am about, but it serves better than most.

Those who are converted to Christianity often feel that the standards to which they aspire brook no compromise. In an age that is seen as hostile to Christianity, it is the ideal of sanctity and often a personal refusal to accommodate to this world that is most attractive. Even if people no longer seek monasticism, the personal ideal of internal asceticism or a denial of the allure of the world is very attractive to many. A person might be someone with an ordinary job, house, family, but as a Christian they live as though the world was passing away. Hence the appeal, also, of Christian businesses, media and communities where the true commitment demanded by Christ can be worked out. The narratives of the Christian community in this vision are powerful enough that they can subdue those of the secular world, which are false narratives of competition, violence and individualism. This is neither an evangelical nor a Roman Catholic phenomenon, for it is common to many aspects of contemporary Christianity. Those who are seeking greater discipline in their lives may argue that the act of making disciples by the churches they join (whether, as I say, it is through being made a disciple under the pastoral care and guidance of Opus Dei or evangelical house churches) is not rigorous enough. Now it would be unfair to deny that this movement has produced great self-sacrifice, giving to charity, and lives of holiness. But it sits at such a distance from the commercial and industrial world in which most people live that it seems to say that one can only be a Christian if one withdraws from that world altogether, at least in one's own self-discipline.

I am seeking a different path forward, that speaks of vocation and a sense of meaning in one's work, but does not abandon the everyday life altogether as a place where the Spirit of God might speak of God's redeeming grace. Such an ethic, or vocation, for daily life must draw on the theological underpinning for this action, for it is not my desire to say that 'the creed and the colour don't matter, were you there?' It is perfectly obvious that for many people creed (beliefs and values, often in a religious form) and colour (ethnicity or race) matter a great deal.[2] Ignoring that point leads to a series of catastrophic misjudgements: the media that does not understand Islam, the civil servant who does not know how to relate to a religious (faith) group, academics in ivory towers with their utilitarian and consequentialist ethics that consider religious beliefs irrelevant, and so on. Yet we cannot just assert that religious faith matters. We must go the long way round, and ask what it is in each faith that leads to political action or has ethical implications in society. Hence a renewed attention to a vocation in secular life must also pay attention to the particularity of each faith, or the tradition, which has shaped that particular religious community.

My topic is Christianity, and in particular modern theology. In other words, I am asserting the importance of religious particularity, distinctiveness, cultural and religious tradition, and sometimes the sheer incompatibility of traditions. The easy smoothing over of differences because of the need for action will not do. We moved too fast 40 years ago, and it has come back to haunt us. But we cannot retreat to a religious ghetto. So what is distinctive about a Christian theology of identity? Ford speaks of the self as being characterized in many ways. We find an ethical self, a self without idols, a worshipping self and much more. Basic to his strategy is that the self is polyphonic. He works out this strategy by dialogue with Dietrich Bonhoeffer. It expresses itself in many ways but at its heart are three things. These are the importance of community, the relationship between faith and obedience to God, and above all the relationship to the natural. By this he means 'all the ordinary elements of human existence (material, social, cultural, economic, moral and so on) which are not about ultimate matters but which make up a great deal of ordinary life.'[3]

There are two reasons why this mattered in the 1940s and why in a different way it matters now. First, so much theology considers the relationship of God to self in such a way that it becomes so ultimate that the penultimate of ordinary goodness was played down. That has certainly been a theme of Lutheran theology in the past, and it is seen now both in Pope Benedict's writings and in much evangelical preaching. There is a turning away from the concerns of the vocation of the Christian in the ordinary world as a matter of primary importance. It is the emphasis which concerns me here. Of course there is much writing, preaching and talks on the need to be involved in daily life as a Christian. But it is seen as secondary, derivative, after the primary work of fundamental theology in Catholic scholarship, or justification/sanctification in Protestant theology.

Second, the Nazis led 60 years ago an assault on ordinary goodness which meant that the task of discriminating among human actions was imperative. The three crucial areas, which they undermined, were those of justice, freedom and human life. It would be preposterous to suggest that the difficulties of contemporary society have a gravity and weight equal to the assaults of the Nazis: they plainly have not. Yet across the Western world we inhabit there is perplexity about justice and a feeling that the demands of security take precedence. It is also the case that there is a widespread view that freedom and human relationships are less easily defended and defined than was the case. In other words, we are not back where we were in the 1940s but there is scope for disquiet, to put it no stronger than that.

It is important to realize that Bonhoeffer's dramatic actions in the last few years of his life were founded on this attempt to relate the ultimate (the self before God, as expounded by Luther) to the penultimate (the everyday, humdrum activities of life). Without a continual awareness of the ultimate the penultimate becomes compromised, engaging in ethical strategies that lack the awareness of God's presence. The ultimate was made up of love, judgement and hope, found above all in the incarnation, cross and resurrection (one might add that Bonhoeffer underplays Pentecost). Each of these aspects of Christ's ministry forms a whole but each allows us to see God in Christ in new ways. The penultimate is made up of the ordinary dimensions of life. Bonhoeffer justified his actions by a belief that in Jesus Christ these two realities, ultimate and penultimate, come together. They come together as we find Christ in the Church as a community in the world, and they demand costly obedience.

Ford draws out the implications of this. First this theology stands in the Lutheran tradition of holding together opposites, such as divine and human, justified and sinner. Contradictions are held together through Jesus Christ. The apparent contradictions held together are the life of joy and the life of free responsibility. They are held together in God's love for the world through the revelation shown in Christ. Joy is not only joy in the ministry of Christ and its victory over death. Joy is to be found in engaging with the natural, and especially in the everyday world of work, relationships and the people we meet. There is no need to retreat to a Christian perfectionism. Second, worship matters. So it is that Ford links Pentecostalism, Taizé and the spiritual songs of Ephesians.[4] There will be varieties of worship, but what matters is that it is good, powerful and moves people. I see this daily among our ordinands who are an eclectic group. Third, and most important of all, Ford claims Bonhoeffer's support for the fact that there can be no overview of the self in modern living. Like a jazz theme, there is no resolution of the music, only continual improvisation in the counterpoints.[5]

Bonhoeffer himself reflects this diversity within himself. There have been many interpretations of Bonhoeffer and his theology.

> Bonhoeffer the saint is as much a construct as Bonhoeffer the radical, Bonhoeffer the liberal, and Bonhoeffer the conservative. Bonhoeffer certainly did not aspire to sainthood. But, like the saints, Bonhoeffer's life and thought draw the eye to Jesus Christ. That is why the centenary of his birth is worth marking.[6]

The diversity of his portrayal of holiness to succeeding generations is very striking. Bonhoeffer does not present a unified
vision of the saint, theologian or activist, even if all his actions
end in the witness of his martyrdom for Jesus Christ.

I feel strongly that the Church has not yet worked out the
sheer importance of the idea of holiness as impossible of being
summed up in particular moral behaviours, types and characters. This leads me into the next section which takes this theme
of untidiness much further. That is the huge changes in the
labour market since 1980. This causes even greater confusion.
The idea of the vocation for life expressed in working practices
is over.

Changes in employment

This can be shown very quickly by a survey of the labour market, and how rapidly it has changed in 30 years. There are six
changes in the labour market since the 1970s which are relevant
to our theme.[7] First, the relationship between GDP (Gross
Domestic Product) and employment has become tenuous in all
OECD counties. Japan's GDP per head grew from 1970 to
1995 by 150 per cent but employment by only 2 per cent. In the
UK, typical of Europe, GDP growth over the same period was
60 per cent and employment fell by 4 per cent. Even in the USA,
which still has a positive correlation between GDP and employment, GDP grew by 50 per cent and employment by 25 per cent.
Since 1995 there has been employment growth in the UK, but
it relies heavily on immigration at the less skilled end of the
labour market. That is especially true of the famous 'Polish
plumber', which has seen 140,000 Poles enter the UK since
Poland joined the European Union, and sent mass figures in
London soaring!

Second, the discrepancy between traded and non-traded
sectors is growing. Traded sectors include financial services and
manufacturing. Non-traded areas include health care and criminal justice. Both seek higher productivity, but the traded sector
generally sees a contraction in employment, at least in the UK.

Traded areas may move offshore as well. Non-traded sectors in theory can provide unlimited employment opportunities.

Third, there has been a change within all OECD countries in typical employment patterns. With a sharp decline in full-time, dependent employment without time limits – what was once called a job for life – it is probable that less than half of Western European employment fits this pattern. In West Germany, 84 per cent of those in dependent employment in 1970 had such contracts. By 1995 it had fallen to 68 per cent. Today it would be well below 50 per cent in the united Germany.

Fourth, then, there is a variety of employment, including part-time, time-limited, contract, self-employed, paid self-employed, home workers and others that defy description. There is also a great deal of expenses only activity, especially in the voluntary sector. All this was well surveyed in *Unemployment and the Future of Work*, the CCBI report written by Andrew Britton in 1997.[8] However, it is worth noticing that the growth in the economy since then has certainly increased employment but it has also further fragmented the labour market.

Fifth, there has been a trend until very recently for retirement to take place earlier and earlier in working life. It is not yet realized how much this will have to change if pensions are to be afforded. Adair Turner's report in 2005 is very relevant here. The number of hours worked in most European OECD countries fell by 20 per cent from 1970 to 1995. Retirement figures in 1995 stood at 44 per cent of all 55–64-year-old men in the UK in 1995; 51 per cent of all in Germany; 58 per cent in Italy; and no less than 62 per cent in France.

Sixth, and finally, unemployment has changed its nature. Beveridge aptly described unemployment in 1929 as making people feel totally helpless in their lives. It spread across the Western world in the 1930s, and it was Beveridge's policies which curbed its power. Before the twentieth century people had alternative means of survival (even arguably in 1909 there was a tradition of voluntary relief) but by the time the CCBI report was published, it was probably 20 years too late for its publication in the UK, for all its deeply impressive analysis and prescriptions.

What we have now is unemployment as a Continental phenomenon, or a factor in inner city areas allied to racial prejudice and
low skills. For most people unemployment is a phase between
jobs, as indeed I have experienced it.

Implications for self-identity

The adoption of the market economy has brought a huge rise in
living standards for the Western world, and increasingly is
doing so in India, as a recent edition of the *New Statesman*
pointed out. It is hard to imagine just how constrained daily life
was in Britain 40 years ago, and how much personal freedom
was limited by the decisions of those who controlled the economy. It was extremely hard to get a mortgage, a loan to start
your own business, foreign currency to travel abroad, or indeed
to buy whatever it was that expressed your identity. The
rationing of mortgages and loans, and the assumption that taste
would be shaped by the few on behalf of the many, was one of
the deepest resentments in the 1960s, along with a belief that
traditional moral standards were to be unquestioned. All this
was swept away in the economic, social and political upheavals
from the 1960s. Christian witness should not seek to bring back
that stultifying culture.

Nevertheless there is another side of capitalism. Richard
Sennett's book *The Corrosion of Character: the Personal Consequences of Work in the New Capitalism*[9] has haunted me for a
long time. Sennett is no old-style socialist. He sees the benefits of
capitalism, but he also knows how the beast has to be tamed. He
writes

> the ethos of teamwork, with its inner suspension and ironies,
> takes us far away from the moral universe of Virgil's grim,
> heroic farmer. And the power relations contained in team-
> work, power exercised without claims to authority, is far
> distant from the ethics of self-responsibility, which marked
> the old work ethic, with its deadly serious, worldly affections.
> The classic work ethic of delayed gratification and proving

oneself through hard labour can hardly claim our affections. But teamwork should have no greater claim, in its fictions and its feigning of community.[10]

Sennett knows that there is no shared narrative of life in modern capitalism, no common story of difficulty and shared fate, nothing other than the accidental working of investment decisions. Some post-modern philosophers accept that the self is therefore an illusion: 'the self-awareness of the individual is only a flickering in the closed circuit of historical life'.[11] Sennett believes that family life is disoriented by work, and migration is symptomatic of the global age. He takes a cultural, or perhaps anthropological, view of the challenge posed by modern capitalism. What late capitalism requires of individuals is, first, how to manage short-term relationships, and perhaps give up a sustained sense of self, for institutions no longer provide much continuity. Second, people need to retrain every decade or so. What is sad about this is that the ideal of craftsmanship (doing one thing really well, and doing it for life) is increasingly not valued, except in a niche craft market, for those who can afford it. Third, people have to let go of the past, and instead look to the future for new ideas and creativity. Sennett believes, almost certainly correctly, that most people are not like this. They value past experiences, they like to be good at things, and they seek for continuity in the story of their life.[12] But late capitalism has a logic of its own. In almost every Western culture, and increasingly in Eastern ones as well, the market brings wealth and a sense of wellbeing to many, especially to the young who are successful.[13] That would be true of most students, for instance. But this reward has its price. The price is that individuals lose their sense of self, especially those who are older and less mobile or adaptable to the new technology. If that is so, we are not surprisingly a society that finds its escape in the luxuries of modern capitalism: drink, consumerism, and the rest for those who can afford them. One answer to this world of constant change is the counter-cultural Christian story that turns its back on the culture of our contemporary society. I wish to resist this option. Instead I believe there must be an alliance of those who have a different vision. Christians can unite with other community groups and indeed humanists in seeking to find some sense of a civic culture that can give human beings dignity and meaning. In an interesting comment David Marquand has argued that what we need is 'a marriage between the social democratic emphasis on civic solidarity and the social liberal emphasis on pluralism, decentralisation and autonomy'.[14] There is much more to be said in this vein.

A renewed Christian vocation at work: theology and employment change

It is obvious that the old patterns of working life, which offered an identity, are dead. The issue which concerns me is whether in the fluidity of employment, the establishment of teams, the growth of project-based work, there can be any sense of identity. There are two clear answers to this dilemma. One is structural reform of the labour market, in ways that address the issues raised by Dahrendorf, Sennett and Marquand. That is, however, an article for another day. The theological challenge is how a Christian can live out their life in this world. White suggests that as religious people we have to carry our identity with us through time. We cannot freeze moments of time, and say this is who we are, and will be for the foreseeable future. Instead we have to take both roles and relationships and see how in a post-modern world we can allow these to be fluid enough to accommodate all the changes I have mentioned and yet relate them to the God who gives us identity in God's faithfulness. That brings me back to Bonhoeffer and to polyphonic living. 'The apparent contradictions held together are the life of joy and the life of free responsibility. . . . there can be no overview of the self in modern living. Like a jazz theme, there is no resolution of the music, only continual improvisation in the counterpoints.'[15] This quote from the earlier part of the article was surprising enough in 1945. It will no doubt be resisted even more by conservatives, whether in the Roman Catholic Church or in evangelical churches. White points to the pain in 'the inexorable passing of the moment . . . The possibility lies in the memory of the moment with its strange capacity to universalise the particular . . . The very particularity of the moment and the place is the route to universality, perhaps the only route.' [16]

A renewed understanding of vocation turns to a theology of diversity, where polyphonic living is the norm. However, thanks to the empowering of the Spirit individuals can find creativity in many different aspects of employment. Just as the Spirit of God could empower both individuals in the Jewish and Christian scriptures with skill, ability and a sense of meaning, so that can be so today. If God calls people to purposeful living, then the nature of employment must be shaped so that this can take place. The development of moral capacities alongside practical and intellectual skills can make a person feel more human, more themselves. This is the fruit of the spirit, for the charisms of God's grace are not given only vertically from above. Instead vocation can be nurtured as people interact with others, develop their potentialities, and become whom God has made them to be.

This chapter has argued that what matters to people today is to find meaning in their work, and that work can confer identity. Nevertheless the whole burden of this chapter is that the identity given today is insecure. A religious vision that can meet this need, without drawing individuals off into a religious ghetto, is the greatest challenge for Christianity. The theologian Miroslav Volf has written that such a theology would focus on three things. One would be the call of God. The second would be the good of the community. The third factor, and for the sake of this chapter the crucial factor, is to pay close attention to the gifts which a person has received. A Spirit-based theology of work would see the Spirit developing those gifts at work, morally, practically and intellectually. He writes:

One discovers what work God is calling one to do by reflecting on the gifts one has received, not simply by examining one's life setting. For God does not call a person to do anything for which God does not give the ability. It is not, therefore, her duty to do whatever morally acceptable work the situation in which she lives might demand of her. It is her privilege to do the kind of work which God's Spirit has guided her.[17]

A vocation at work has to find a way of making work meaningful, humane and nourishing of each person's own gifts. That is a huge, and daunting, task. It means tackling the inhumanity which employers can inflict on individuals and groups, and helping each individual to discover their own gifts. That task takes Christianity back to its roots, for again and again in history Christianity has spoken to oppressed groups about their dignity. However, it is because the Christian faith sees each person's gifts as a gift of God through the Spirit that these gifts can be nurtured. To return where we began, this is not a simple blessing of human endeavour as being worthy irrespective of the biblical understanding of human vocation, where work is related to service, and to the wider community (1 Corinthians 12). Christ meets us with the gift of the Spirit in calling us to serve one another, find meaning in work, and develop one's gifts. What is not promised is stability of life or freedom from rapid change. That is why I find Bonhoeffer's appeal to polyphonic living such an attractive vision, for it speaks powerfully to the restless mobility of modern employment, and yet the need to value our gifts and to serve one another in the Spirit.

In a day recently at this college Ken Leech reflected on his two curacies in the 1960s. One, in Hoxton, was a solid working-class parish where everyone knew everyone, and the church was part of the rhythm of life, expressing a deep stability so long as clergy and people did not shun the pubs of the area, for that was where community was found (he had no problem with this!). The second curacy was in Soho, with its clubs, bars and the offer of anonymity for those who had been ostracized in the communities where they grew up, because they were gay, Chinese, or whatever it might be. Ministry was done fleetingly at 4 a.m., and that conversation might lead to a deep ongoing pastoral relationship. At the time, said Ken Leech, Soho seemed strange and Hoxton felt the norm. Today it is increasingly the opposite across towns in Britain; the norm is a rootless community. The point of this illustration is to suggest that the working life of modern capitalism is equally anonymous. There can be community there, but it can also (as Sennett shows so well) corrode character. The issue is how to respond. Dahrendorf's statistics reveal the sheer intensity of the change we have lived through in working life. So my suggestion is that in Bonhoeffer's theology of Christian living there is the germ of a response to fragmented post-modernity. Christian life allows of no overview; it is a polyphonic living, where all one can do is fling oneself into the whole of life; but what sustains it is the depth of worship, the knowledge of God's faithfulness, and above all the fact that a Christian vocation is made possible by the meeting of the ultimate with the penultimate in every moment. There are great political, and social, implications of how a market economy might be made more humane, but that is not the drift of this chapter. Rather it is to affirm that in the daily living in office work, the service economy, and the dynamism of the market, Christ's faithfulness might be found. It is no steady working out of a lifelong vocation, but the fragmented pieces of daily life in employment that offer us a road in which to find, and be assured of, the presence of God. The challenge for the churches is whether they cling with nostalgia to the older forms of community, finding in that security something of the security of God's love. I may be wrong, but I fear that is the confusion which bedevils our ministry today.

Notes

1 David F. Ford, *Self and Salvation*, Cambridge, Cambridge University Press, 1999. David F. Ford, *The Shape of Living*, London, Fount, 1997.

2 Ken Leech, *Race*, London, SCM Press, 2005.

3 Ford, *Self and Salvation*, pp. 246–8 is the source for all quotations that follow unless otherwise indicated.

4 Ford, *Self and Salvation*, p. 126.

5 Ford, *Self and Salvation*, p. 261, quoting D. Bonhoeffer, *Letters and Papers from Prison*, London, SCM Press, 1971, p. 347.

6 David Moore's comment on Bonhoeffer's centenary exhibition. I owe this reference to John Kennedy. The lecture by Stephen Plant on Bonhoeffer's centenary in February 2006 at Hinde Street Methodist Church is also important.

7 Ralf Dahrendorf, *New Statesman*, 15 January 1999. The article summarizes his *Equality and the Modern Economy*, London, Smith Institute, 1999

8 *Unemployment and the Future of Work*, London, CCBI, 1997.

9 Richard Sennett, *The Corrosion of Character: the Personal Consequences of Work in the New Capitalism*, London, Norton, 1998.

10 Sennett, *The Corrosion of Character*, p. 116.

11 Hans-Georg Gadamer, *Truth and Method*, 1975, p. 245, cited Sennett, *The Corrosion of Character*, p. 147.

12 Richard Sennett *Respect*, London, Penguin, 2003.

13 See my article 'A Christian Reflection on Economic Change' in *Prosperity with a Purpose*, London, CTBI, 2005.

14 David Marquand, 'The Fall of Civic Culture', *New Statesman*, 13 November 2000.

15 Ford, *Self and Salvation*, p. 261, quoting *Letters and Papers from Prison*, p. 347.

16 Vernon White, *Identity*, London, SCM Press, 2002, p. 135.

17 Miroslav Volf, *Work in the Spirit*, Oxford, Oxford University Press, 1991, p. 200, and the chapter 'The Work Ethic' where I discuss Volf's ideas in P. H. Sedgwick, *The Market Economy and Christian Ethics*, Cambridge, Cambridge University Press, 1999.

Part 2

Concluding Reflections:
Hope for the Task Before Us

13. Emerging Directions for Christian Social Ethics and Political Economy

JOHN ATHERTON

Setting the scene for purposeful conversations

This book and particularly this conclusion bring together a collection of individual contributions and shared understandings developed at a residential consultation and all purposefully influenced by the agreed task of developing faiths' contributions to economic affairs in the early twenty-first century. Although as a concluding note, it is the work of one of the editors, all the contributors reflected on it individually and collaboratively, and gave their warm support to it as a valuable reflection of their individual and co-operative efforts and understandings. It builds deliberately on the current spate of Christian reflections on economic matters, whether from different denominational churches, ecumenically and regionally or as individuals. Some of these are noted in the Introduction. It is also set in the long history of Christian tradition's engagement with modern economies and economics from their origins in the late eighteenth century to the present. It is the empiricism of tradition which will illustrate and reinforce the following exposition wherever it is appropriate and relevant. It suggests both recurring signposts for the future and justifications of past performance.

Much of what the book argues through the conclusion reflects that continuity. For example, it develops what at first sight are often well-rehearsed arguments and experiences concerning such economic matters as market economies, competition and co-operation. Yet some of it reflects more innovatory developments particularly as more distinctive faith alternatives to mainstream economics. Both will be explored further in this concluding chapter.

Importantly, both continuities and innovations reflect, but also will contribute to, decisive changes in the contemporary economic and religious contexts. Yet this is not to repeat detailed well-rehearsed interpretations of the dramatic transformations our context has undergone in the last 40 years, or indeed in the last decade. The first has witnessed change in extent and intensity unparalleled in human history. Whether in world production, research and development, population growth or environmental crisis, we encounter regularly the startling comment that more has been achieved since 1945 than in *all* previous history. The second has witnessed growing prosperity in advanced economies and increasingly in emerging economies led by China and India. The distance between two ecumenical reports, the deprivation of *Unemployment and the Future of Work* in 1997 and the economic success implied by *Prosperity with a Purpose* in only 2005, illustrates this accelerating progress. This is despite the gap between the richest and poorest within nations like Britain and the USA, and between all nations, which has continued to grow, and the fact that happiness has failed to accelerate in tandem with economic growth. It is profoundly a context of complex paradoxes, whether of prosperity or inequality. Yet this is no longer a sufficiently adequate understanding of that contextual change, a process which has rightly continued to be essential for developing adequate contemporary Christian social ethics. For an additional dimension of contextual change needs to be engaged with which alone makes these contributions different from past endeavours.

On the one hand, the development of Christian arguments for and against the market economy and mechanism has gained a new urgency and significance because we are all inhabiting an increasingly globalized economy dominated by capitalist market economies. In such debates, often profoundly divisive, Christians are, and always have been, strong participants. We have a most important job to address in this conclusion. For we need to test out whether and how such often fiercely divided opinion can be held in some kind of conversational relationship of mutual respect. We accept and value difference, as demonstrated by the different contributions and perspectives in this book. And yet, we have also searched for overlaps and models connecting the differences. But this is certainly not the same as achieving a consensus covering all the issues raised. That, we believe, is neither achievable nor desirable. The challenge therefore begins to emerge which is to hold together in a continuously interacting tension both workable overlaps and likely persistent differences.

On the other hand, the religious context has changed and is changing at least as decisively as the secular. Indeed, it often interacts profoundly with globalization processes; for example, witness the astonishing world growth and spread of Pentecostalism, a truly global religion. It is a rise, or better resurgence, of a globally furious religion, focused particularly, but certainly not exclusively, on Christianity and Islam. Although we continue to experience some unease over the use of 'furious' to describe current religious experience, we have become reconciled to its value almost like Martin Buber did with the word 'God'.[1] Continuous misuse does not override the utility of well-proven tradition. This accommodation is confirmed by our growing recognition that furious religion in the contemporary context represents a continuum or spectrum, from fundamentalism and religious intolerance to the rediscovery of strongly faith-based traditions and communities often critical of liberal secular or religious experience, and at times suggesting alternatives to it. Such furious religion stands in sharp contrast to or juxtaposition with the continuing decline of mainstream churches in the West (more significantly outside the USA) epitomized so graphically by Callum Brown's *Death of Christian Britain*,[2] and various predictions, given current trends, of the effective collapse of some mainstream denominations by the middle of the twenty-first century. It may well be, however, that such a dualistic picture of contemporary world religion, of a spatially different rise and decline, is merging into a more coherent whole. For religion in the West, particularly Christianity, *may* be reformulating, influenced by its increasing interaction with a globally furious religion (not least through communication systems, technologies and migrations) with its historic and present assumption of faith's strong public role. It is that intrusion into the West which combines with the emerging and growing recognition of the substantial contribution of faith communities, particularly as Christianity, not simply to the social capital of people, neighbourhoods and societies, but to an emerging argument for that faith contribution to be defined as *religious capital*. The work of the William Temple Foundation in Manchester is developing a major contribution in this field, not least as a powerful example of a living Christian tradition, closely linked to the earlier seminal work of Archbishop William Temple in the field of Anglican and ecumenical Christian social ethics. Based on its current research into local churches and communities, its provisional conclusions are drawing the important distinctions between social capital (as good neighbourliness) and religious capital, as reflected in Chris Baker's chapter. The latter, religious capital, is defined as 'the practical contribution to local and national life made by faith groups' energized by and inextricably bound to spiritual capital's 'value system, moral vision and basis in faith.'[3] More importantly, it concludes that from a church-based perspective 'religious capital represents a *progressive* spiral of influence and growth that contrasts with the apparently *regressive* spiral of institutional decline'. Clearly, what is happening in the West is not best described as the extension of furious religion, but it may well warrant being described as a *reformulation* of religion as it becomes more involved in the public realm. And that development will certainly be contested, not least because of the power of secularization processes in media, government and academia, and because of the justifiable criticism of religious extremism. Yet it will not be stopped. So the task becomes one of influencing it for the better, as a constructive faith contribution to the common good of society. Hannah Skinner's introductory chapter reflects these agenda-forming features, strongly informed by her work for the William Temple Foundation.

Importantly, this book, and particularly this conclusion, addresses this task. It develops both the contribution of that reformulated faith to economic affairs in the early twenty-first century, and also recognizes the complexity which makes up that reformulated faith. This now includes what faiths share with governments in promoting the public good, but also how faiths challenge such mainstream orthodoxies both as critique and as generating distinctive faith alternatives to mainstream economics. In our contributions, the promotion of Islamic interest-free banking and Christian fair trade illustrate these latter developments. How we try to get a purchase on all of them, and then communicate and promote them for the public good, is one of the key objectives of this conclusion.

It will have become clear that we believe that contextual changes, interacting with the developments of faiths, produce a decisive change in our conversations on the contributions of Christianity to economic affairs. Understanding this emerging significance of faith traditions (as Christian beliefs) and of faith communities (as churches) is both essential for the churches in the West, so overwhelmed by decline or false dawns, and for other bodies, including government, media, academia and the general public, so often and too easily seduced by very dubious secularization theories. For this objective, understanding this reformulation of faith is one way of at least recognizing what is actually going on, and acquiring some knowledge of religious literacy. In many ways, these tasks mesh in well with the discoveries of this project and book. Many of the contributors were certainly shaped by the mainstream liberal traditions of churches and Christian social ethics[4] (which Malcolm Brown has described so well) of emphasizing the role of reason above Scriptures and tradition. Much of mainstream churches and theology still operate in this way, with some of our contributors being closer to this than others. Yet there is a strong argument that the reformulation of religion in Britain must still include recognition of the contributions of liberal traditions to human wellbeing. Indeed, some of our contributors argue that Christianity has a renewed duty to defend secular liberal space. This includes acknowledging its manifestation in Christian social ethics, particularly as interdisciplinary working, and as a distinctive part of Christianity, as much distinctively religious as the faith-based contributions which we will explore later. Adapting Lonergan's work in the Roman Catholic tradition, it should be described as an essential contribution to the development, noted above, of a religious literacy in different horizons of meaning. Yet given or despite this renewed commitment to liberal Christianity, many have also developed into post-liberal or radical Christian positions. What is clear is that all of them have moved significantly, in that all see the need to take Scriptures and wider tradition much more seriously, as Hannah Skinner so strongly reminds us, certainly recognizing the role of reason (some more than others), but all recognizing the need for faith tradition and faith community to occupy a more central position in this reformulation of religion in the West, including in its conversation with economics. To summarize this development is therefore helpful both to ourselves as contributors, and for the churches, *but* also for partners in other disciplines and arenas of society, whether government, business or civil society. Essentially, therefore, the reformulated Christianity which is emerging in Britain and the West is struggling to hold together a more mainstream and renewing liberal tradition, emphasizing collaboration with other disciplines and partners, with a more resurgent Christianity emphasizing a more distinctively different Christian position often acting as critique and alternative to other disciplines and partners. Certainly the mainstream liberal tradition includes those who may move beyond it but not breaking decisively with its virtues including among our contributors myself, Malcolm Brown, Peter Sedgwick and Patrick Riordan. They are more likely to place greater emphasis now on Scripture and tradition, in critical conversation with more resurgent religion. This has encouraged them, for example, to reformulate the distinctively Christian insights – searching for the added value of faith (added to what is shared with others of good will). For example, it is seen in the development of the Christian understanding of human dignity by Hannah Skinner and myself, now more firmly located in God and Christ, the development of the company as agent of transformation by Peter Heslam, and in the Christian understanding of the Church as the body of Christ, including its consequences for a distinctively different Christian community and polis this inspires. That, of course, through Northcott's radical view of fair trade, leads also to the strong interpretation of the politics of Jesus, in terms of its engagement with empire, and the consequences of that for Christian engagement with global capitalism and empires, including the decisive role of the USA and Christian Right, in supporting such adventures but also of the deep opposition to them. Both Wilde and Northcott have developed these understandings further in their recent publications,[5] as well as strongly incorporating such perspectives in their contributions to this book.

In all these examples, we are presented with a reformulated Christianity which clearly includes very different perspectives, yet which is increasingly engaging with the distinctive understandings embodied in its faith traditions and faith communities. All these insights have informed our 12 contributions and the 24-hour consultation discussions. What we attempted to do in the latter, is not to come to an overriding consensus. The nature of global Christianity, especially in its reformulated Western form, but also of the contemporary global context, including in its economic nature, both *precludes* such a consensus being reached, and, indeed, suggests the undesirability of so doing. In other words, we accept that we will not agree over the legitimacy of market economics as capitalism, or the emergence of one overwhelming dominant tradition in Christianity's engagement with economic affairs, whether radical distinctive or mainstream overlapping liberal, or between faiths. Yet, since we are facing together the challenge of daunting global problematics such as poverty, environment and security we are committed to enquiring as individuals and as collaborators (as in this project – as an example of a way of faithful working today) into the possibilities for some shared understandings, including models and typologies that consciously link our differences, future conversations between our different understandings, and pursuing theoretical and practical projects, like this faithful journeying.

With this task in mind, reflecting on the 12 contributions for this conclusion begins to suggest a clustering of our material to reflect *connections* between them as an emerging agenda for developing the contribution of Christianity to political economy in the early twenty-first century. The first part of this conclusion, discussions or arguments over market economies, economics and capitalism, is the biggest, and includes both macro-economics and economic systems, and micro-economics, for example as competition. The second part examines ways of developing relationships between the different Christian approaches to economics as revealed in the first part. This is particularly done through the development of models and typologies for Christian social ethics in such a reformulated Christianity, and their link to ecclesiological models as different ways of being Church. This is a quite essential development, in the light of our contributions and discussion, of the recognition at the beginning of this chapter of the renewed and new importance of both faith traditions and faith communities for engaging global change, including in its economic dimensions. Addressing issues raised by such typologies, including how to face up to differences, this part ends with a reflection on the nature and implications of collaboration. It is these two parts which include the meat or major results of our collaboration, because they incorporate our response to our declared task of investigating what kind of political economy for the early twenty-first century our faith suggests, and what are the implications for the development of Christian social ethics.

Part One. Faith contributions to political economy. Are market economies and economics, including capitalism, the preferred option for an ethically sustainable political economy in the early twenty-first century?

The arguments over market economies and economics, and especially as capitalism, have existed in some form or other since the late eighteenth century – back to the beginnings of industrialization and urbanization. The arguments have crossed disciplines, from economics to sociology, and politics, from the Liberal Party to the Labour Party and Marxism. And they have been conducted on, among other things, ethical and religious (in this case Christian) grounds. Indeed, the relationship between religion (Christianity) and capitalism has been an important contribution to an evolving tradition in British Christian social ethics, which, because of its focused relevance for this project, is worth elaborating in detail, including with reference to contemporary examples of the stages in this tradition.

It is a tradition which begins with R. H. Tawney's *Religion and the Rise of Capitalism* (1926). Written as a critical response to Max Weber's seminal *The Protestant Ethic and the Spirit of Capitalism* (1930 edition), the centenary of its publication in original article form we have recently celebrated. Tawney modified Weber's thesis linking the rise of capitalism with the emergence of Protestantism in the sixteenth and seventeenth centuries. Whereas Weber emphasized Calvinist attitudes to predestination as revolutionizing Protestant trade, Tawney argued they essentially confirmed existing business values. Written in the 1920s in the midst of great economic and political turmoil, Tawney's devastating critique of Christianity's inability to continue to engage critically the emerging new socio-economic order inspired his own efforts to promote the development of an adequate Christian social ethics for the inter-war period. His scathing judgement on the seventeenth- and eighteenth-century churches still holds good today: 'The social teaching of the Church had ceased to count, because the Church itself had ceased to think'.[6] His response was to work denominationally and increasingly ecumenically in developing a resurgent Christian critical engagement with economics and capitalist systems, which has numerous recent impressive equivalents, though often lacking Tawney's subtlety and realism or pragmatism. For example, in Britain, Tim Gorringe's *Capital and the Kingdom* (Orbis-SPCK, 1994) and *Fair Share: Ethics and the Global Economy* (Thames and Hudson, 1999), Wilf Wilde's *Crossing the River of Fire* (Epworth, 2006), and Philip Goodchild's *Capitalism and Religion: The Price of Piety* (Routledge, 2002), Peter Selby's *Grace and Mortgage: The Language of Faith and the Debt of the World* (Darton, Longman and Todd, 1997), Antonia Swinson's *Root of All Evil: How to Make Spiritual Values Count* (Saint Andrew Press, 2003) and Ann Pettifor's, who led the Jubilee 2000 campaign, editing of *Real World Economic Outlook: The Legacy of Globalization; Debt and Deflation* (Palgrave, 2003) all continue that tradition of a religious-based radical critique of global capitalism. In Europe, out of the German Lutheran tradition, Ulrich Duchrow, through links with Latin American liberation theology, has similarly developed a strong theological critique, which has been particularly influential in the ecumenical tradition of Christian social ethics in the World Council of Churches (WCC) and in the global Lutheran World Federation: his *Global Economy: A Confessional Issue for the Churches?* (WCC, 1987) continues Tawney's theological opposition to capitalism, and moves from critique to reconstruction in his *Alternatives to Global Capitalism: Drawn from Biblical History, Designed for Political Action* (International Books, 1995), and *Property for People, Not for Profit: Alternatives to the Global Tyranny of Capital* (Zed Books, 2004). In the USA, the work of Douglas Meekes' *God the Economist* (Fortress, 1989) provided an early example of the attempt to construct a radical theologically grounded political economy. Much more recently, and linking explicitly to the growing awareness of globalization, Richard Gillett's *The New Globalization: Reclaiming the Lost Ground of our Christian Social Tradition* (Pilgrim Press, 2005) presents a more socio-political critique of global capitalism, but very clearly tradition-based. Importantly, the American feminist radical critique of global capitalism and search for faith-based alternatives is represented by the work of Cynthia Moe-Lobeda's *Healing a Broken World: Globalization and God* (Fortress Press, 2002), and Rebecca Peter's *In Search of the Good Life: The Ethics of Globalization* (Continuum, 2004).

The second stage of this tradition in British Christian social ethics' engagement with the religion and capitalism debate was provided by V. A. Demant's *Religion and the Decline of Capitalism* (Faber and Faber, 1952), written out of the seeming triumph of socialism in Britain, Europe, the Soviet Union, China and much of the Third World. Demant's work almost announced the emerging end of capitalism, not least because of its intrinsic contradictions. These included its profound erosion of those virtues like trust and benevolence (both historically religious, as in Weber, and contemporarily as in social and religious capital) seen as external to the free market yet on which it so powerfully depended. It is a tradition or theological perspective which has powerfully re-emerged in the resurgent form of today's radical orthodoxy, and especially in D. Stephen Long's *Divine Economy: Theology and the Market* (Routledge, 2000). Its reformulation as a neo-Thomism, promoting a just price and wage, and condemnation of usury (interest), provides important connections with medieval Christian tradition's subordination of economics to theological ethics, but also with the contemporary resurgence of Islamic faith-based economics. Both are also linked as traditions through Aquinas' dependence on Muslim translations of Aristotle in the thirteenth century. Both appear in our book, with the work of Zahid Hussain and Michael Northcott.

By the late 1970s, it was clear to Ronald Preston that a third stage in the engagement with capitalism had emerged with his *Religion and the Persistence of Capitalism* (SCM Press, 1979), followed by his *Religion and the Ambiguities of Capitalism* (SCM Press, 1991). As an economist as well as theologian, Preston both acknowledged the continuing significance of the market mechanism for human living in contemporary societies, and also the ability of capitalism to transform itself in relation to continuing contextual change. Announcements of the death of capitalism have always been and probably continue to be premature. The blessed (or bloody) animal will not lie down. Following in the tradition of Preston and Reinhold Niebuhr, and picking up the paradoxical nature of our book's title, Richard Harries wrote *Is There a Gospel for the Rich?: The Christian in a Capitalist World* (Mowbray, 1992).

My own research, therefore, will try to develop this tradition in British Christian social ethics a stage further, in relation to the rise of global capitalism in the early twenty-first century. The task is likely to be focused on the contribution of religions as faiths to the transformation of capitalism (SCM Press, 2008).

There is a large additional literature relating Christian social ethics to economics which reinforces our contributions to this debate. For example, Bob Goudzwaard's *Capitalism and Progress: A Diagnosis of Western Society* (Paternoster Press, 1997) develops an important distinctively Christian critique of capitalism out of the Dutch neo-Calvinist tradition. Peter Heslam had early connections to this tradition. Other evangelical contributions engage in a most constructive way with market economies, particularly the patient work over the years by D. Hay, from his *Economics Today: A Christian Critique* (Apollos, IVP, 1989) to his *Christianity and the Culture of Economics* (editor) (University of Wales Press, 2001). Hay was an important player in the Association of Christian Economists. The mainstream liberal tradition of Christian social ethics is best represented by J. P. Wogaman's work, including his *Christians and the Great Economic Debate* (SCM Press, 1977).

Interestingly, this material also represents a journey that reflects theological differences connecting to our contributors, as I have begun to note. So Demant, and to a lesser extent Tawney, represented a Christendom tradition that pursued a *distinctively Christian* sociology, with links as I have observed to today's radical orthodoxy. Preston, in contrast, was the doyen of the mainstream liberal tradition of Christian social ethics. Again, what takes such conflicts and arguments over capitalism into a new and different stage is the contemporary context with the emergence of three interlocking features. First, the rise, however contested, of globalization, centrally informed by the integration of a growing global economy, itself domi- nated by a capitalist market economy. Here we recognize that, as Wilf Wilde argues, this includes a series of different capitalist market economies, deeply informed by their political and cul- tural – civilizational – histories. Another of our contributors, Peter Heslam in his *Globalization and the Good* (SPCK, 2004), has edited a very useful introduction to some of the leading viewpoints on globalization. All were agreed, as with our Project, that 'ethical and economic concerns cannot and should not be separated'. Second, the peculiar prominence or domi- nance of capitalist market economies in a global context was reinforced by the collapse in 1989 of the communism of com- mand economies, the only feasible alternative to capitalism. This has led some, like Fukuyama, to argue that liberal capital- ist democracies now represent *The End of History*.[7] Most com- mentators, however, including Christian, while recognizing the sharp dominance of the capitalist market economy in the current global context, do not regard this as the conclusion of historical change. Indeed, as I have noted above, they have been stronger on criticism, weaker on alternatives, and rarely con- structively supportive of or engaged with the market economy. Exceptions to this rule include Michael Novak's work in the USA, particularly his very influential *The Spirit of Democratic Capitalism* (London, IEA, 1991), and Brian Griffiths in the UK, and his *Morality and the Market Place: Christian Alternatives to Capitalism and Socialism* (Hodder and Stoughton, 1982). Third, there are arguments which suggest that such a global dominance by capitalist market economies is so interlinked with the geopolitical dominance of America as to suggest descriptions such as global empire. Some commentators, say Hardt and Negri, collapse these arguments into a definition of a new empire of essentially global capitalism, and American led. Their deep and radical critique of such a reformulating capitalist empire of global political economy ends with what is essentially a secular appeal to a form of Franciscan spirituality as the basis for an alternative to contemporary globalization. It is, as I have noted above, an anti-globalization, empire and capitalism which has attracted strong theological support from a variety of what we may need to see as a series of interconnecting religious perspectives and traditions around that common *anti* theme.[8]

In other words, such a new and changing context gives particular prominence to the historic debates with religion about market economies and economics, including as capitalism, which will necessarily involve some continuities of arguments with the past but also new departures. I have therefore divided this first part into two sections covering theological conversations over contemporary global capitalism, and conversations over the market economy and economics.

1 Searching for a way forward: Conversations over contemporary global capitalism and market economies

Many Christian reflections on economics have not seriously addressed this agenda, including contemporary reports like *Unemployment and the Future of Work*, *Prosperity with a Purpose* and the recent report of the Commission for Urban Life and Faith, *Faithful Cities* (2006), or they have sided, for Christian and other reasons, with either the unequivocal condemnation or approval of capitalism. Since I have already referred to these debates and some of their leading protagonists, I will only briefly acknowledge them here but do so in conversation with our contributors. At first sight, for example, the critics of capitalism present the most vocal if not strongest case. Yet they must be balanced by the next section, representing the bulk of British theological work, which engages constructively with the market economy, the basis of capitalism itself.

As critique of capitalism, the most attractive, persuasive and most strongly rooted in a detailed interpretation of Christian tradition continues to be epitomized by Tawney's work. His condemnation of the religion of capitalism as contradicting basic Christian beliefs still stands as a classic expression of this tradition: 'Compromise is as impossible between the Church of Christ and the idolatry of wealth, which is the practical religion of capitalist societies, as it was between the Church and the State idolatry of the Roman Empire.'[9] Yet Tawney was also equally acerbic in his dismissal of the liberal intelligentsia's wild denunciations of capitalism, not least because they had no feasible alternatives to offer. A careful reading of the Tawney archives in the London School of Economics, which my own PhD research required, reveals the presence of a much more nuanced approach, tempered with a realism and pragmatism, at the service of his radical visions. It is this powerfully moral case against capitalism, so often, unfortunately, without that realism and pragmatism, which continues to be made today. So Rebecca Peters and Cynthia Moe-Lobeda continue to express an argument which in the end rejects the capitalist market economy as fundamentally, including ethically and religiously, unacceptable. Like Gillett, their strengths reflect a deep rejection of the harm done to particular individuals and communities by the forces of economic, including global, change. Their limitations are their inabilities to construct a feasible alternative in a disciplined conversation with economics which takes the local seriously but increasingly in a global context.

In our contributions, Wilf Wilde particularly continues this radical critique, confirmed by his *Crossing the River of Fire* (2006), and focuses on the link between global capitalism and empire, especially through oil. Although his is essentially a rejectionist stance, it is, unlike the scholars mentioned above, one that is deeply aware, like Marx, of the valued and essential contribution of capitalism to the human journey. His task, in some ways close to mine, is to *transcend* capitalism, but through and beyond its midst. To do this, he usefully constructs a link between empire and capitalism, which allows him to develop a condemnation of them from the basis of an exposition of the Jesus of Mark's Gospel as Christ's stance against empires. That theme is strongly present in much contemporary biblical scholarship, including Tom Wright's work on St Paul.

It also links strongly with Yoder's *Politics of Jesus* (Eerdmans, 1972), itself closely linked to our other contributor's work, Michael Northcott's, also seen in his *An Angel Directs the Storm: Apocalyptic Religion and American Empire*, and how he develops an exposition of a biblical-Christian tradition understanding of the body of Christ as paradigm for Church and secular polities. What emerges is a distinctively Christian stance which represents both critique of contemporary economics, including global capitalism, and the development of faith-based radical alternatives to the present order. What is important is the connection of this domestic version of global furious religion with its wider phenomenon, particularly resurgent Islam. This is often linked with the stance against a US-led globalization or Westernization, and the development of alternatives to such processes, with religions often making important contributions to them. There are important signs of this Islamic construction of a religious-based political economy which critiques both capitalism and socialism, almost as a religious third way between them in Zahid Hussain's contribution. This has interesting resonances with the third way in Catholic social encyclicals from *Rerum Novarum* in 1891 to *Centesimus Annus* in 1991. There are connections, too, with early ecumenical Christian social ethics, for example the Second Assembly of the WCC at Evanston in 1954, and its search for a responsible society, transcending both communist East and capitalist West, but thereby able to speak to each in terms of balanced critique.[10]

What these contributors all manifest is an interpretation of religion which brooks *no* division between private and public, material and spiritual, religion and political economy. Instead they argue for a *decisive* role for religion and theology in the formation of economics and politics. It is worth remembering that what might seem odd, if not reactionary, to much Western liberal, including Christian eyes, in fact represents the *norm* in recorded history, and today, in most of the world (outside the West).

2 Searching for a way forward: Conversations over the nature of market economies and economics

This section, arranged under seven headings, includes the bulk of our contributions. Essentially, in contrast to the previous section, they accept and work with capitalism as market economies, at least on the basis that they provide the least harmful way of operating modern economies – that is, other ways are more harmful. Some go further, and argue for the ethical adequacy of the market economy.

Recent theological commentary in this field includes the work of some of our contributors. For example, Peter Sedgwick's patient and detailed ethical explorations of the workings of the market economy include *The Market Economy and Christian Ethics* (CUP, 1999), and, with the economist Andrew Britton, *Economic Theory and Christian Belief* (Lang, 2003). Ian Steedman's *From Exploitation to Altruism* (Polity Press, 1989) similarly contributes to this field. Interestingly, Patrick Riordan's related exploration of selfishness, self-interest and the market resonates with an earlier piece of work on self-interest, similarly by a Jesuit scholar, in essays commemorating Ronald Preston's work: Gerard J. Hughes, 'Christianity and Self-interest', in M. Taylor (ed.), *Christians and the Future of Social Democracy* (Hesketh, 1982). Malcolm Brown's contribution draws strongly on his detailed work in *After the Market: Economics, Moral Agreement and the Churches' Mission* (Lang, 2004). In both, he offers theology a way of constructively critiquing market mechanisms, and particularly the philosophies and ideologies associated with them. My own work includes *Christianity and the Market: Christian Social Thought for our Times* (SPCK, 1992) which argued theologically for the importance of the market economy and mechanism as the least harmful way of operating a modern economy given a world population approaching 6 billion. Its significance was heightened, elaborating as it did my earlier *Faith in the Nation: A Christian Vision for Britain*, (SPCK, 1988), because it represented the liberal tradition of Christian social ethics coming to terms with the economic and political transformations of the 1980s. *Faith in the City* (CIO, 1985), so significant for the churches' commitment to urban regeneration and as critique of Thatcherism, singularly failed to understand or accept these changes in terms of their strong values. It could only see their deep limitations. Interestingly, the latest Church report, *Faithful Cities* (2006) repeats this failure to recognize the significance of wealth creation and economic growth for human wellbeing and the reduction of poverty.

Importantly this section also covers arguments about the ethical nature of market mechanisms, particularly in the work of Riordan and Brown, and competition and co-operation, through Kennedy and Steedman – very much, as Steedman reminds us, in the economist's field of micro-economics. Yet it also includes contributions on how a market can address the environmental crisis (Kennedy), and the role of companies (Heslam). Although much of this material applies to the relationship between Christianity and market economies and economics in general, the fact that they have survived to play a dominant role in the global context means that these agendas have continuing significance. Failure to recognize and understand this will seriously impair any effective and adequate way forward for a global economy. Some of these features will be elaborated in a little more detail than others, not least because they have been recognized as significant by contributors but not necessarily developed in detail.

1. Can markets be morally justified? Can Christians justify, and in what ways, the operating of a market economy and economics, including the market mechanism? Three members made important contributions to this debate, essentially reflecting a conversation between Riordan and Steedman, with Brown. The former highlight the theological, ethical and economic justifications for the role of the market mechanism in offering, in Steedman's words, 'a solution to the truly enormous "co-ordination problem" of co-ordinating the production and consumption activities of billions of individuals, who, with few exceptions, know nothing of each other.' Whatever the market's failures may be, it must be asked: 'what system of pure world-wide co-operation would be able to co-ordinate billions of people and their myriad economic activities better than (or even as well as) the market?' And, as Steedman then continues to argue: 'Pointing to the market's failures (which are many), would do *nothing* towards answering that vital question.' In other words, what is the feasible alternative to such a mechanism, in a world of now over 6 billion consumers, and many millions of producers? Importantly, that argument for the market mechanism is elaborated theologically in important ways by Riordan, including his refusal to associate the self-interest of most producers and consumers in the market with selfish greed, so regularly highlighted by Christian moralists. Rather, the operating of the market mechanism contributes decisively to the common good through the coordination of such self-interests. It is at this point that Brown develops an argument that seeks to free Christians and theology from this justification which he interprets as the disconnecting of ends from means, the latter, as market mechanism, being regarded by some as independent of faiths, yet as justified ethically by Riordan and economically by Steedman as 'the proper mechanism for addressing questions of value and distribution of goods in a society' – as Bentham's 'society of strangers' – the anonymous mass of individuals, consumers and producers of Steedman and Riordan. Rather, Brown seeks to develop a way of working ethically and theologically which allows a shared moral critique of the market mechanism, essentially a *constructive* critique as distinguished from the *rejectionist* critique of Wilde and Northcott. Importantly, he develops an argument for what he has called 'a post-liberal dialogic traditionalism' which includes, most importantly, an elaboration of post-liberal virtues essential for supporting, resourcing and promoting such a critique of the market mechanism. This links strongly with Peter Sedgwick's reformulation of what the Christian vocation of individuals can now mean in such an economic context. This features strongly at the end of this conclusion in a discussion of the role of individuals and local communities in such a global context.

2. *Is the market based on greed?* Closely linked to these arguments over the ethical adequacy of the market mechanism are two other related issues: one, is the attempt to justify ethically the market mechanism and the role of individuals in it, in the end a justification of materialism, and two, its links to the issue of the ethical role of competition (this latter will be dealt with next).

The argument for capitalism, as market economics and economies, including the justification of materialism, hedonism and acquisitiveness, has a long history. It certainly figured prominently in Tawney's rejection of the 'religion of capitalism' as incompatible with the religion of Christ (itself regarded as incompatible with the Emperor worship of the Roman Empire – an interesting linkage with our contributors Wilde and Northcott's arguments over the unacceptability of empire and capitalism). The rejection of such mammon-worship of materialism as a justification for rejecting Christian commitment to the market mechanism is discussed by Riordan and Steedman. For them, the theoretical model of the market does *not* presuppose greed in its description of the economic argument. This refusal to collapse market behavioural motivation into an argument justifying greed, materialism and acquisitiveness also links to the recently emerging arguments over the paradox of prosperity in my chapter, which certainly recognizes the crucial importance of a reasonable income for the attainment of happiness, and by elaboration also of human fulfilment and flourishing. Yet it also includes a growing recognition that above a certain level of income, as achieved by most in the West, increases in that income do not deliver a commensurate increase in happiness at all. That happiness is dependent on other, often non-material, factors such as relationships (including marriage and family life), community life, health, and most interestingly, a philosophy of life (especially religious). In other words, like the case developed by Riordan, these arguments confirm the importance of the material as income, but also its limits, therefore requiring a balanced constructive approach to the market mechanism. In some respects, the Muslim argument in Hussain similarly condemns greed and materialism but not legitimate self-interest as wealth creating and profit-seeking.

3. Is the market wrong to promote competition? Should Christian opinion condemn the market mechanism because it promotes profit-oriented competition? Here the contributions of Steedman, with Riordan, Kennedy and Brown, figure prominently. Again, the arguments *against* competition and *for* co-operation figure large in Christian tradition from the nineteenth century to the present. For example, competition was regularly, though mistakenly, seen as the opposite of co-operation to the extent that F. D. Maurice roundly condemned competition as 'a lie' because it contradicted the brotherhood of men as derived from the fatherhood of God.[11] Yet, as Steedman reminds us, the actual opposite of competition in economics is monopoly, with all its damaging consequences for human prosperity.

The ethical attack on competition also links to its association with greedy profit-seeking. A recent collection of essays on interfaith ethics was actually entitled *Subverting Greed: Religious Perspectives on the Global Economy* (Knitter and Muzaffar, Orbis, 2003). Yet as we have noted above, that reduction of economic motivation to greed is highly questionable. And its association with competition is equally dubious for Steedman. For him, the evaluation of competition as the antithesis of co-operation fails, for example, to do justice to the co-operation within teams and companies essential if they are to compete effectively. For Kennedy, the contribution of competition, guided and protected by a strong state, was a foundation of the social market economy in West Germany in the post-war years. Just as strong competitiveness was the basis of German prosperity in overcoming the dire poverty and social dislocation immediately following World War Two, so it now becomes equally essential for facing up to the contemporary challenge of the global problematic of environmental crisis. This could be achieved not least through the market stimulation of those technological innovations so essential for reducing CO_2 emissions. He also links this to the use of the market mechanism to reshape moral behaviour in radical ways supportive of environmental sustainability. This connecting of competition and environment has an additional significance in terms of encouraging the conversations between market economics and environmental concerns. For Heslam, similarly, the market mechanism is an economic and moral prerequisite for the flourishing of companies, an essential basis for their proposed transformative role.

4. *Companies for transformation?* The role of companies in the creation and distribution of wealth has been the bedrock of commercial, financial and industrial systems since the Middle Ages. Throughout this long history, its form has evolved to include today the transnational corporations. Particularly as the latter, they have become major battle grounds between proponents of global capitalism and globalization, and those deeply opposed to them, including anti-capitalist and anti-globalization arguments and movements. Christians have been deeply involved in both camps, sharing their strengths and limitations, whether it be the demonization of transnational corporations or their blessing, including viewing them as sacramentally significant. The demonization is revealed in such WCC work as *Transnational Corporations* (1982), and in the Church of England's report *Transnational Corporations: Confronting the Issues* (CIO, 1983) – with a revealing reference, in Tina Wallace's chapter on 'The damaging impact of TNCs on the Third World', to Ngugi's *The Devil on the Cross* (Heinemanm, 1982), and its critique of TNCs in Kenya. The theological affirmation of TNCs features in the work of Novak, and his *Spirit of Democratic Capitalism*, but particularly in Stackhouse's earlier work *Public Theology and Political Economy* (Eerdmans, 1987) which he has usefully developed into today's global context: *Christian Social Ethics in a Global Era*, M. Stackhouse, P. Berger, D. McCann and D. Meeks (Abingdon Press, 1995).

Careful thought can begin to dissect these complexities,

particularly in relation to the arguments of the other contributors to this project. Such reflections suggest:

- The deep and strong relationship between companies and market mechanisms – what Heslam calls the 'mechanisms of production'. This links to Steedman's recognition of the important role in wealth creation played by incentives, including their relation to innovation and entreprenurial activity. (One of Sedgwick's earlier works was titled *The Enterprise Culture*, SPCK, 1992.)
- The need to focus Christian opinion on the broad reality of what the company actually is. For example, the ease with which some Christian thought focuses on the moral obviousness of the great transnational corporations, and their dominant contribution to global production, needs to be set alongside the fact that the overwhelming number of corporations employ fewer than 50 people (99 per cent even in the UK). These provide the major contribution to actual employment, and therefore to happiness – as noted in my chapter – and particularly in developing economies.
- The arguments over the role of the company in the economy are linked to a number of our contributors, from Sedgwick, as providing an arena for the exercise of individual Christian discipleship, to its essential contribution to poverty reduction. This is a reminder that the more just distribution of wealth, particularly seen as the overall responsibility of government, has to be accompanied by an efficient wealth creation process which is best achieved, historically and contemporarily, by the operations of the market mechanism in the context of a free socially constrained market economy.
- The creative argument by Heslam that the company as a prime agent of theological and secular transformation can come within the remit (in the following reformulated typology for Christian social ethics and what it means to be Church) of the more mainstream liberal and hybrid types. It is therefore apparent that the transformative role is not the peculiar preserve of the more radical faith-based approach, not least

because the latter does not accept the basic contribution of the market economy to poverty reduction and human flourishing. Instead, the transformative role accepts the markets' fundamental legitimacy, but also suggests the need to reform it, because of its obvious limitations.

5. Promoting fair trade. Is fair trade the only ethically justifiable means of exchange? The case for has been strongly supported by the powerful advocacy of such theologians as Gorringe in his *Fair Shares: Ethics and the Global Economy* (Thames & Hudson, 1999) and Northcott's *Life after Debt: Christianity and Global Justice* (SPCK, 1999). A more cautious and economically-based argument is found in Finn's *Just Trading: On the Ethics and Economics of International Trade* (Abingdon Press, 1996). It is a case which has to be located in a context in which increasing trade has played a central part in the astonishing progress of the remarkable economic growth which has so shaped our contemporary world. And that contribution has accelerated, like so much else since World War Two, including production, consumption and income per capita, all so essential for human wellbeing. It has featured prominently in ethical debate over economics, from Cobden's arguments in the 1840s, that free trade between nations is an essential contribution to peace between them, to current proposals for fair trade. Fukuyama has brought that argument into the present, in his case for liberal capitalist democracies that they do not make war with each other. Both incorporate the 'comparative advantage' arguments of economists that a nation should focus its efforts on what it can best produce that others will buy, and using the wealth created to purchase what else it requires. It is at this point that Northcott takes issue with this argument of classical economics, when it is linked to what he argues is the manipulation of the WTO for the benefit of the most powerful and richest nations, especially the USA. The price of such profound injustice is paid particularly by the poorer and economically weaker nations, who are thereby increasingly marginalized from the global capitalist economy. This drives him to argue instead for *fair trade*, a key development in the churches, and resourced by such Christian-inspired business organizations as Traidcraft. This could be usefully buttressed by the classic medieval arguments for the just price and wage and the condemnation of usury, all of which feature in the case for fair trade. Yet for him, the argument against current global trading patterns and for fair trade instead becomes much more significant – for it develops into a faith-based radical critique of trading relationships in a global capitalist empire economy, and the promotion of a faith-based alterative to that empire through developing an ethically based alternative trading system. ·

6. *The challenge of poverty reduction.* Not surprisingly, the attack on poverty has occupied a prominent place in current Christian apologetics both in the British Church and theological academy. (This allows me to be very selective in a complex of fields which include urban theology, liberation theology and world development and poverty.) Poverty reduction features strongly in the major Church report *Faithful Cities* (2006), itself celebrating the twentieth anniversary of the seminal report *Faith in the City* (1985). Both focus on poverty in Britain, and its links with increasing inequality. My work provides a link between the two, including a more economically oriented contribution to the latest report. (Unfortunately, the Commission overplayed the material on poverty and inequality, and underplayed the material on economic growth, thereby repeating the mistakes of *Faith in the City*.) This report also reflects the paradoxes of prosperity and poverty in my chapter in this book, building on my earlier work on *Marginalization* (SCM, 2003), itself a return to the theme of my first publication *The Scandal of Poverty: Priorities for the Emerging Church* (Mowbray, 1983). It also links with the growing importance of Church or faith-based pressure groups such as Church Action on Poverty. Its earlier chair, Hilary Russell, combining this experience with her secular academic expertise on urban regeneration, produced a fine study of deprivation, *Poverty Close to Home: A Christian Understanding* (Mowbray, 1995). Like myself, Brown,

Baker and Skinner, she is actively involved in the work of William Temple Foundation, a Christian faith-based research institute particularly focusing on economy, marginalization and urban regeneration.

All the contributors to this book accept the centrality of poverty reduction as a primary objective for the Christian engagement with economics. It is equally foundational for Muslim economics as Hussain indicates so strongly. Both Christians and Muslims link the campaigns to reduce poverty and marginalization with the central commitment of faith to the promotion of justice and the rejection of injustice. Both are seen as central to the Scriptures and the Qur'an, and to the wider sacred traditions of Islam and Christianity, and to the *practice* of their respective faith communities and members. Clearly, particular contributors reflect both the identification of key commitments in economics to poverty reduction, but also the arguments over their respective value to that poverty reduction. These differences can often be traced back to the debate over the theological and ethical acceptability, or otherwise, of market capitalist economies. The challenge itself is starkly identified by my use of Layard's research to explore the strong linkage between the $15,000 per annum per person above which increasing income does not commensurately generate increasing happiness ($20,000 in Layard's book as against $15,000 in his lectures) and the West's minimum income. Below this people are effectively marginalized from effective participation in advanced economies. This stands in stark contrast, to the 1.3 billion people who live on $365 or less per person per year. To reduce that absolute poverty and to generate income sufficiency is the key moral task for people and faiths. And, although much progress has been made, not least through the recent efforts of India and China, so much has still to be done if the millennium goals of reducing the absolute poverty of those living on less than $1 a day by 50 per cent are to be achieved by 2015. The contributions to that poverty reduction are likely to come from engaging the economies of the least developed economies in the global economy, particularly by carefully opening them to trade and investment, and the role of competition and strong government in this, as Kennedy reminds us from the example of post-war West Germany, supported by the current achievements of East and South East Asian economies. Yet it is at precisely this point that Northcott is so critical of the current trading and production practices of global capitalism, and its dominant institutions like the World Trade Organization, World Bank and International Monetary Fund, and the undue influence of the American empire on them.

These arguments are precisely a reminder of the importance for poverty reduction, first, of the need for and feasibility of promoting actively increasing prosperity. In itself, therefore, this is a stark reminder of the scandal of the persistence of the scale of absolute poverty. Second, it is also a reminder of the growing significance of government in both modern post-war economies in general, and particularly in emerging economies. This in itself relates to the sharp polarization of economic systems throughout most of the twentieth century between the free market of capitalism and the state-dominated command economy of communism. This importance of government has featured strongly in a number of our contributors' chapters, including in their wider work. It involves the need to balance government with the free operating of the market through competition – as Kennedy argues. In my *Marginalization*, government was observed as playing a major role in reducing those sharp and increasing inequalities which so obstruct poverty reduction strategies, and for developing health care and education for all, including through pro poor economic growth strategies. The latter significantly embraced the encouraging of the participation of the marginalized in especially local decision-making. Women, as the poorest of the poor, feature centrally in such programmes as their involvement is a key solution in poverty reduction.

7. *Developing ethical economics*. Through all these reflections on market economies and economics a clear ethical dimension has been present. It has been both intrinsically part of any

discussion on, for example, competition, poverty reduction and trade, but also because the engagement by Christian social ethics of political economy inevitably includes the elaboration of ethical understandings. What is especially important is that this ethical concern is also part of the development of economics from its formation as a discipline in the late eighteenth century to the present, and particularly reflecting the distinction between what the contemporary economist Sen has called *engineering* (or positive, scientific, fact) and *ethical* (normative, values) economics. Sen has also rightly bemoaned the fact that in the twentieth century, the more scientific understanding increasingly dominated and marginalized the ethical, a trend which Wilde has noted. The contributions of Riordan, Steedman, Skinner and myself have also reflected on this ethical aspect of economics. They recognize, with Sen, that the task is to restore the significance of ethical economics in debates over economic affairs, for '(t)here is no scope at all . . . for dissociating the study of (technical) economics from that of ethics and philosophy'.[12] To that task, Christian social ethics, churches and faiths both *should* contribute, and recognize that they have much to contribute. Faith traditions, including Christianity and Islam, have ethical foundations in terms of the character of God and what God requires of humankind. For example, both are profoundly committed to poverty reduction because people have an intrinsic dignity in and through the Creator God, but also because so often large-scale absolute poverty in the midst of great wealth is associated with an injustice which a just and righteous God – and therefore his disciples – condemn. This contributes both to our liberal or reformist Christian critiques of global market capitalism and to the more radical critiques.

The promotion of such ethical economics has particularly figured in my recent work on *Marginalization*. In this, I begin to try to reformulate a religious tradition of Christian political economy, in critical conversation with its origins in the late eighteenth and early nineteenth centuries.[13] Ethical economics play a central role in this, along with more faith-based economics. The role and nature of the former has been particularly resourced by my strong contacts with Uppsala University, and the impressive work of Professor Carl-Henric Grenholm. His seminal interdisciplinary research project delivered 12 reports exploring detailed aspects of the engagement between (Christian) ethics and economics. Some of this material appeared in his valuable 'Justice, Ethics and Economics' in *The Future of Christian Social Ethics: Essays on the Work of Ronald H. Preston, 1913–2001* (Continuum, 2004). My chapter, introduction and conclusion in this book develop all this material further, in addition to my foreword, 'Why developing tradition is a matter of life or death' in *The Church and Economic Life* (Epworth, 2006). Taken altogether, they suggest an emerging cumulative programme seeking to promote the development of a tradition of ethical economics strongly related to Christian social ethics. That instinct is interestingly recently confirmed by Stiglitz's encouragement of what he calls 'moral growth – growth that is sustainable, that increases living standards not just today but for future generations as well, and that leads to a more tolerant open society.'[14]

Connected to this commitment to supporting the role of ethical economics in the development of political economy today, is the continuing debate over the significance of ethical and engineering economics, and the appropriate nature of the relationships between them. Clearly, Christians too easily reinforce the ethical dimension, for example in therefore promoting the moral superiority of co-operation over competition. But Steedman and Kennedy have reminded us that such a stance can be both economically ill-informed and empirically inaccurate. So Steedman is clear that an adequate Christian social ethics for today will engage both engineering and ethical economics. It will not promote one at the expense of the other. And it is at precisely this point that these arguments for such a balanced judgement are critiqued by those like Northcott and Hussain who would, as of faith, assert the supremacy of the ethical over the engineering. But that conversation runs through the contributions, and this first part of the conclusion on the market capitalist economy. How to address that argument is one of the key tasks which Christian social ethics is required to engage through its development of contributions to an emerging political economy for the future. What is clear is that in both sections in this first part of the conclusion, arguments over contemporary global market capitalism, and then over the nature of market economies and economics, are integrally part of a task which I have earlier called 'searching for a way forward.' For this certainly addresses the fundamental question of global capitalism, but also engages with the details associated with operating modern political economies. Both constitute what is the emerging contribution of faith to a political economy of the early twenty-first century. Yet in addressing the crucial task of how to connect the two sides of that coin, it is the following Part Two, as the contribution of Christian social ethics, which provides the best way forward for such an exploration. And that will be to the mutual benefit of political economy and Christian social ethics.

Part Two. Faith as Christian social ethics. Making sense of the contributions of Christian social ethics (and faith contributions) to political economy

The 12 contributions to this Project have much in common, not least their strong commitment to developing the contribution of Christianity (as Christian social ethics and as interfaith ethics) to political economy today. We are strongly agreed that such a task will be of mutual benefit to churches, faiths and society. In our reflections, and emerging out of our consultation together, some of these agreements on the features of a market economy and economics have been identified. These include the priority of poverty reduction and the value of competition and co-operation. They have been written up in the first part of this conclusion. That is of some importance, because it illustrates the significance and indeed growing necessity of identifying and elaborating convergences or overlapping consensuses, which the sheer pressure of global problematics will increasingly require of us all. Yet what has also become evident from reflecting on the contributions is the divisions between them regarding both particular issues, for example trade, but also underlying matters, for example, the ethical acceptability or not of market economies. The latter so often greatly inform our stances on these issues. As important, there are divisions, certainly over economics, for example over the relative strength of ethical as against engineering economics, but equally, and sometimes more so, over theological and ethical priorities in relation to economic affairs.

How to address such existing differences and desired convergences is likely to become one of the key issues for Christian social ethics, theology and religions in their engagement with the emerging global context. For Hollenbach, the most challenging question raised by the phenomenon of globalization is 'how to achieve effective and universal respect for the common humanity of all people even in the midst of their differences'.[15] It is a question which certainly figures large in Brown's, my own and Baker's contributions. Yet I recognize that this task is reflected in and emerges from a consideration of all the contributions, particularly when read together. It is, in fact, perhaps the key question which has to be addressed as we consider what kind of Christian social ethics for what kind of political economy today.

Reflecting on the convergences and divergences which the contributions embody begins to suggest, among other things, the possible value of developing ways of locating the different contributions on a broad tapestry or map. We could then see their distinctive contributions but also where they are located in relation to each other, including the likely connections between them. That is to recognize that the contributions do not simply reflect differences, but also shared understandings. It is also to recognize that the deep contextual changes in the global economy and religions, identified at the beginning of this conclusion, have begun to result in the reformulation of religious traditions in the West. They can then no longer warrant description by the old traditional distinctions alone, but are also often in the process of being reformulated, so opening up the

possibility for new connections between traditions, and therefore for new formulations.

For example, Brown, myself, Baker, Skinner and Sedgwick
recognize the value of the reformulated virtues of mainstream
liberal theology, but equally the need to engage with the growing arguments for greater theological distinctiveness. Old divisions no longer dominate the field to the exclusion of everything
else. It is a field with much blurring of the edges and of interactions between particular traditions and understandings,
epitomized in John Reader's study *Blurred Encounters: A
Reasoned Practice of Faith* (Aureus, 2005) (he too is a WTF
partner). Maps or tapestries that seek to allow the recognition
of such differences, but also such linkages, therefore become
increasingly relevant and necessary for the development of
Christian social ethics.

And that is, importantly, quite fitting, because there has been
a long tradition in scholarship in general, and in Christian
social ethics in particular, including in our contributors, of
developing the contribution of typologies to the task of both
interpreting contemporary contexts and also in developing the
praxis-responses to them. For our contributors, the task could
become ways of describing existing and emerging traditions to
enable us to see what is going on in the broad, in the terms of
clustering traditions, in the differences and possible collaborations, and in what is new. And, most importantly, we can
connect a typology for contemporary Christian social ethics, as
revealed by our contributions, with a typology identifying
different forms of what it means to be Church. The latter, for
example, features prominently in Northcott, Baker and my contributions. This recognizes the changing evolving nature of faith
contributions and the centrality to them of faith traditions
(Christian social ethics) *and* faith communities (churches),
including in terms of developing religious identities. In an
important editorial introduction to an edition of *Crucible* dedi-
cated to ecumenical social ethics,[16] and currently edited by
myself and Peter Sedgwick, Stephen Platten observes how the
Anglican tradition of moral theology forged significant connec-

tions with Anglican ecclesiology from the seventeenth century to the present. The latter includes the Anglican and Roman Catholic bilateral agreed ecumenical statement on morals, *Life in Christ: Morals, Communion and the Church* (Church House Publishing, 1994). This therefore locates our findings in this Project in the centre of ecumenical understandings and ethics. The following two typologies reflect all these experiences.

1 An emerging typology for Christian social ethics; what the contributions suggest

In terms of what the particular contributions reveal, in terms of underlying convictions, two such clusters immediately come to mind, which essentially represent the two ends of a continuum or spectrum:

- *From overlapping consensuses*: that is, Christians co-operating with others, whether faiths, government, business or civil society, in the promotion of economic policies which Christian beliefs can justify. These include, for example, the belief in human dignity, in terms of the nature of the Creator God and God the incarnate Christ ensuring and requiring that as God participated in the human so the human now participates in God. It is such beliefs which drive Christians into such poverty reduction programmes as pro-poor economic growth and, conversely, human flourishing programmes as noted in my chapter. This type is particularly associated with the mainstream liberal tradition of Christian social ethics, as observed and critiqued particularly by Brown. Yet as Brown argued, and other contributors confirmed, the Christian apologetic for liberal values remains essential not least because it is so strongly rooted in Christian beliefs and traditions. As we argued earlier in this conclusion, this warrants the description of an overlapping consensus as distinctively Christian as the other end of this spectrum.
- *To promoting understandings and practices in economic affairs which are distinctively different from the mainstream*

in Christian social ethics and economics, and which embody unique Christian and religious understandings in contemporary economic contexts as both *critiques* of and *alternatives* to these mainstream consensuses. It is here that we see, in our contributions, the greater likelihood of a rejection of capitalist market economies and economics, and the struggle to develop faith based alternatives (sometimes linked to radical political economic analysis, for example by Wilde). Here we also see Northcott's work on fair trade and the body of Christ, Wilde on a Jesus-based political economy rejecting the empire of global capitalism, particularly as seen in oil, and Hussain's elaboration of Muslim interest-free banking.

Yet given the fluctuating religious and economic contexts, and the pressures on some to reformulate religious tradition in the West, it becomes possible also to identify, in some of our contributions, one other type which stands between and more importantly *interacts* the overlapping and distinctive types. So it will, as Brown argues, recognize and engage the significance of the *distinctive* religious contribution and its basis in Scriptures and tradition, yet it will seek to engage constructively with the mainstream liberal tradition, for example in developing a reformulation, through interacting overlapping and distinctive, of the virtue of tolerance. In this, as essentially a post-liberal position, it contrasts strongly with the Hauerwas and Yoder critique of the liberal. This interacting position is also strongly present in the work of Baker, my own, Sedgwick's and possibly in Hussain's. They use it to allow the recognition of the strengths and limitations of overlapping and distinctively different in a *continuing interaction* which becomes so substantial as to suggest a new type. It is essentially more flowing, fluid and blurring, what Sedgwick creatively refers to as polyphonic, yet nonetheless sufficiently cohesive as to warrant definition as an additional type.

2 An emerging typology for what it means to be Church: What the contributions suggest

Reflecting on our contributions as they engage with the emerging global economy has strongly emphasized the need to hold together, in terms of the foundations of Christian identity in such a context, faith traditions (as theology and Christian social ethics) *and* faith communities (as churches and other faiths). It should not therefore surprise us that the implications of our reflections on Christian social ethics for ecclesiology are particularly sharply defined and underlined, including as strong spiritual and religious contributions to and resources for the formation of Christian social ethics. Importantly, and not surprisingly, such an ecclesiological typology has strong resonances and indeed parallels with the Christian social ethics typology. So we move:

- From a broad understanding of mainstream liberal Church, including working with other disciplines (including economics) and with other partners in practical policy making. This view of Church fits with mainstream denominations in Britain, and the ecumenical movement. It includes many of our contributors, from Kennedy to Riordan. Indeed, Heslam argues that this type equally has the potential for transforming capitalism.
- To a more sectarian view of the Church as essentially embodying the distinctively different in religion. So Northcott embodies his important and creative Hauerwasian interpretation of the Church in a trading economy radically different from mainstream economics. Wilde similarly develops a high Yoderian politics of Jesus which leads easily into an alternative ecclesiology. It stands as critique and alternative to mainstream capitalist economics and theology. Again, as with the equivalent Christian social ethics type, there is a strong linkage between this type and furious religion. And Hussain, through the basis of Islamic beliefs, develops a radical critique of and alternative to mainstream finance and economics rooted in his faith community.

As with Christian social ethics, these two ecclesiological types are both necessary for describing the work and implication of some of our contributors, but yet they are also insufficient – because the work of Baker, Brown, Sedgwick and my own and maybe Heslam seeks to develop a type of being Church that stands between broad mainstream liberal Church and the more sectarian view of Church. (There may also be signs of this in Hussain's Islamic tradition's use of a 'third way'.) For Baker, this is best described as a *hybrid* type of being Church, rooted in his two case studies from local Manchester churches (as organized Christian presences). For him, 'a hybrid church is not ideologically wedded to one way of achieving outcomes [my two ends of the spectrum], but is prepared to learn from a wide variety of models, and to be creative in the different people and groups it can gather together.' Importantly, it is the overlap between the ethical and ecclesiological types which suggests the possible value of doing further work on them.

Of course, the key task is, in the light of such mapping, to what extent they allow the development of further resonances between the typologically located contributions, and how to engage those differences which persist. This leads on, therefore, to a brief discussion of what it can mean to collaborate.

3 The implications of the Project for the development of more collaborative ways of working

It is certainly possible, and increasingly necessary, to explore the possibilities for either further collaboration between the types or testing the feasibility of maintaining some kind of relationship between them, certainly when agreement or consensus is clearly not achievable. It is at this point that the findings of the Project for the nature and purpose of various forms of collaboration moves from being rather a mundane task to being rather strategic (for the development of Christian social ethics and its contributions to Church and society). The role of a multifaceted collaboration becomes important in addressing this, and includes:

1. Embodying collaboration in the Project. This Project itself has suggested the possibility and significance of collaboration:

- The 12 contributors intentionally represent very different religious and theological traditions and forms of Church and faith. It is these differences which have been exploited to generate, for example, the findings of this concluding section. Yet the respect for differences as a most positive and constructive experience is also complemented by two intentional pressures for collaboration, including shared and differing understandings. On the one hand, we all began with the same brief: *what for your religious tradition or perspective are the defining principles and ideas for the contours of an ethical political economy for the twenty-first century?* On the other hand, we also reflected together at a residential consultation on these different contributions and their implications if any, for shared and different understandings. We have taken into account these conversations for the final drafting of our individual contributions and this concluding chapter.
- The origins of this project also demonstrate the value of a collaborative way of working:
  - from the partnership between the Church of England's Mission and Public Affairs Council (MPA) and the ecumenical William Temple Foundation to jointly fund and oversee collaboration on economic affairs, resulting in the appointment of Hannah Skinner, joint editor of this book. It is here that the Project was conceived and its organization focused.
  - and recalling and continuing an earlier partnership between the CCBI and the WTF to follow up the CCBI report *Unemployment and the Future of Work* (1997) with the jointly funded and published report *Putting Theology To Work* (1998).
  - to the promotion of the present Project and its follow-up, with strong CCBI and MPA support.

2. Promoting public theology through churches and academy.
The Project represents the importance of developing collaboration between the churches and the academy (as theology) in this
promotion of public theology (through economic affairs) as the
interaction of churches, academy and society (including as
economy) hopefully for their mutual benefit.

One aspect of such collaboration is likely to be of particular
importance, namely promoting a constructive relationship
between churches and academies in terms of sharing research as
theoretical and practical experiences, and in terms of recognizing the importance (now renewed by the impact of globally
furious religion and local religious capital discoveries) of connecting faith communities and faith traditions which academies
and churches can so easily disconnect to their mutual disadvan-
tage and impoverishment. The demands of a rapidly changing
context globally and locally, and religiously and economically,
are regularly increasing the pressure on such disconnections
and dislocations. Equally, this collaboration draws renewed
attention to the importance for the theological task of theological reflection on *praxis* (as practice embodying theory) and
the consequent need for it to be *performative* in that by their
fruits you shall know them. Both are emerging key features in a
credible public theology and Church.[17]

*3. Extending social ethics from ecumenical to interfaith col-
laboration.* There has been a significant emphasis in the contributions on the importance of inter- and multidisciplinary
ways of working, including the need to ensure the inclusion of
disciplines wider than theology and economics in the tasks of
engaging the contemporary global economy. Another form
of collaboration has been the recognition of the importance of
gradually extending that collaborative working *from* work
within Christian churches and denominations *to* ecumenical
working, and now also *to* interfaith working. We see this form
of collaboration as a *continuing process*, never therefore forgetting the significance and contribution of each arena, and recognizing that we are only on the threshold of collaboration

as interfaith social ethics (and recognizing its fundamental importance for engaging political economy matters in a global economy). This has been particularly focused in the work of Hussain, essentially suggesting a conversation between economics and Islam as alternative theories. The Manchester Project, noted in the Introduction, involves three of the participants in this Project, Hussain, myself and Steedman. While addressing the theoretical conversation, it also involves a more praxis-oriented approach involving local financial schemes. These include Christian and Muslim theory, geared particularly to the poor, and offering alternative finance to mainstream financial systems. Usefully, such work can now engage with interfaith explorations on economics found say in *Subverting Greed: Religious Perspectives on the Global Economy* (2002),[18] Susan Buckley's *Teachings on Usury in Judaism, Christianity and Islam* (Mellen, 2000) and Rodney Wilson's *Economics, Ethics and Religion: Jewish, Christian and Muslim Economic Thought* (Macmillan, 1997).

4. Involving faithful individuals and local faith communities. A most significant contribution of faith traditions and communities to engaging political economy is their recognition of the profound and seminal importance of the contribution of faithful *individuals* to and in faith communities and society. Sedgwick has powerfully restated what such individual faithful economic activity means through a reformulation of Christian vocation. We recognized the importance of Christian involvement in politics, business, profession, services and manufacturing as both exemplar of Christian discipleship and as role models for emerging generations. To that should be added Baker's reflections on the contributions of *local* faith communities to political economy, linking to Northcott's reflection on fair trade and local congregations. The renewed significance of the local, given the particular pressures of global contexts, has led us to a rediscovery of the strategic value for Church and society of *global localities*, epitomized by Baker's and Sedgwick's contributions. These powerfully underwrite and confirm the growing significance of faithful individuals in faith communities for the development of social capital. The William Temple Foundation's reformulation of this as *religious capital*, discussed here by Baker, links to furious religion, as the suggested reformulations of British religion. Interestingly, this connects to my own work on happiness and life satisfaction, and the powerful and formative role in that of both social capital but also religious capital (as the central importance for human fulfilment of a philosophy of life – and especially of the role of religion in that). What this adds up to is an emerging renewed confidence in faith traditions and communities as essential resource for engaging the emerging global political economy. Our project has hopefully, through its contributors and collaborations, also suggested the possible directions such an economy should engage with for its ethical sustainability. In doing so, it has also offered important clues for the future development of Christian social ethics. The two futures are therefore now in a profoundly and continuing interactive relationship. That is how it should be, and always has been, when both political economy and Christian social ethics have been pursued to their mutual advantage. It offers, we believe, a most interesting, creative and exciting way forward for faith traditions, communities, and political economy in this twenty-first century.

Notes

1 M. Buber, *Eclipse of God: Studies in the Relation between Religion and Philosophy*, New York, Harper and Row, 1957, pp. 3–9.

2 C. Brown, *The Death of Christian Britain: Understanding Secularization, 1800–2000*, London, Routledge, 2000.

3 C. Baker and H. Skinner, *Faith in Action: The Dynamic Connection between Spiritual and Religious Capital*, Manchester, William Temple Foundation, 2006, pp. 9 & 47.

4 See Introduction.

5 See M. Northcott, *An Angel Directs the Storm: Apocalyptic Religion and American Empire*, London, I. B. Tauris, 2004 and SCM Press 2007, and W. Wilde, *Crossing the River of Fire: Mark's Gospel and Global Capitalism*, London, Epworth Press, 2006.

6 R. H. Tawney, *Religion and the Rise of Capitalism*, Harmondsworth, Penguin edition 1966, p. 188.

7 F. Fukuyama, *The End of History and the Last Man*, Harmondsworth, Penguin 2002.

8 M. Hardt and A. Negri, *Empire*, Cambridge, MA, Harvard University Press, 2000.

9 Tawney, *Religion and the Rise of Capitalism*, p. 280.

10 R. H. Preston, *Confusions in Christian Social Ethics: Problems for Geneva and Rome*, London, SCM Press, 1994.

11 F. Maurice, *Life*, London, Macmillan, vol. 2, p. 32.

12 A. Sen, *On Ethics and Economics*, Oxford, Blackwell, 1987, p. 3.

13 See Atherton, *Marginalization*, London, SCM Press, chapter 6.

14 J. Stiglitz, 'The Ethical Economist', in *Foreign Affairs*, Nov–Dec 2005.

15 D. Hollenbach SJ, *The Common Good and Christian Ethics*, Cambridge, Cambridge University Press, 2002, p. 238.

16 *Crucible*, October–December 2006.

17 See J. Atherton, 'Marginalization, Manchester and the Scope of Public Theology' in E. Graham and E. Reed (eds), *The Future of Christian Social Ethics*, London, Continuum, 2004.

18 P. Knitter and C. Muzaffar (eds), *Subverting Greed: Religious Perspectives on the Global Economy*, Maryknoll, NY, Orbis, 2002.

Index of Names and Subjects